IMAGES
of America

ARDMORE

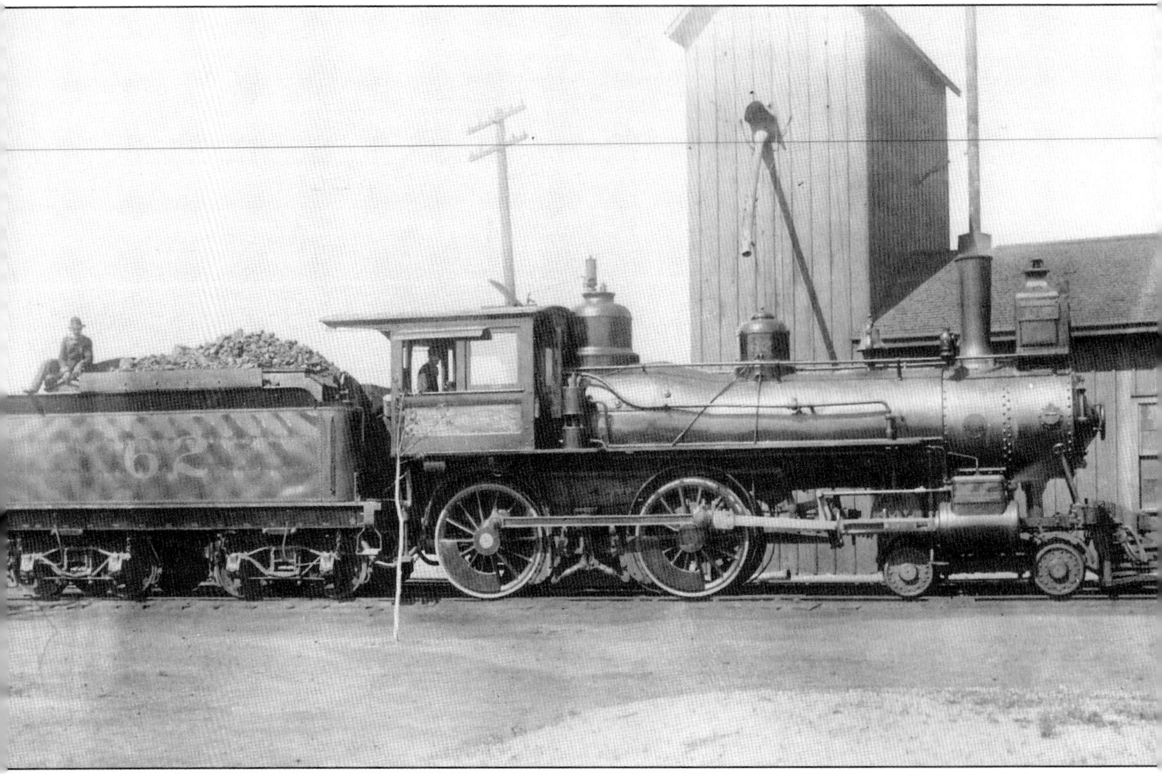

Ardmore began as a railroad town, and the railroad is still an integral part of the city. The old union depot, which stood abandoned for many years, has been refurbished and again serves as a passenger platform for the *Heartland Flyer*. It is also home to Ardmore Main Street Authority, which sponsors many community activities in the Ardmore area. (Courtesy of Ardmore Main Street Authority.)

On the cover: The silver cornet band was formed in 1890 and performed in the Ardmore area for a number of years. A local production of a Tom Thumb wedding was performed to raise money for the band uniforms. (Courtesy of Greater Southwest Historical Museum.)

IMAGES
of America

ARDMORE

Charlsie Foust Allen

ARCADIA
PUBLISHING

ISBN 978-0-7385-6085-4

Published by Arcadia Publishing
Charleston, South Carolina

Printed in the United States of America

Library of Congress Control Number: 2008941582

For all general information contact Arcadia Publishing at:
Telephone 843-853-2070
Fax 843-853-0044
E-mail sales@arcadiapublishing.com
For customer service and orders:
Toll-Free 1-888-313-2665

Visit us on the Internet at www.arcadiapublishing.com

CONTENTS

Acknowledgments 6

Introduction 7

1. The Intruders 11
2. An Incorporated City 29
3. Disasters 61
4. The Builders 79
5. The Players 109

ACKNOWLEDGMENTS

Special appreciation is extended to Dr. Paul N. Frame for his book *A History of Ardmore, Oklahoma, From the Earliest Beginnings to 1907*, which provides a wealth of information about the city from prehistory until statehood in 1907. He wrote the manuscript in 1949 as his master's thesis, and it was published in book form in 1995. Much of the factual information about the pictures in this volume comes from Dr. Frame's book.

Appreciation and thanks are extended to Sally Gray for her encouragement, her invaluable information, her love of local history, and for access to her private photograph collection, which includes many people and buildings.

Ardmore Main Street Authority opened its collection of photographs, which includes a historical look at downtown buildings and businesses throughout the city's history, including many photographs of the great fire in 1895 and the 1915 railroad tanker explosion.

The Greater Southwest Historical Museum made available its photograph collection, which includes the earliest known photograph of Ardmore as a tent city as well as churches, schools, and the original two-story Carnegie Library.

Ardmore Public Library has been very helpful in allowing access to the McGalliard Collection, which is an extensive compilation of photographs, memorabilia, and artifacts by William A. "Mac" McGalliard from Ardmore's earliest history through most of the 1900s. Of great importance in the collection are the notes that identify people, pictures, and events that otherwise may have been forgotten.

Special thanks to Ted Gerstle, my editor, for his continued encouragement and support in completing this volume.

This book is dedicated to the intruders, whose desire to take the land and build upon it helped create a state; to my grandparents Charley and Lillie Cole Palmer and Wilbert and Lula Collins Foust; and to my great-grandparents George Washington and Nancy Jane Williams Cole and Jerry and Diretha Barnes Collins, all of whom lived through the events in this book.

Introduction

Ardmore had been a city for 20 years before Oklahoma finally became a state. When the first inhabitants arrived on the prairie where the town would be born, buffalo bones still lay among the tall clumps of native grass. The 700 Ranch had been established by Alva Roff, an intermarried citizen, about 1880 in what is now southeast Ardmore. Located in the largest county of the Chickasaw Nation, the ranch was controlled by Roff, then Bill Washington, followed by Dan Fitch and Richard McLish—all citizens or intermarried Chickasaw citizens. The cowboys who worked for the 700 Ranch were the first residents of the area.

More than a year before the population arrived en masse, the town that would be born here had already been named. When the Santa Fe Railroad Company changed direction of its line from west toward New Mexico to the north toward Indian Country, the financiers met together and on a map marked and named seven towns that would be created after the railroad crossed the Red River into Chickasaw Indian lands: Marietta, Overbrook, Ardmore, Berwyn, Wynnewood, Paoli, and Wayne. All these cities were established as station stops on the Santa Fe as it moved northward and were named after cities on the Pennsylvania line just to the west of Philadelphia.

Entrepreneur Samuel Zuckerman applied to the Chickasaw Nation for a permit to sell merchandise at the Ardmore station, and the permit was issued on June 13, 1887. Earlier that same year, the Frensley brothers, Bob and Frank, had received a permit and established a business at Dresden, near present-day Gene Autry, but they moved south as the railroad laid track toward the Ardmore station. These early merchants were the first to arrive, and they continued doing business in Ardmore for many years. They were there when the first train pulled to a stop on July 28, 1887, next to the spot where the Ardmore station would be built. That date has been recognized and is celebrated as Ardmore's birthday.

Every businessman who moved into Ardmore built his store, warehouse, and home on land that did not and could not belong to him. All land in the Chickasaw Nation belonged to the Chickasaw citizens in commonality. Any citizen could claim a ranch or farm site and a home site, and they could lease the property; but they could not sell the land. Most of the businessmen were glad to pay a lease of $5 to $15 a year in order to build their homes and stores. After a few years, however, the businessmen realized their investments might be in danger should the Chickasaw Nation intervene and reclaim the land upon which their buildings sat.

The intruder population continued to grow. Intruders were those white and black noncitizens who moved into tribal lands all over Indian Country. At first, these intruders followed tribal laws and secured sponsorship of a citizen who then registered the noncitizens' location and collected a permit fee of about 25¢, which helped fund the nation's treasury.

As the number of intruders continued to grow, many of them failed to find a citizen sponsor, and even more discontinued paying the permit fee. The flood of intruders was so heavy in Pickens County that the rest of the Chickasaw Nation often referred to it as the "Free State of Pickens." It is estimated that before statehood, intruders outnumbered citizens more than 10 to 1 in Pickens County.

It is not surprising, then, that the intruders felt a need to protect their interests. Noncitizens congregated in small communities around the railroad stations, but they had no legal standing. They could not enter into contracts or even get married. In order to obtain a marriage license, a couple had to travel south across the Red River into Gainesville, Texas. Communities could not elect city government or collect taxes to establish law enforcement and fire protection. The people living at the Ardmore station were mostly intruders into the Chickasaw Nation without any legal standing. The Ardmore Board of Trade was a voluntary organization that attempted to help the merchants of Ardmore; but beyond collecting a small fee for membership, the Ardmore Board of Trade had little power other than suggesting certain actions. It did, however, hire a night watchman to guard the town at night.

Even though farms and communities of people were few and far between in the early days, circuit preachers rode the trails and organized brush arbor camp meetings. Churches also entered Pickens County. They came first as missionaries to the tribal citizens throughout Indian Country. The first church in Ardmore was built by the Methodist Episcopal Church, South. They organized in 1888 with 12 members and evolved into the First Methodist Church of today. Also in 1888, the Baptists established a church that divided and then reunited to become the First Baptist Church of today. What was to become the First Christian Church also began in 1888. By 1898, the First Presbyterian Church, St. Mary's Catholic Church, St. Philip's Episcopal Church, First Church of Christ, and Temple Emeth were serving the spiritual and social needs of Ardmore's growing population. By the mid-1900s, Ardmore had 52 active churches.

As early as October 1890, an incorporation petition was filed in the Third Judicial Division of Indian Territory for Ardmore, but it was denied; and the effort was not attempted again until 1895 when a second petition was also denied. Both of these petitions were filed in the judicial system of Indian Territory, which did not favor actions that would weaken the tribal governments. The third endeavor to incorporate Ardmore was successful probably because the petition was filed under a different authority. The Statutes of Arkansas had provided the only legal redress for United States citizens living in Indian Country since the mid-1800s. Judge Hosea Townsend used the Statutes of Arkansas to declare Ardmore an incorporated city on April 16, 1898.

As an incorporated city, Ardmore blossomed. A city election was held on July 5, 1898. The welfare of the new city superseded politics: of the 30 men who ran for public office, not one declared a political affiliation. By September, 46 ordinances had been passed, including the establishment of city government, fire department, city engineer, street commissioner, and post of city scavenger. It was the scavenger's job to clean up the streets and alleys, some of which were piled 10 feet high with trash. The seventh ordinance required males between the ages of 18 and 45 to clean streets five days a year with a few exceptions, which according to Dr. Paul N. Frame's research for *A History of Ardmore, Oklahoma, From the Earliest Beginnings to 1907* included "invalids, ministers of the gospel, teachers while teaching, and firemen." Citizens passed bond issues to install a water supply and sewer facilities and establish public schools.

Setting up a public school system was one of Ardmore's finest achievements before statehood. Prior to incorporation, the community had no authority to levy or collect taxes. Children who could afford it attended one of the several subscription, or private, schools with tuition about $1 or $2 a month per child. After incorporation, Ardmore City Schools were organized, and bonds built four elementary schools with grades one through eight and a high school.

One thing citizens could still not do after incorporation was own the land on which their homes and businesses were located. It would not be until the Dawes Commission's work was completed and individual allotments were made to tribal citizens that leftover lands would be offered for sale to the intruders.

As the new railroad station continued to grow, downtown merchants were cognizant of the fact that fire was a very real danger. Three wells were dug in the middle of Main Street to provide a supply of water, but most of the buildings were made of dry, highly combustible cottonwood lumber. In 1895, the disaster that had so been dreaded finally occurred. The great fire of 1895 began in the middle of the night in a livery stable. During the next six hours, 86 buildings west of the railroad station were burned—the heart of downtown Ardmore was almost completely destroyed. Within a few months, however, most of the buildings were reconstructed as Ardmore rose from the ashes. The next year a similar fire broke out east of the railroad tracks. Most new construction had been west of the tracks for several years; and few businesses destroyed in this second fire were replaced. Another fire in 1922 broke out in the C. P. Hall Furniture Company, and a two-block area was destroyed, including the Brooks Burner Stove factory and a boardinghouse where one man was killed. Numerous other fires have destroyed landmark buildings in Ardmore during the last century.

Much of Ardmore's early history is recorded in the pages of the myriad of newspapers that flourished beginning in 1888 with the *Ardmore Weekly Courier*. At least four other newspapers had published in Ardmore before the *Daily Ardmoreite* was established on October 28, 1893. Under the leadership of Sidney Suggs, who bought the *Daily Ardmoreite* in 1897, the first linotype machine in Indian Territory was installed. After 115 years, the *Daily Ardmoreite* continues to publish as a daily paper, and the presses also print for several area weekly newspapers.

In 1915, Ardmore was reduced to ashes again. When the railroad storage tanker exploded on September 27, 1915, splinters of wood and burning ash rained down over most of the city. The terrific boom shook the town, and the force of the explosion flattened numerous buildings both east and west of the depot. The depot was severely damaged. Several women and children were killed when the Madden Store collapsed. A man and his team crossing the tracks near the explosion were basically vaporized. Another man and his team were completely buried when the wall of a store collapsed on them. Altogether, 43 people were killed, and a couple of them were never identified. In a tour of the downtown historic district, one can see on several buildings that the east wall is of a different composition than the west wall after damaged buildings were repaired with different materials.

Throughout Ardmore's history, those businessmen who became highly successful invested their money back into the community, creating new business opportunities. From earliest days in 1887 until after the dawn of the 20th century, the main farming enterprise was cotton. By 1900, the five cotton gins were producing more than 60,000 bales of cotton per season, and Ardmore was billed as the largest inland cotton market in the world. Cotton buyers came from more than a dozen foreign countries to secure the fiber for their textile mills and arrange shipment south along the railroad to Galveston for shipment on to Liverpool, England.

The people who came to Ardmore came from all walks of life and all economic and social backgrounds. Only a small segment of the intruders belonged to the criminal element. Many were poor laborers looking for simple jobs. Small farmers came in search of virgin soil. Professionals such as attorneys and physicians sought a place to establish a practice. Businessmen, entrepreneurs, and speculators came with money hoping to make more in this new land. Whether coming from the north or the south, many of them came because the Civil War had destroyed their family ties to the eastern half of the United States. Nearly all of them were honest, upright, hardworking Americans who brought their families to the Indian Country to wait until the land would become available for purchase. Even though they came into the land illegally, they came with a desire to build and prosper; and their grit and determination made stronger this land called Oklahoma.

One

The Intruders

Since the beginning of this nation, people have been moving west. White people had already settled southeastern Oklahoma while it was still part of Arkansas Territory. With passage of the Indian Removal Act of 1832, those settlers were notified they would have to vacate the land that had become part of the Choctaw Nation.

The settlers burned their homes, barns, communities, and the courthouse with all its records and moved back to Arkansas. Each of the five tribes used a permit system to bring artisans, skilled workers, and professionals into tribal lands to build businesses, provide education to tribal children, and establish professional services. The permit system opened the floodgates to a white invasion. Pickens County was one of four counties in the Chickasaw Nation along with Pontotoc, Panola, and Tishomingo with the nation's capital located in Tishomingo. Approximately 5,000 Chickasaw citizens occupied the four new counties. All land was owned by the tribe communally, but a citizen could establish farming or ranching rights to any portion of land so long as he or she occupied the land being claimed. It was common practice for white men to marry Chickasaw women, and in fewer numbers white women also intermarried, in order to gain tribal citizenship. They could then claim large tracts of land for running cattle or lease small portions of land to white and black settlers who entered the nation under the permit system.

As word of the many opportunities in Indian Country circulated in the United States, more and more people poured into the land. By 1890, there were approximately 50,000 intruders and 5,000 citizens in the Chickasaw Nation with the preponderance of intruders located in Pickens County in communities along the railroad tracks. The intruders established businesses and cities, cultivated the land, and ran large herds of cattle on the open plains. The rest of the Chickasaw Nation often referred to this area as "the Free State of Pickens." The intruders made their own laws and virtually took the western half of the Chickasaw Nation for their own.

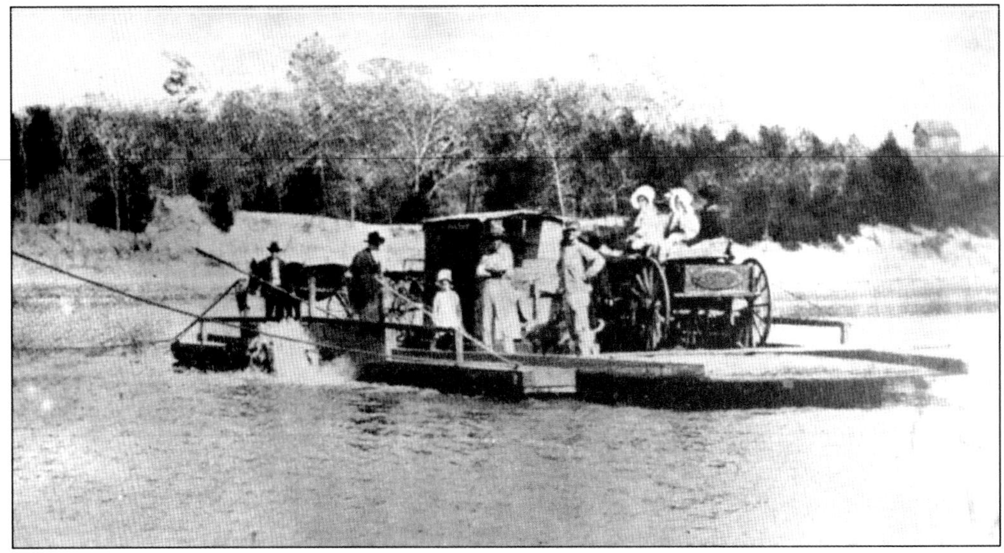

Colbert's Ferry was a popular entry point into Indian Territory. Ben Colbert, a Chickasaw citizen, established a ferry across the Red River north of Dennison, Texas. White settlers entering the Choctaw Nation filtered west toward Pickens County and north toward the Unassigned Lands soon to open for settlement. This picture was made about 1900. Colbert's Ferry operated from 1850 to 1899. (Courtesy of the McGalliard Collection, Ardmore Public Library.)

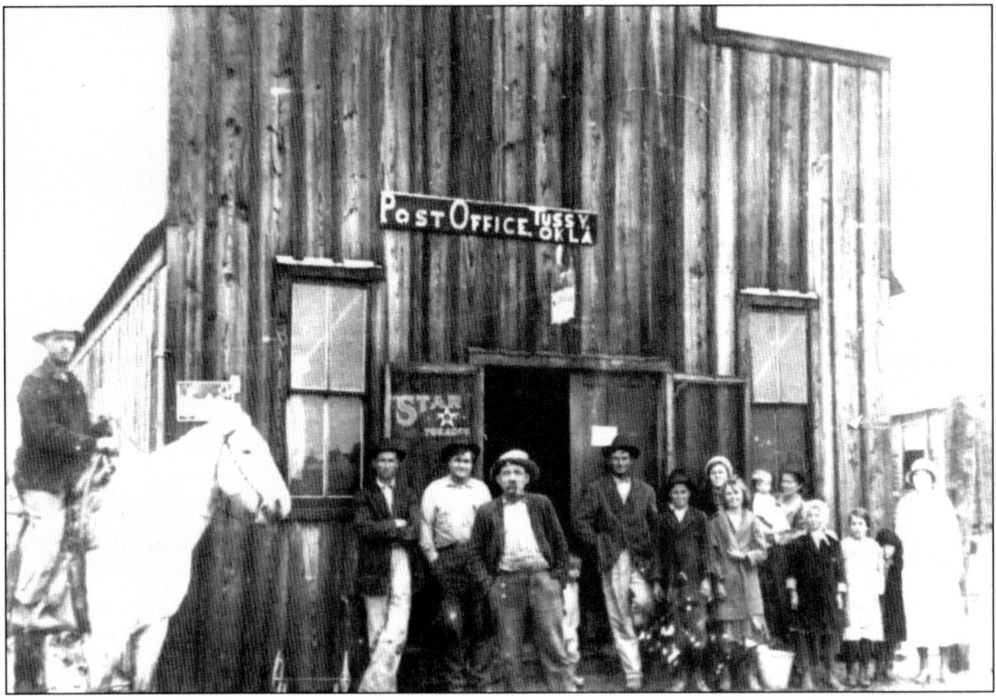

Henry Baker Tussy entered Pickens County in 1869 working for the Addington Ranch northwest of Ardmore. In the *Indian Pioneer Papers* interview, Tussy remembered that "federal militia would not let us think about settling. They called us 'nesters.' The militia cut the wires and [drove] our cattle back across the Red River." He is seen here mounted on the white horse. (Courtesy of Betty and John Stanton.)

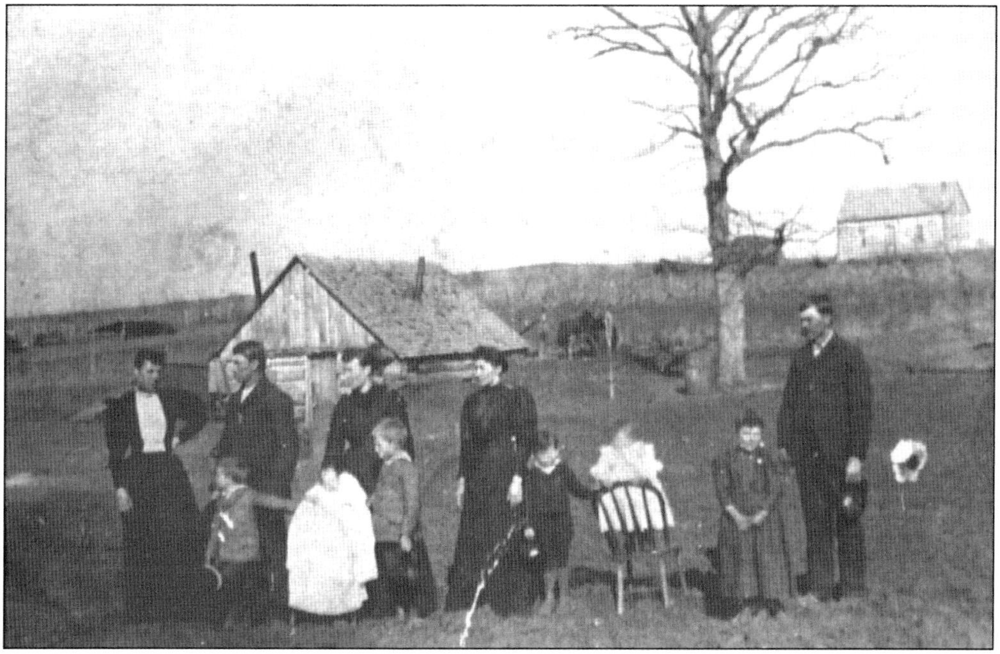

This unidentified family is typical of the intruders. They simply moved onto the land, built homes, and began to raise livestock and crops. The photograph was probably made in western Chickasaw Nation because of the scarcity of short, stubby oak forests common in the eastern areas. On the left the house is built against a small hill and may include a dugout room. (Courtesy of Sally Gray.)

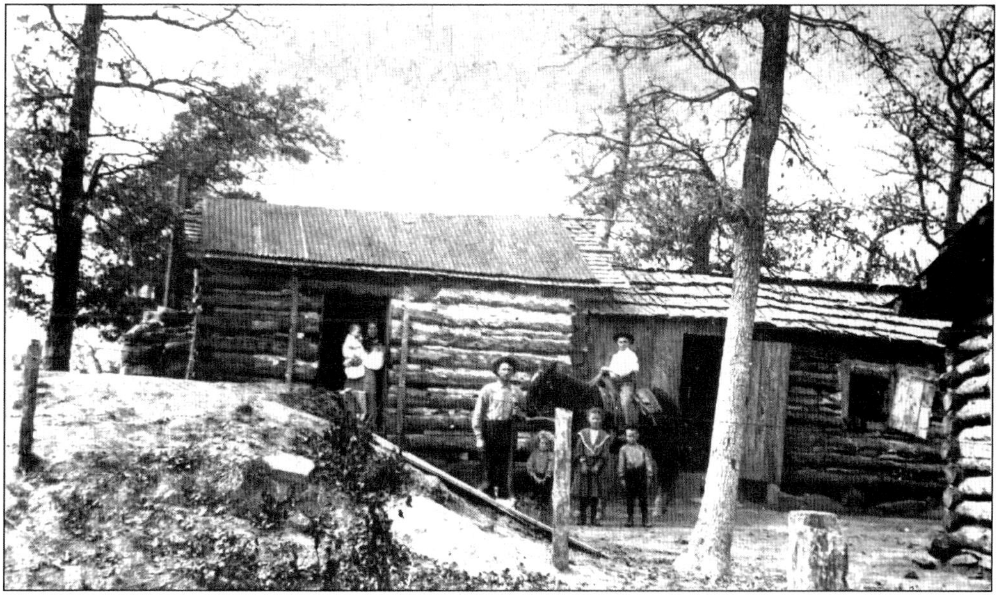

Early homes were made of logs. The open spaces between the logs were filled with mud, sometimes mud with chopped hay stubble, and later with cement. Many settlers dug cellars into the earth. These cellars were used to store root vegetables and home canned meats and vegetables as well as a shelter from the tornado storms, and sometimes they served as an extra bedroom. (Courtesy of Sally Gray.)

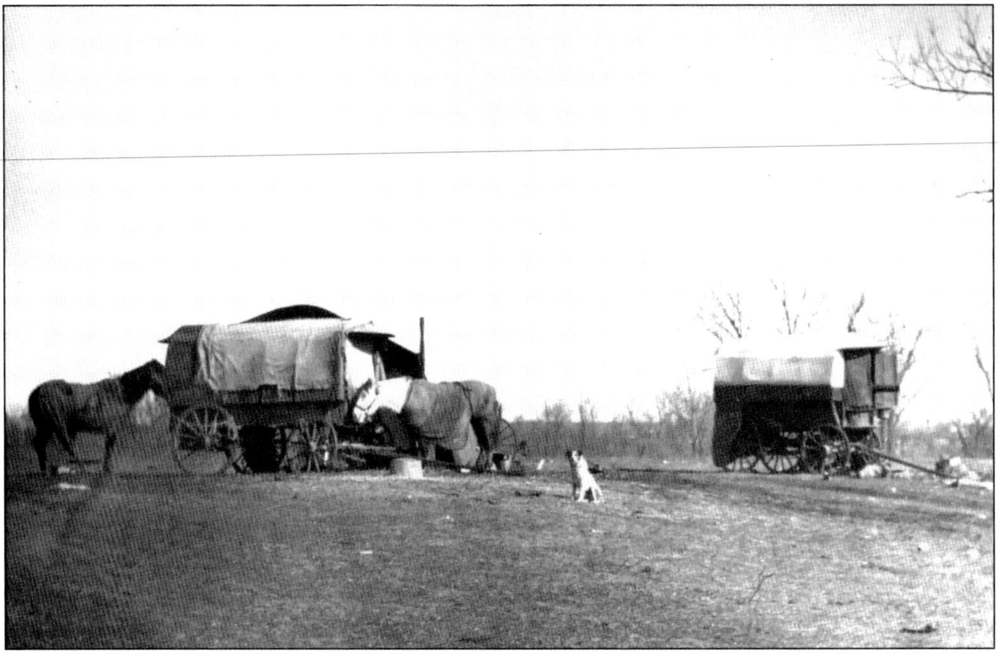

These covered wagons parked on the winter prairie probably served as home until a house was built. Sometimes the decision of where to settle was determined by a breakdown in the wagon or the death of a horse. There appears to be a house behind the wagon on the left, and the family dog poses in the center. (Courtesy of the McGalliard Collection, Ardmore Public Library.)

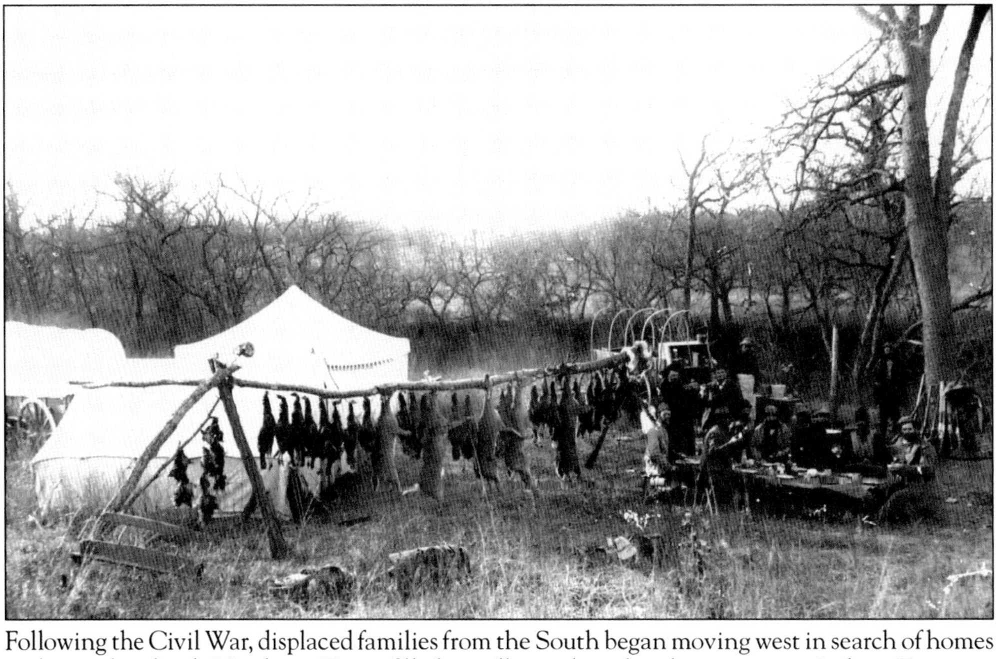

Following the Civil War, displaced families from the South began moving west in search of homes and new farmland. Northern Texas filled rapidly, and settlers began to eye Indian Territory. Small parties of men scouted the area living off the land, supplying their camps with deer, rabbit, and wild turkey. Some of these scouting parties never left. (Courtesy of the McGalliard Collection, Ardmore Public Library.)

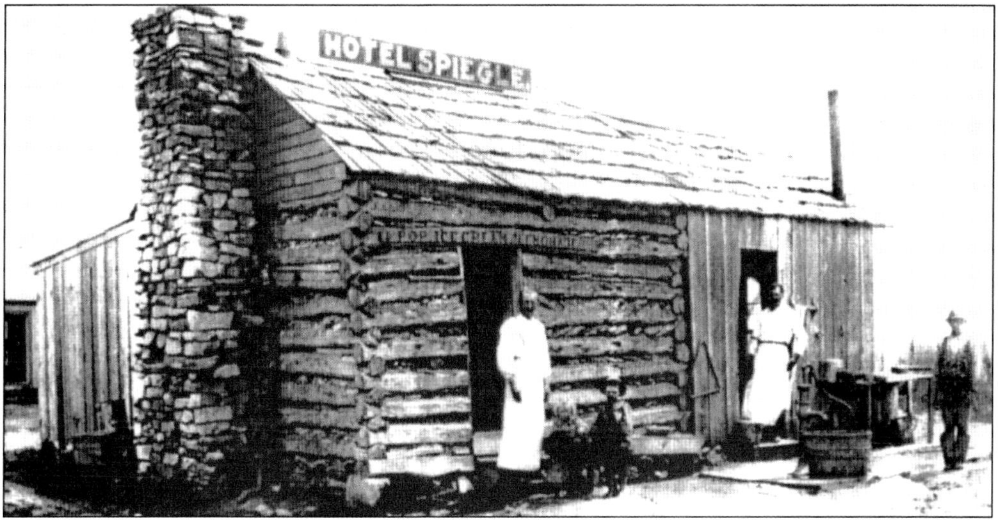

The Hotel Spiegle was open for business in 1887 and may predate even the Buckles Hotel, which is usually considered Ardmore's first hotel. This photograph was donated to the Ardmore Main Street Authority collection by Mrs. V. Sutton. The hotel appears to be a family affair, probably doubling as the family home. A sign above the door offers "Pop, Ice Cream, and Lemonade." (Courtesy of Ardmore Main Street Authority.)

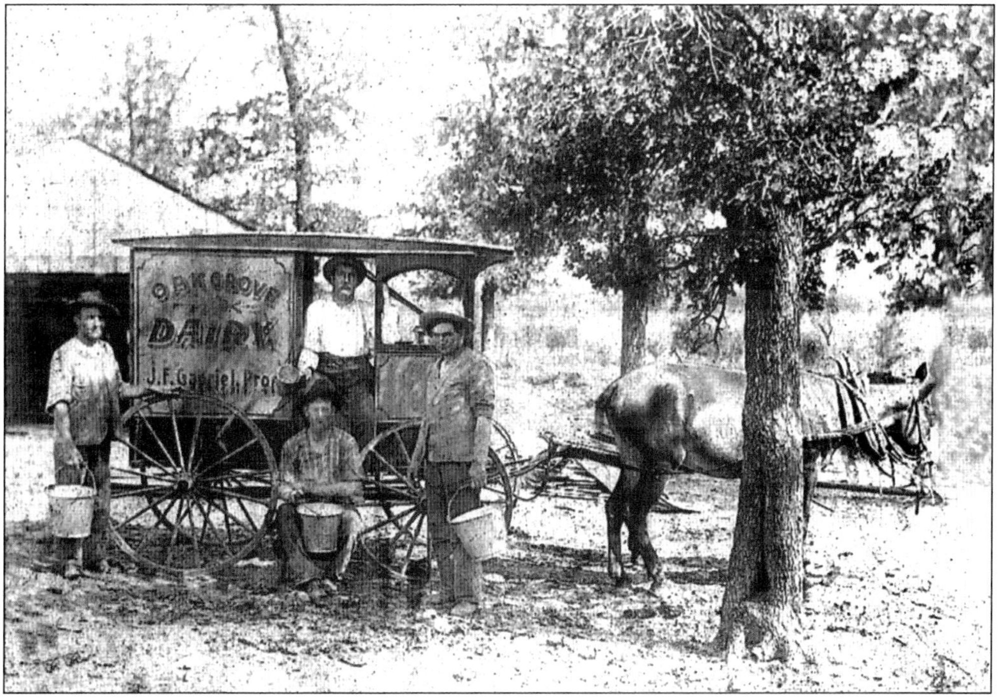

Although the location of Oak Grove Dairy is unknown, the photograph provides a look at an early delivery business. Milk was collected in open buckets and may have been transported in them or poured into larger 5- or 10-gallon milk cans. The cart would then drive up and down residential streets filling orders door-to-door, sometimes by simply pouring milk into the homemaker's pitcher. (Courtesy of Sally Gray.)

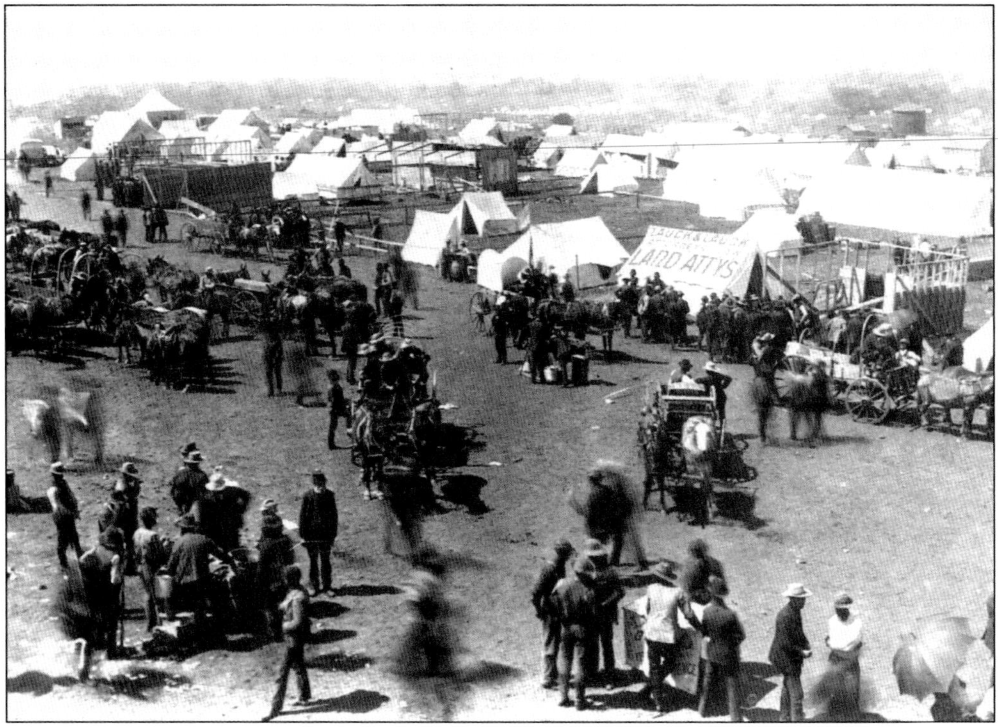

Within 24 hours, tents had been erected along Main Street laid out and named by Jim Staples. Some of the first professionals to arrive were Lauck and Lauck, land attorneys. The first wooden structures were built by the Frensley brothers, with lumber brought on the first train to arrive at the Ardmore station, and later by Samuel Zuckerman, merchants already in business when the train arrived. (Courtesy of Greater Southwest Historical Museum.)

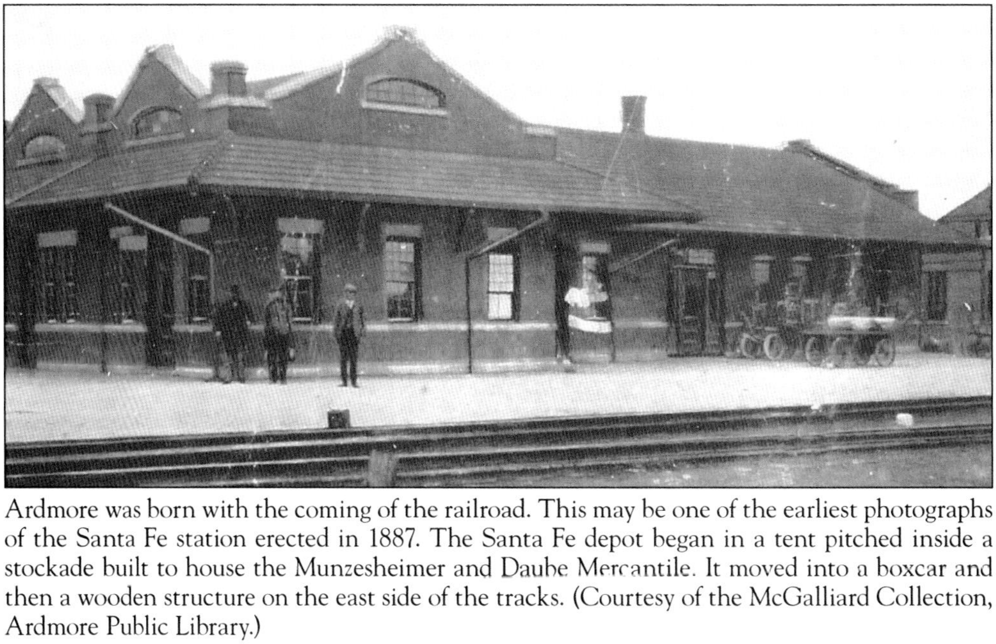

Ardmore was born with the coming of the railroad. This may be one of the earliest photographs of the Santa Fe station erected in 1887. The Santa Fe depot began in a tent pitched inside a stockade built to house the Munzesheimer and Daube Mercantile. It moved into a boxcar and then a wooden structure on the east side of the tracks. (Courtesy of the McGalliard Collection, Ardmore Public Library.)

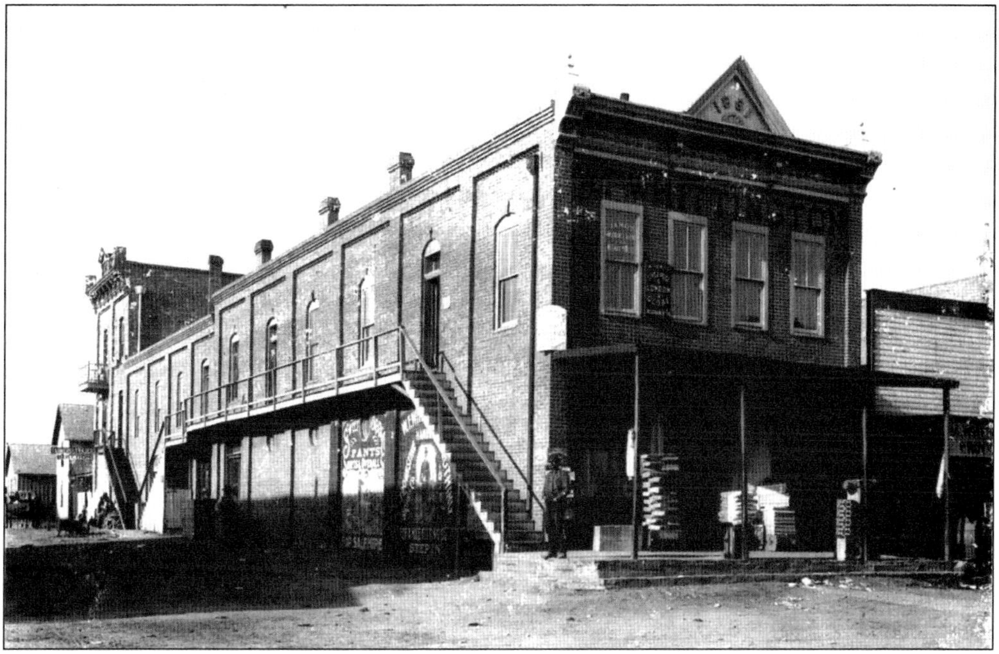

W. F. Whittington was one of the earliest businessmen in Ardmore. Recognizing the immediate need for general merchandise by new settlers, he opened the Whittington Store about 1890. Most early stores were credit stores, meaning the merchant bought the farmer's yearly crops and stock and recorded the purchase as credit against which the farmer could draw all year. (Courtesy of Greater Southwest Historical Museum.)

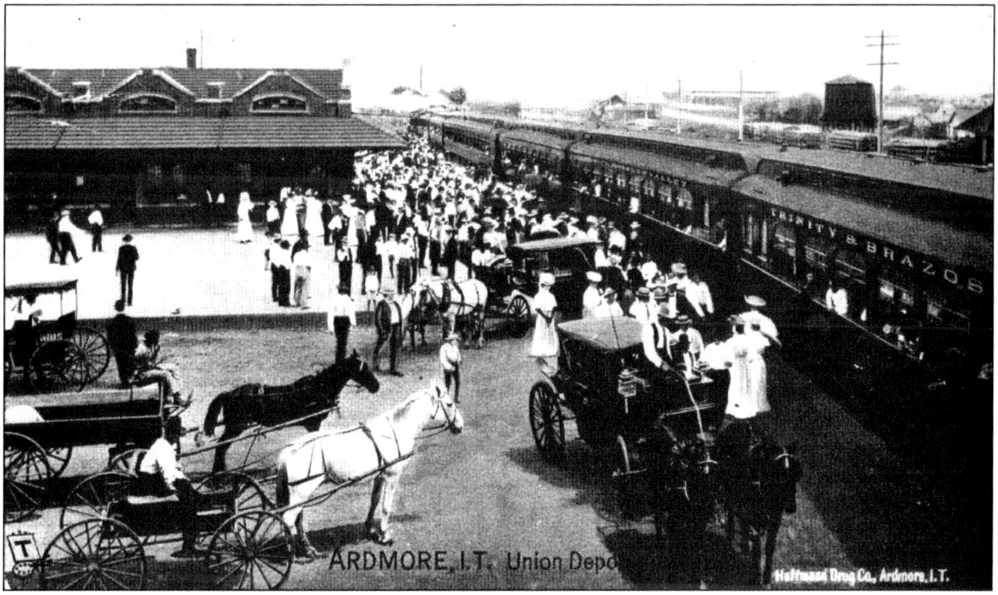

This postcard was made for "Hoffman Drug Co., Ardmore, Indian Territory." It was addressed to Clemie Crawford, Wynnewood, Oklahoma, asking if she had received her teaching certificate yet. It was mailed after statehood, but the picture was taken about 1900. In the lower right corner is the famous red and yellow coach that ran between the train and the Wisnor Hotel. (Courtesy of the McGalliard Collection, Ardmore Public Library.)

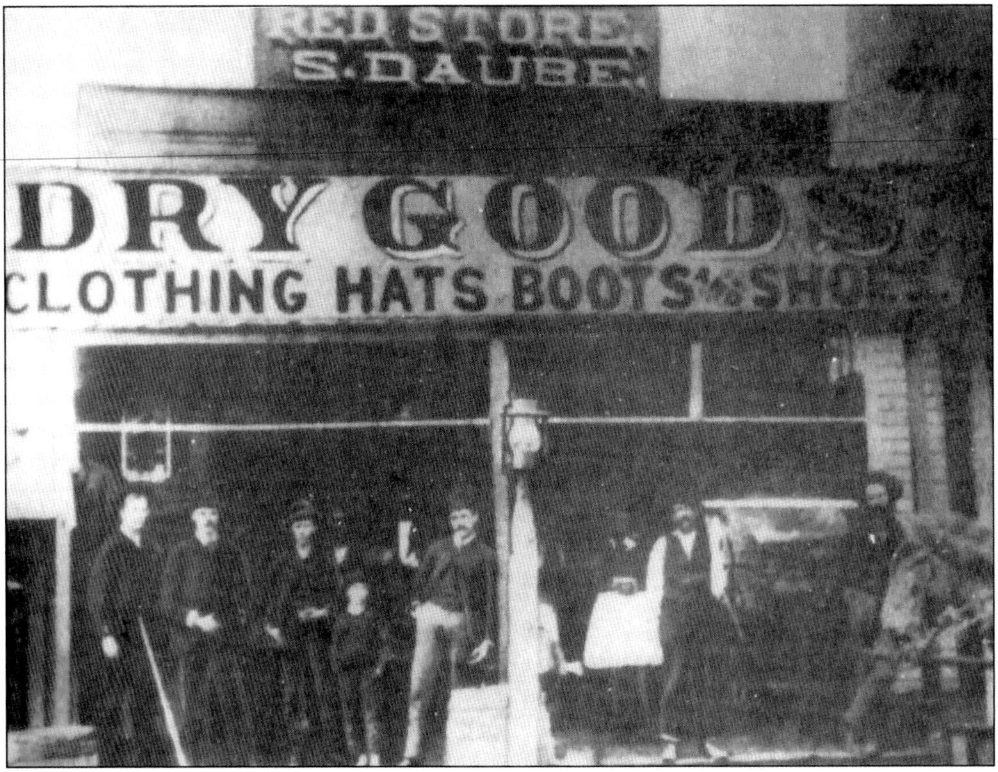

The Red Store was established by E. S. Wiseman in 1888. Later Sam Daube became a partner in the Red Store. Samuel Zuckerman sold his store to Max Munzesheimer. Daube and Munzesheimer became partners and operated the Iron Store, named for its iron siding, which for several years was the largest store in Pickens County. Settlers came from almost 100 miles to shop in Ardmore. (Courtesy of Ardmore Main Street Authority.)

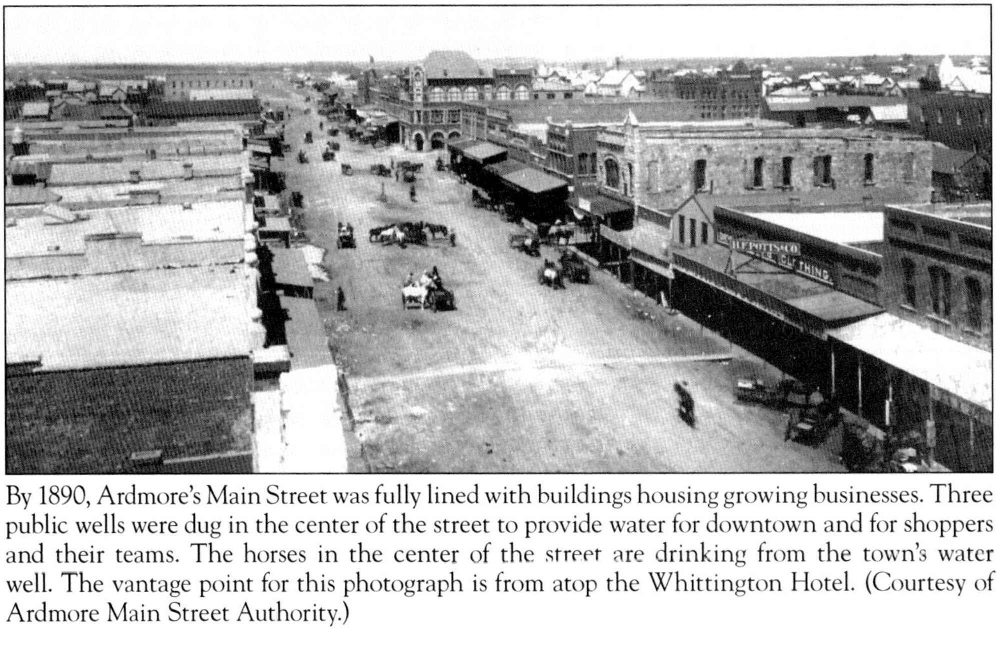

By 1890, Ardmore's Main Street was fully lined with buildings housing growing businesses. Three public wells were dug in the center of the street to provide water for downtown and for shoppers and their teams. The horses in the center of the street are drinking from the town's water well. The vantage point for this photograph is from atop the Whittington Hotel. (Courtesy of Ardmore Main Street Authority.)

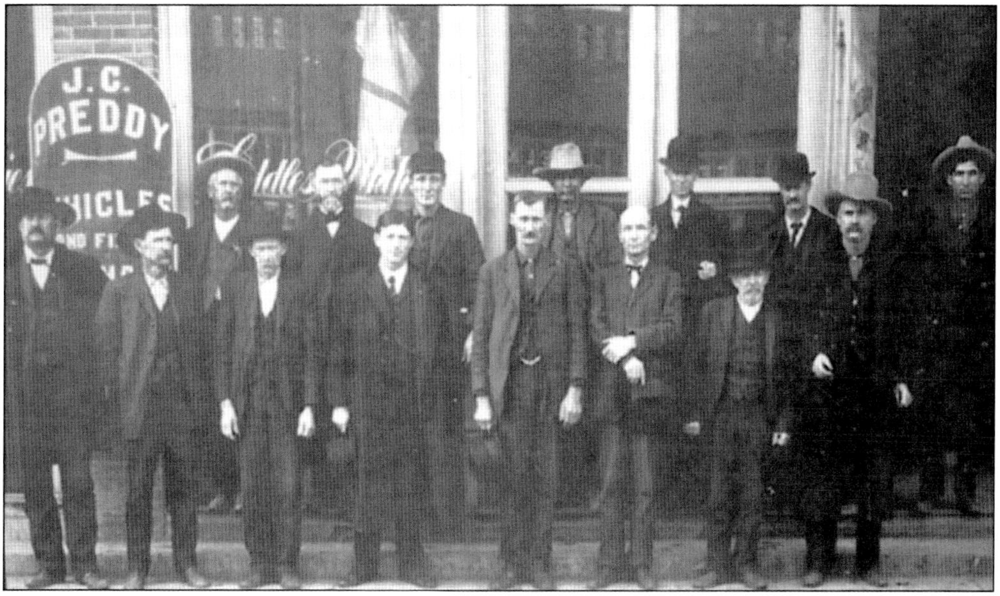

Noncitizens were under jurisdiction of the United States Court of the Western District of Arkansas. On March 1, 1889, a federal court was established at Muskogee. The Organic Act of May 2, 1890, enlarged the federal court to three districts: Muskogee, McAlester, and Ardmore. This picture is the first grand jury to be seated in the new federal court at Ardmore in 1894. (Courtesy of the McGalliard Collection, Ardmore Public Library.)

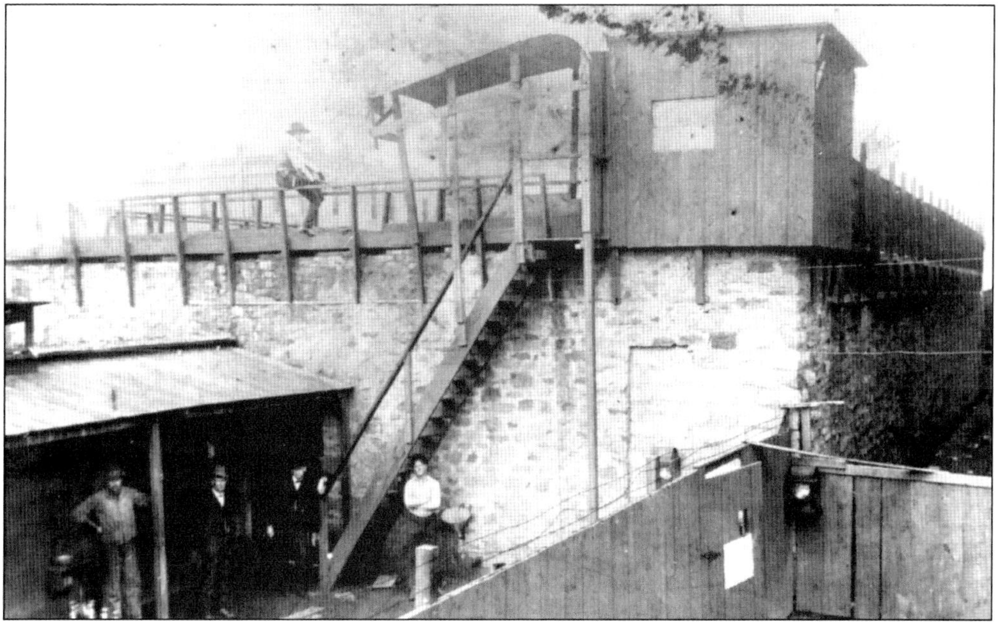

Judge James Shakelford presided over the Third Judicial Division housed in the Broadway Methodist Church beginning on October 7, 1890. In 1891, a wooden stockade was built and a two-story wooden courthouse was built on North Washington Street between Main Street and Broadway. A stone-walled structure was built about 1898 at the intersection of B Street and Main Street next to the new stone federal courthouse. (Courtesy of the McGalliard Collection, Ardmore Public Library.)

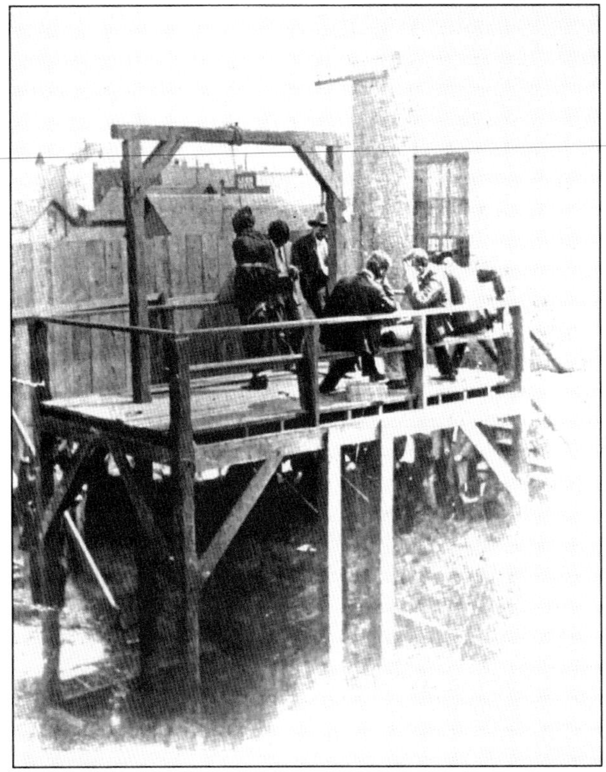

This hanging occurred at the federal jail on Main Street about 1904, the only hanging to be performed at that location. On the back of the photograph is this statement: "The color of the neck being pulled until it popped was of no consequence to the hangman." On the face of the picture is the name Rufus Beuyon; he was hanged for murder. (Courtesy of Ardmore Main Street Authority.)

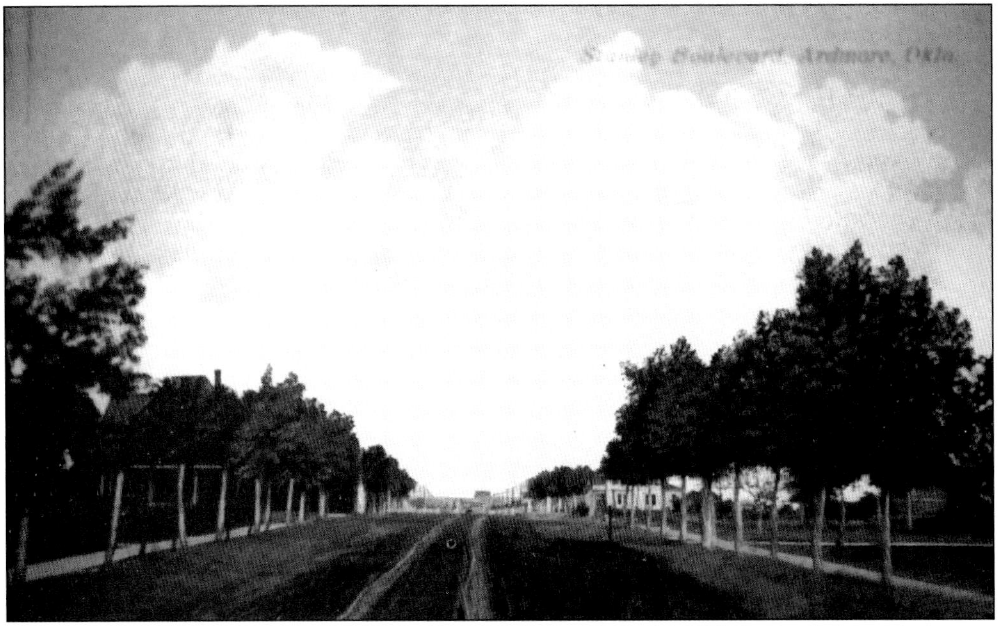

Stanley Street SW is one of the earliest streets in Ardmore. In this old postcard, the wide avenue is still a dirt thoroughfare. It is lined with young trees, which are now more than 120 years old and tower over the wide shady street. Many beautiful homes line this main traffic through street, which transverses the city from South Washington across southwest Ardmore to Sunset Street. (Courtesy of Ardmore Main Street Authority.)

This asphalt mine may be the Chickasaw Asphalt Mine, which opened in 1895. At the height of operations, four mines stripped asphalt from layers of sand northwest of Ardmore, including the Chickasaw, the Downard, the Continental, and the Le Grande. Asphalt was made into paint and also used to pave Ardmore's streets. Fees and royalties paid to the Chickasaw Nation were earmarked for education. (Courtesy of Ardmore Main Street Authority.)

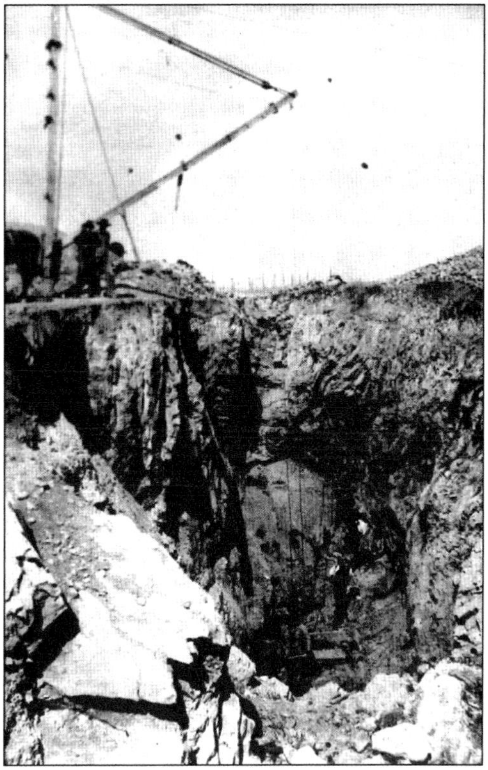

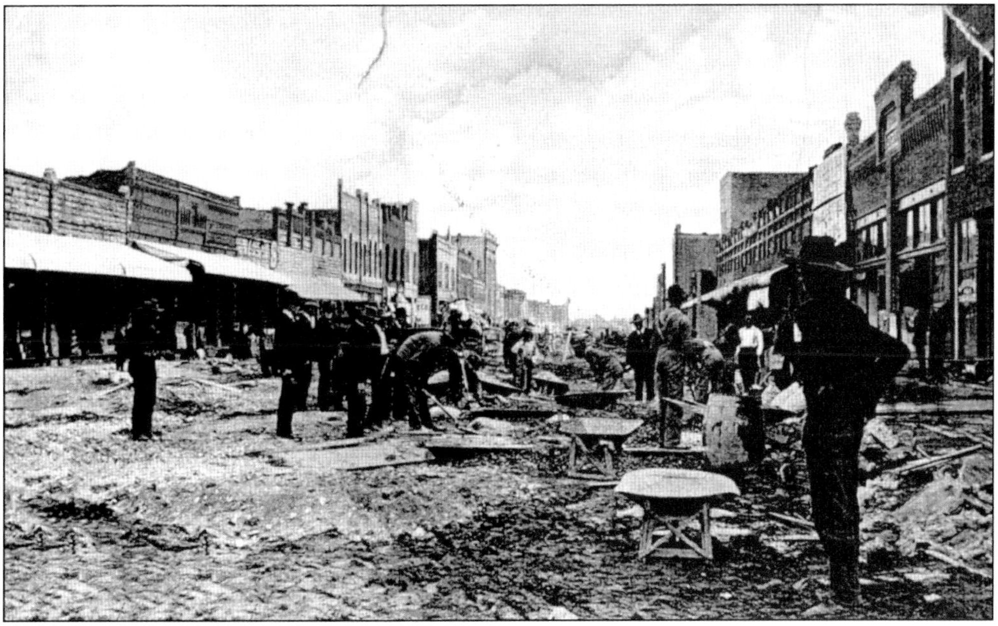

Ardmore streets were chokingly dusty in dry weather and axle-deep in mud during rainy weather. With asphalt so abundant and so near, the city fathers early on contracted to have the streets paved with asphalt. Within two years after incorporation in 1898, the main streets were either paved with asphalt or bricked. This picture shows a crew laying asphalt on Main Street. (Courtesy of the McGalliard Collection, Ardmore Public Library.)

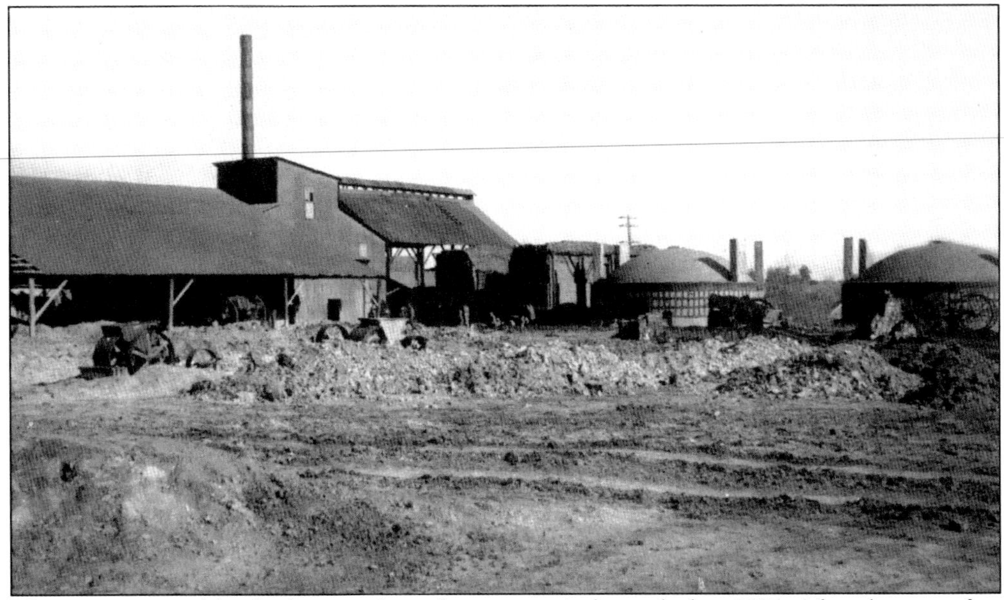

There were several brick plants such as this one in Ardmore before 1895. After the great fire, the ovens went into 24-hour operation to expedite rebuilding the downtown businesses. The original wooden buildings were built with locally manufactured brick. Later these same plants produced bricks, which paved the streets of Ardmore. Some of these streets still exist. (Courtesy of the McGalliard Collection, Ardmore Public Library.)

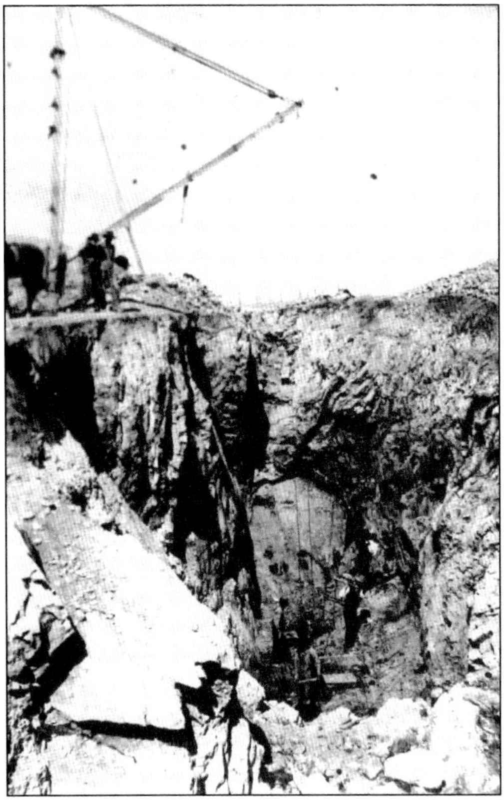

This photograph is of a coal mine located southwest of Ardmore. The Ardmore Coal Company was formed by Samuel Zuckermann, Max Munzesheimer, and B. C. Burney with Sam Daube and Max Westheimer becoming partners. With high sulphur content and vertical veins, the cost of mining outstripped the profit. A fire broke out at the entrance of the mine and burned for two years. (Courtesy of Ardmore Main Street Authority.)

Sam Palmer was an intruder. His three-year-old son, Charley, vividly remembered the day he arrived at the Ardmore station hoisted high against his father's shoulder. With his wife and five children, Sam moved into a batten house similar to the one in this photograph. Sam, a wealthy man when he arrived, secured a lease on land east of town where he raised cattle and built a two-story home. (Courtesy of Flora Palmer Foust.)

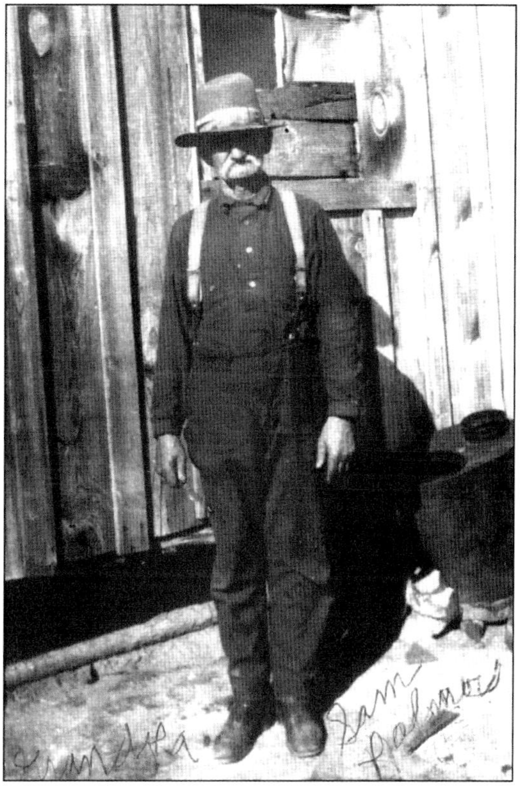

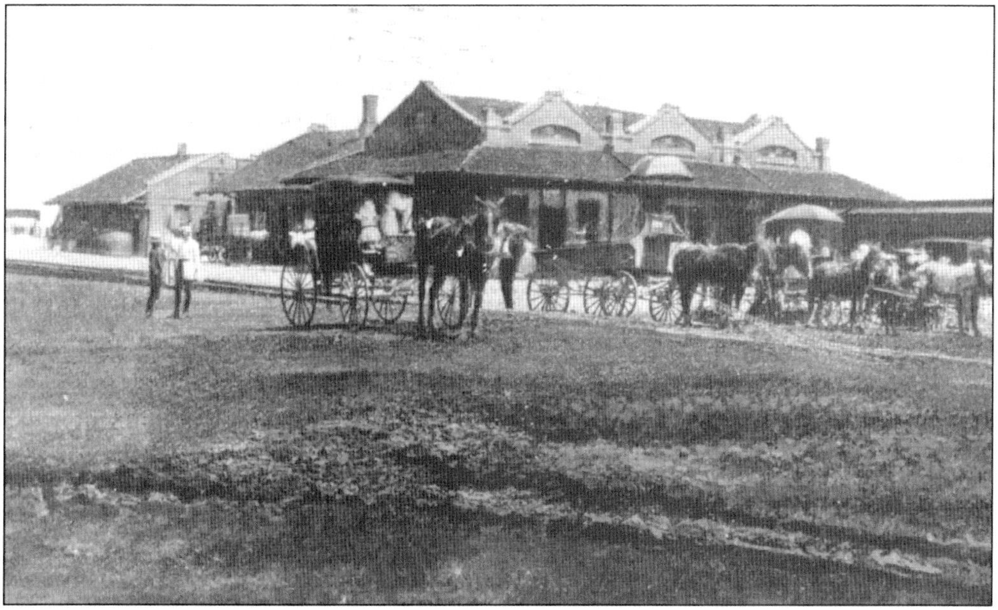

Two tracks have been laid in this later photograph. This is the depot where Sam Palmer arrived in 1894 or 1895. Thousands of intruders stepped off the train onto this station platform coming as professionals such as lawyers and doctors; coming as farmers and ranchers; and coming as businessmen to open mercantiles, newspapers, wagon yards, lumber mills, hotels, restaurants, and a myriad of other businesses. (Courtesy of the McGalliard Collection, Ardmore Public Library.)

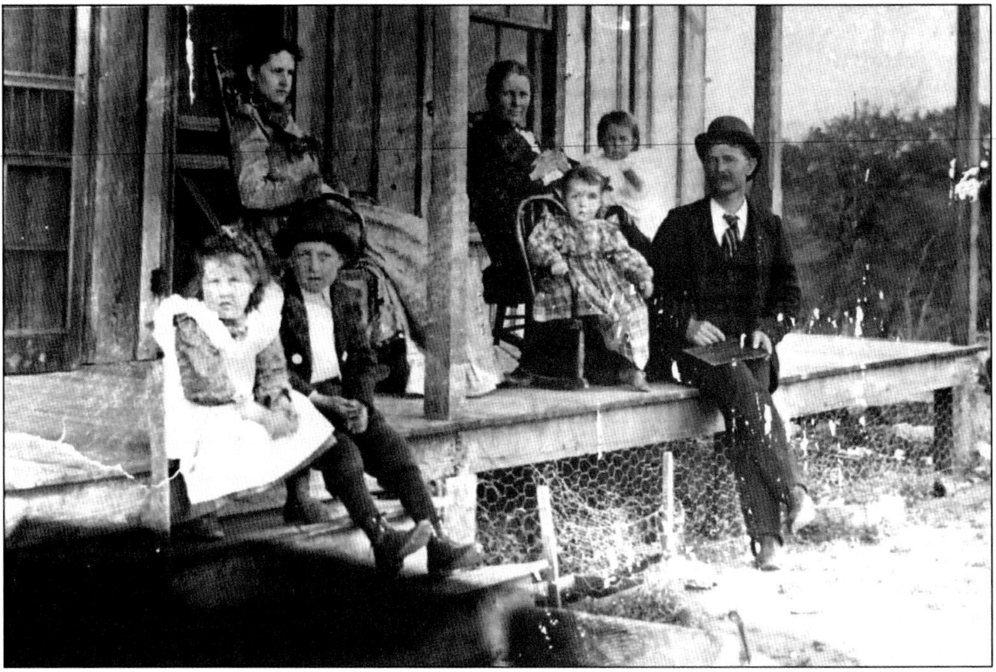

Here is another example of a board and batten house, which was a favorite of intruder families in the Chickasaw Nation because it was quick to build. Notice the chicken wire around the porch. Under the porch was a safe place to put chickens and even young pigs on occasion. Families typically enjoyed the cool of the evening on the porch. (Courtesy of Sally Gray.)

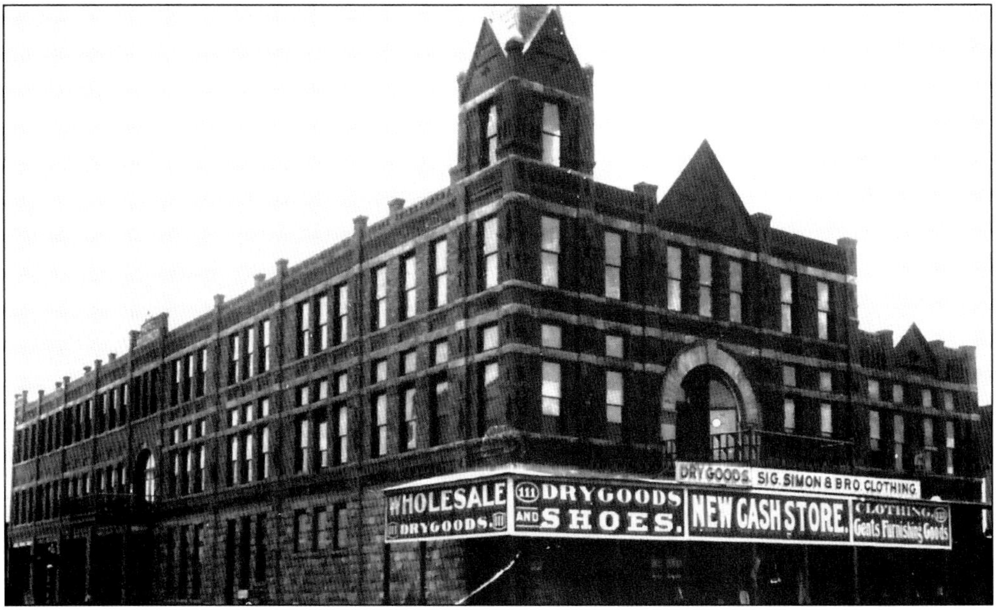

In the decade of the 1890s, many stores in Ardmore were credit stores, which meant that farmers and ranchers would literally sell their cash crop to the store and live off the credit for the next year. The New Cash Store, on the other hand, did not purchase crops and stocks but preferred a cash business, as affirmed in the store name. (Courtesy of the McGalliard Collection, Ardmore Public Library.)

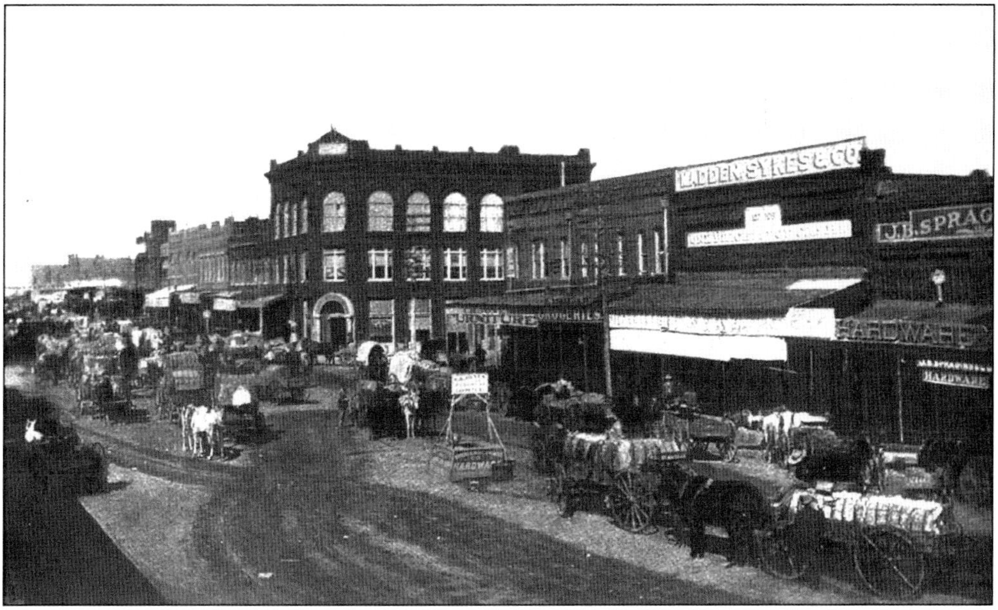

Being a railroad town enhanced the importance of cotton as a cash crop. Between 1888 and 1894, cotton production increased from 800 bales to 25,000 bales. By 1894, two cotton gins and one compress produced 1,000 bales a day. Most of this cotton was shipped via rail to Galveston and loaded onto ships bound for Liverpool, England. (Courtesy of Ardmore Main Street Authority.)

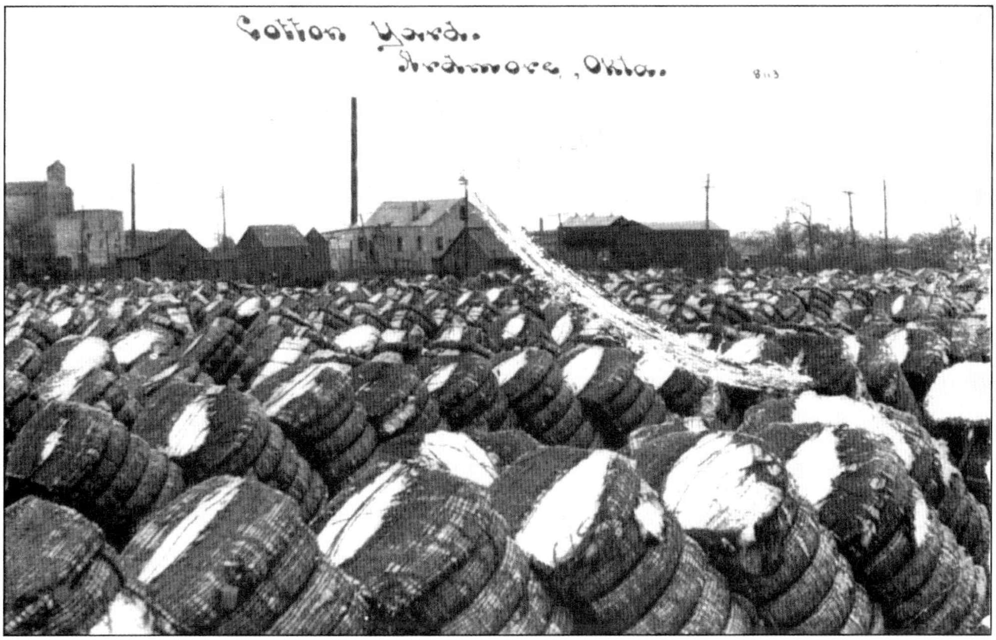

Bales of cotton are stacked in the compress yard waiting for transport. By 1900, more than 65,000 bales of cotton were being produced each season. There were at least five gins in Ardmore, including the National, Palmer, Blanton-Ray, Ball, and Ardmore gins, along with two compresses, including the Chickasaw Compress. Scenes such as this were typical. (Courtesy of Greater Southwest Historical Museum.)

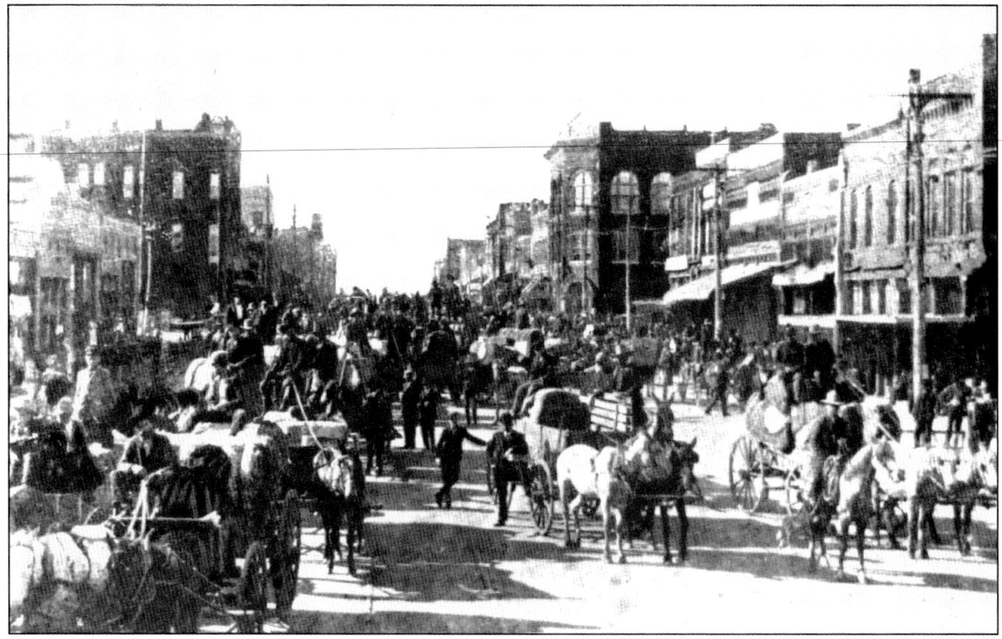

During cotton season, wagons lined up to be weighed in at the gin, congesting traffic on Main Street. Cotton filled Main Street from side to side and as far out as three miles during the height of cotton season. Buyers from foreign countries mingled among the farmers buying their bales and arranging to transport the cotton by rail to Galveston but also occasionally to New York. (Courtesy of Ardmore Main Street Authority.)

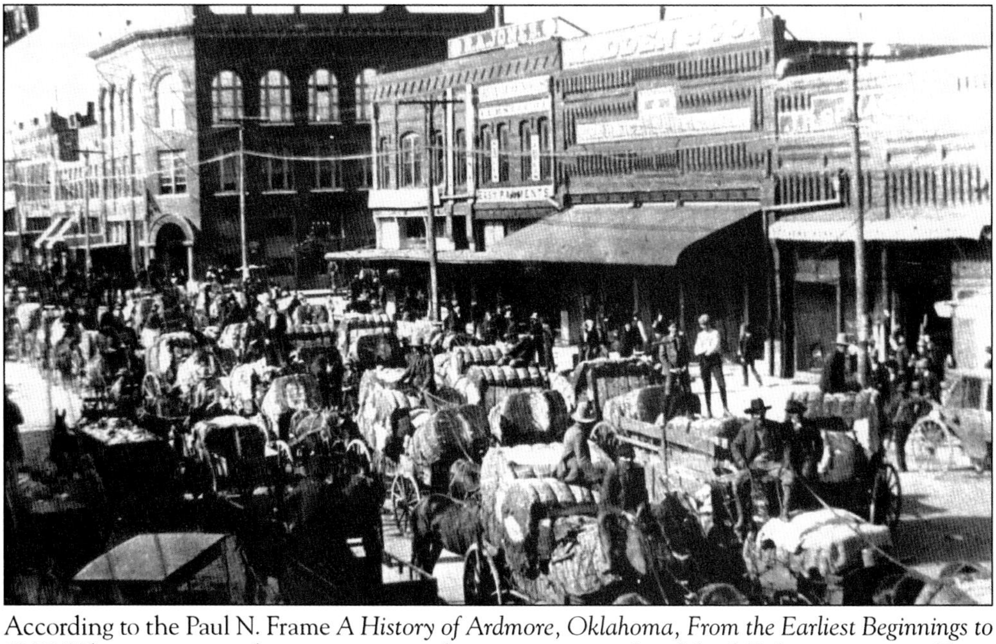

According to the Paul N. Frame *A History of Ardmore, Oklahoma, From the Earliest Beginnings to 1907*, "There was so much cotton in town during certain weeks of the fall that it was possible to walk on top of bales the length and breadth of Main Street without the feet ever once touching the ground." Ardmore was the largest inland cotton market in the world. By 1907, raw cotton sold for about $50 per bale. (Courtesy of Ardmore Main Street Authority.)

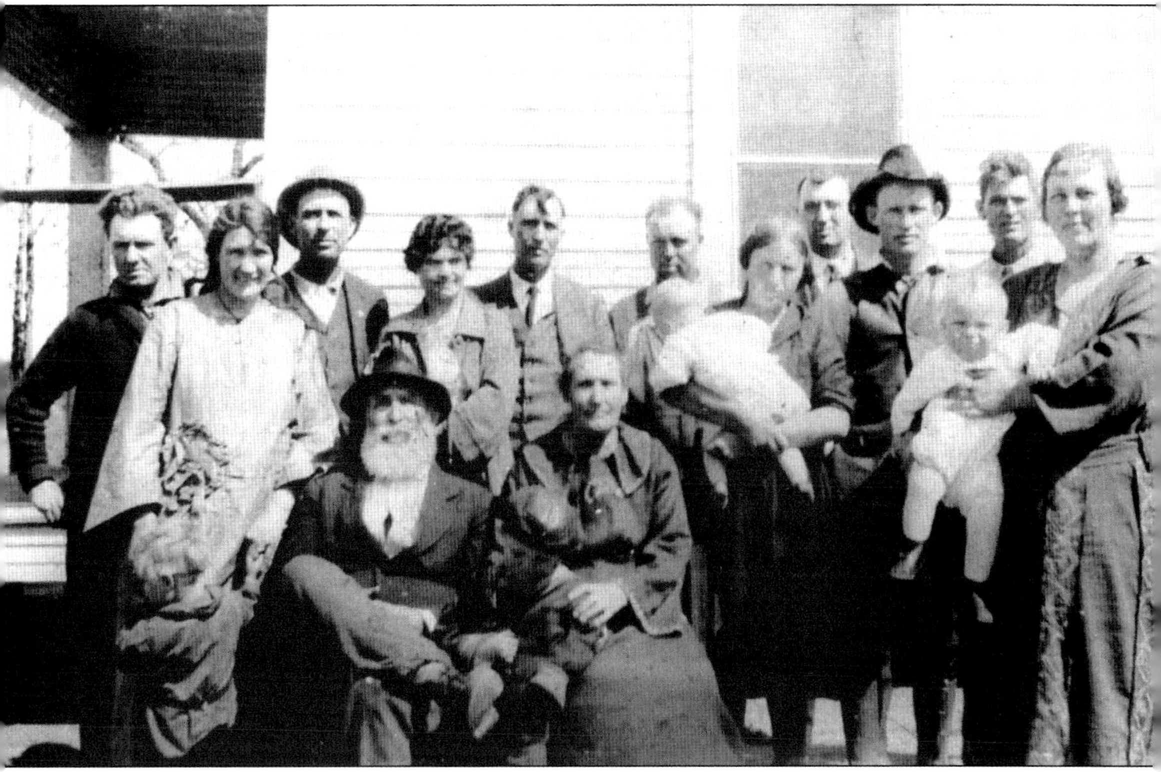

The Cole and Williams families were among the earliest intruders coming into Pickens County in the Ryan, Leon, and Jimtown area where they ranched and farmed. As with all intruders, they could not conduct legal contracts inside the Chickasaw Nation. Therefore, when Nancy Jane Williams and George Washington (G. W.) Cole decided to marry, their families traveled to Gainesville, Texas, to the Cook County Courthouse. G. W. and Nancy Jane raised cotton on land they leased north of Ardmore along Refinery Road. After statehood, G. W. was able to purchase most of the land he had been leasing. They raised 10 children, 7 boys and 3 girls. Sons Riley and Will became teachers; Marvin became an evangelist in the Enon Association. There was a small graveyard, the Yates Cemetery, located on the acreage when G. W. purchased the land; and that is where he and his wife along with several children and grandchildren are buried. G. W. offered 10 acres around this little cemetery to the county commissioners to preserve the burial ground. After G. W.'s death, the name changed to Cole Cemetery. (Courtesy of Flora Palmer Foust.)

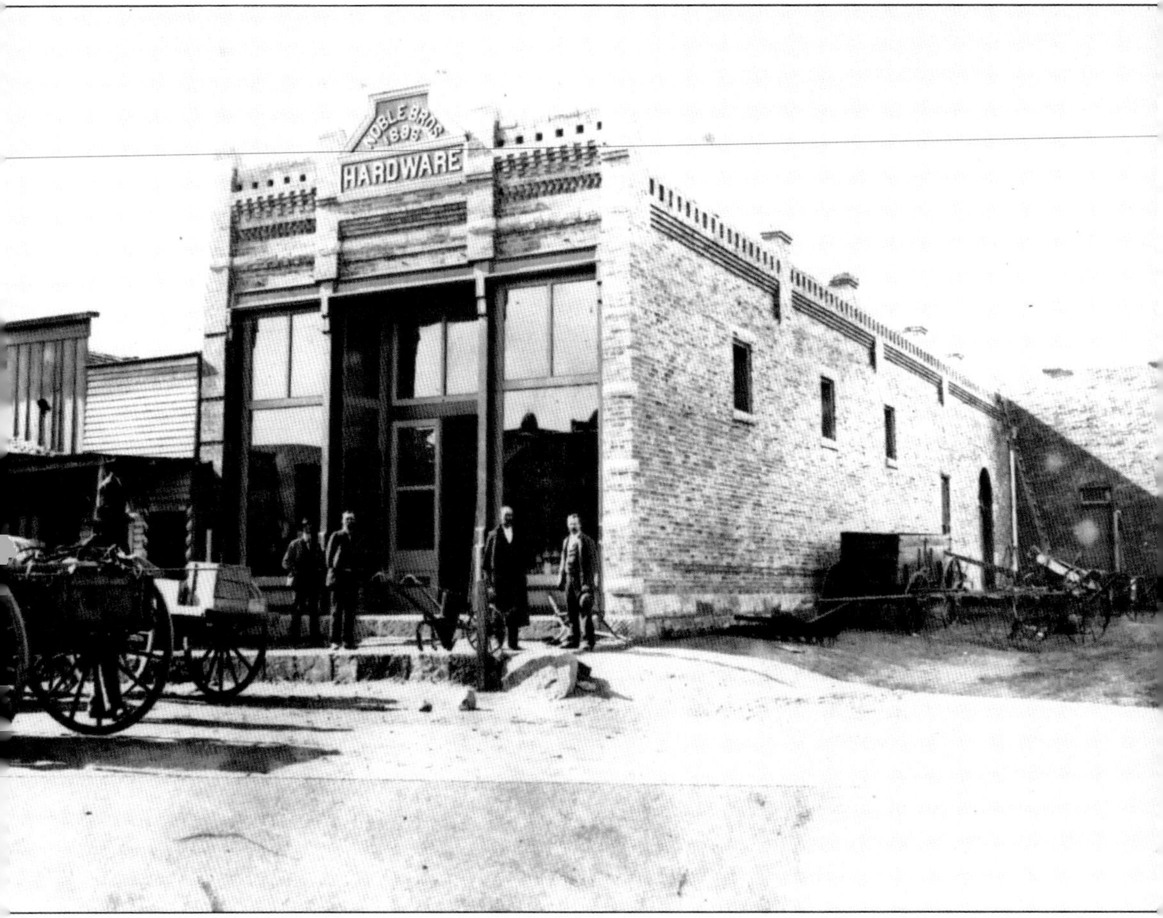

Ardmore was eager to be born in 1887 with the coming of the railroad, and it was eager to be reborn after the great fire. The wooden structures that had burned so quickly in April 1895 were replaced by rock and brick buildings. Rebuilt of stone in 1896, the Noble Hardware store fronted Main Street near the depot. (Courtesy of Greater Southwest Historical Museum.)

Two

An Incorporated City

Because much of Indian Territory had been part of Arkansas Territory prior to 1832, Arkansas statutes were applied to noncitizens (whites and blacks) in Indian Country. Additionally, businesses could file for incorporation under Arkansas Statutes, as did Ardmore's First National Bank. On October 18, 1890, Ardmore leaders, including W. A. Ledbetter and C. L. Herbert, applied for status as a city of the second class under the United States Court for the Indian Territory, Third Judicial Division. A city of the second class had a population more than 2,500 and less than 5,000. The federal court for Indian Territory at Muskogee denied the application. Without incorporation status, a community could not levy or collect taxes to provide such services as city government, public schools, sanitation laws, or fire and police protection. Following the denial for incorporation, prominent Ardmore citizens pushed for the city to provide needed services anyway. The Ardmore Board of Trade had been organized among downtown businessmen. Their powers were limited because the membership could only make recommendations. They did, however, hire a night watchman and attempt to remove some of the many hogs that scavenged on Main Street and lived under many of the businesses. In 1895, a second application for incorporation was filed in the same court and again denied. Finally, in April 1898, Judge Hosea Townsend used the Arkansas Statutes to declare Ardmore an incorporated city.

The first act of the incorporated city of Ardmore was to establish city government. An election was quickly organized, and from a field of 30 candidates city officers were elected. They immediately began the work of writing ordinances that would govern the city. Fire and police departments were authorized. Waterworks, a sanitation system, and a medical board were established. One of the most important acts of the new government was organizing a public school system. Private schools in Ardmore were educating maybe 500 children, but at least another 1,000 were not receiving any formal education. The Ardmore Electric Light and Telephone Company was organized and began installing electric lighting and telephone wires in the downtown area.

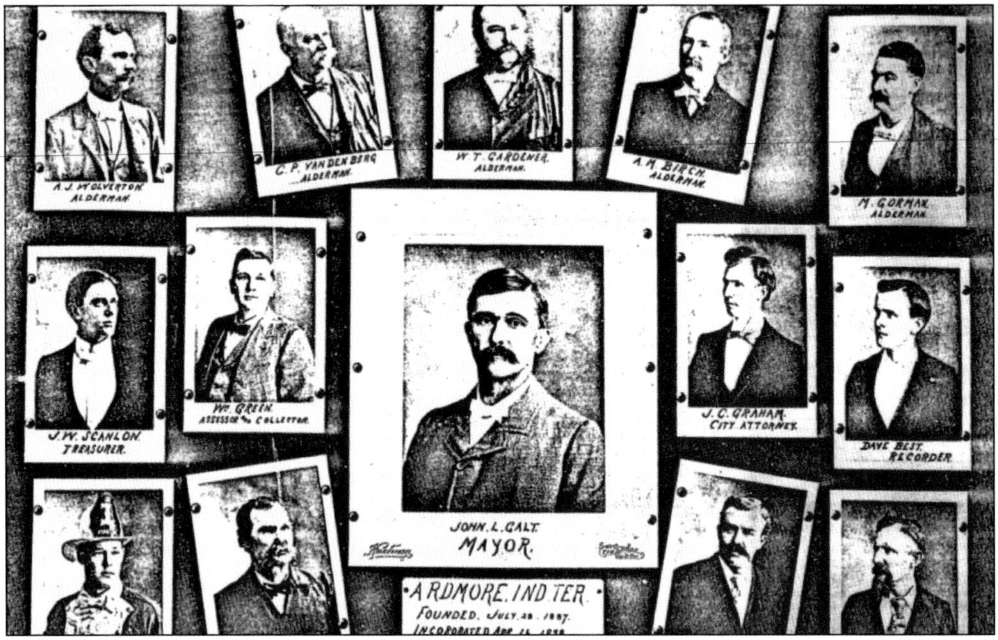

After two failed attempts to incorporate the federal courts in Indian Territory, a third attempt was successful. Judge Hosea Townsend declared Ardmore an incorporated city under the Statutes of Arkansas. On July 5, 1898, John L. Galt was elected mayor with aldermen Dr. W. T. Gardner, Dr. A. J. Wolverton, A. M. Burch, C. P. VanDenberg, and Michael Gorman. The city officials were sworn in on July 6, 1898. (Courtesy of Ardmore Main Street Authority.)

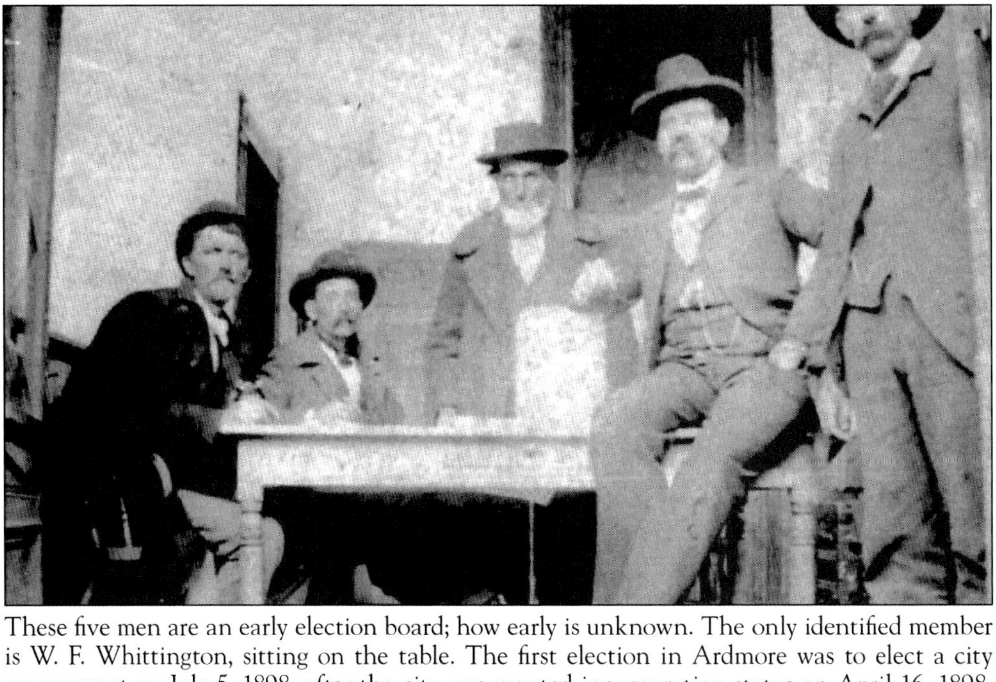

These five men are an early election board; how early is unknown. The only identified member is W. F. Whittington, sitting on the table. The first election in Ardmore was to elect a city government on July 5, 1898, after the city was granted incorporation status on April 16, 1898. The election was set up by W. A. Ledbetter, Alexis Eddleman, and W. F. Bowman, who were the incorporation agents. (Courtesy of Sally Gray.)

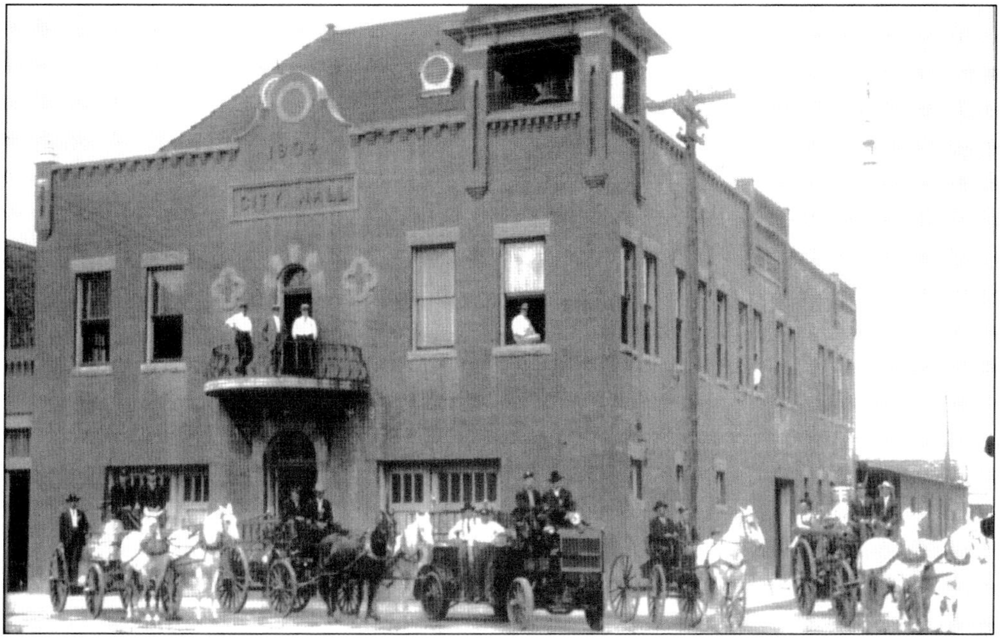

Ardmore's first city hall was built in 1904 at the current location. In comparing this picture and the next, the view in this photograph is toward the west. The courthouse, which sits west of city hall, was not built until 1907. The building in the background may be the jail, paid for by citizen donations prior to statehood and becoming the Carter County Jail after statehood. (Courtesy of Sally Gray.)

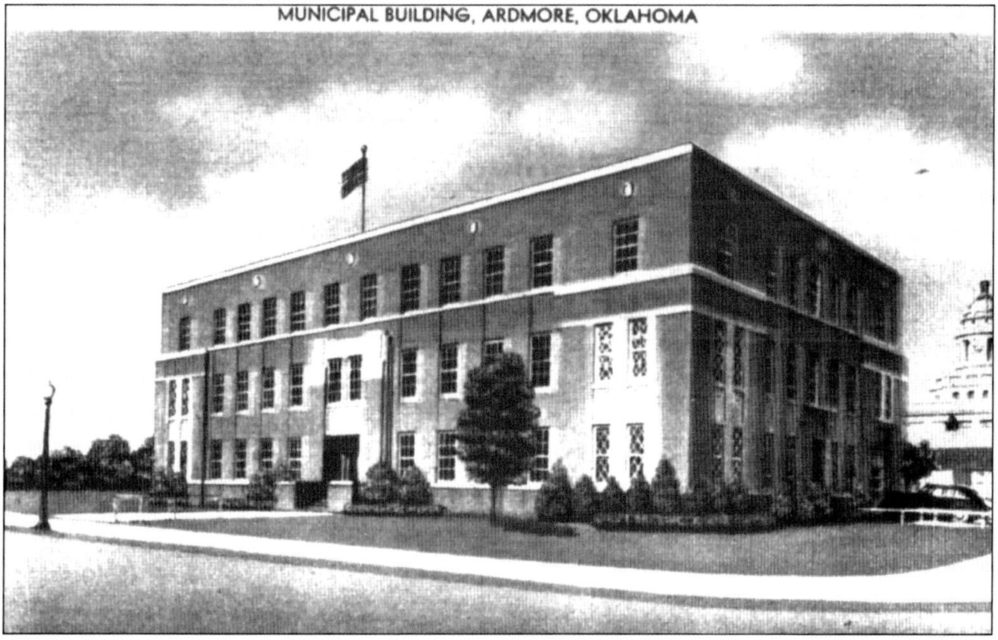

Built in the same location as the original city hall, this building still serves as the Ardmore City Hall. For many years it housed the police department, city jail, and fire department. City offices and the police department remain, but the fire station has moved to the west side of town. (Courtesy of Ardmore Main Street Authority.)

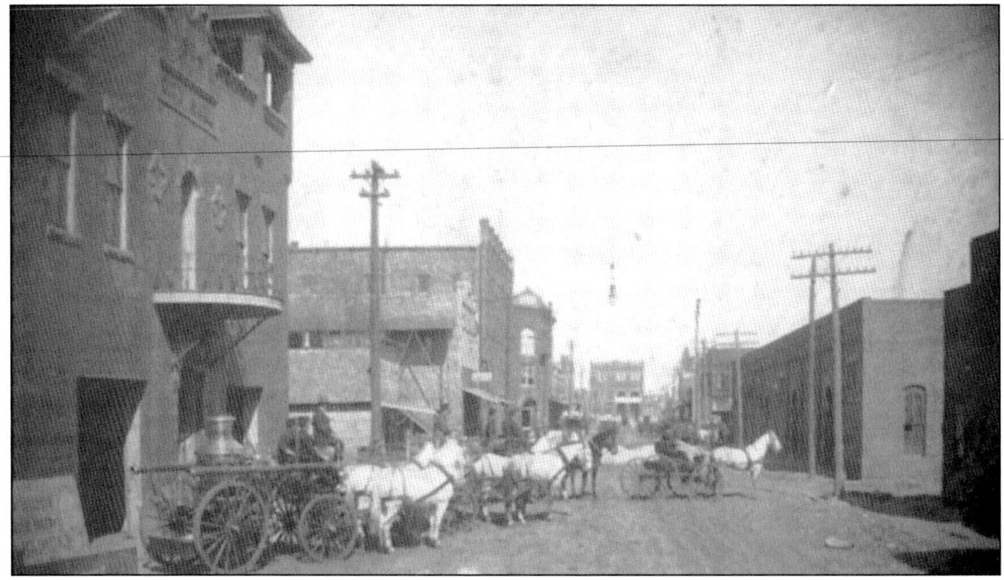

The view is north along Washington Street toward Main Street. New fire equipment is on display. The first fire chief was John S. O'Mealy, who had also been the first stationmaster at the Santa Fe station. The bell tower is visible on the upper right corner of the city hall building, constructed in 1904. City government and the fire department were housed in this building until the 1940s. (Courtesy of Sally Gray.)

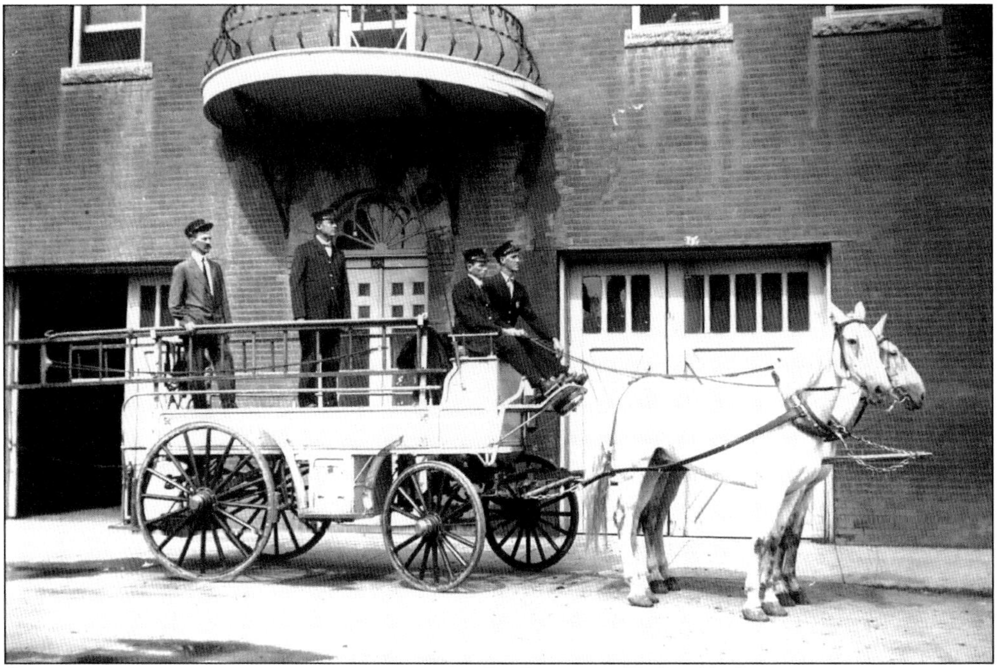

Prior to 1895, Ardmore had no fire department or any other type of formal government. After the great fire, a volunteer fire department began with 23 members. Being a volunteer fireman became a position of social importance for young men. This photograph of a new ladder truck was made sometime after 1904, as the first city hall is in the background. (Courtesy of Greater Southwest Historical Museum.)

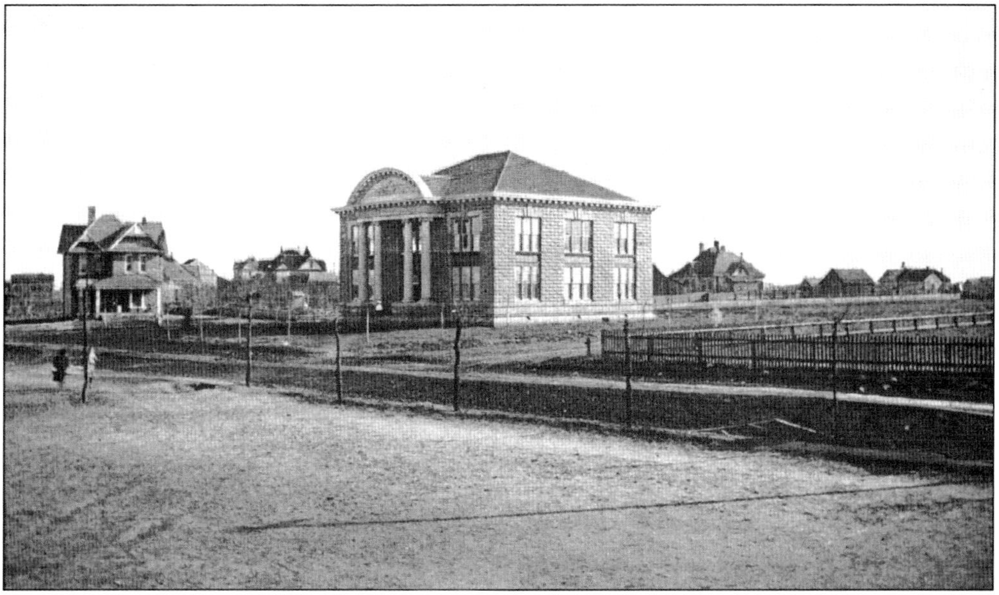

The Carnegie Library, built in 1905, was a two-story building until a tornado tore off the top. Mrs. Hosea Townsend, Dr. Charles Evans, (Ardmore City Schools superintendent), and mayor C. L. Anderson sought funding from Andrew Carnegie. The library sat vacant for a year, during which time it suffered damage from weather and vandals. City funds purchased 300 volumes in 1896. (Courtesy of Greater Southwest Historical Museum.)

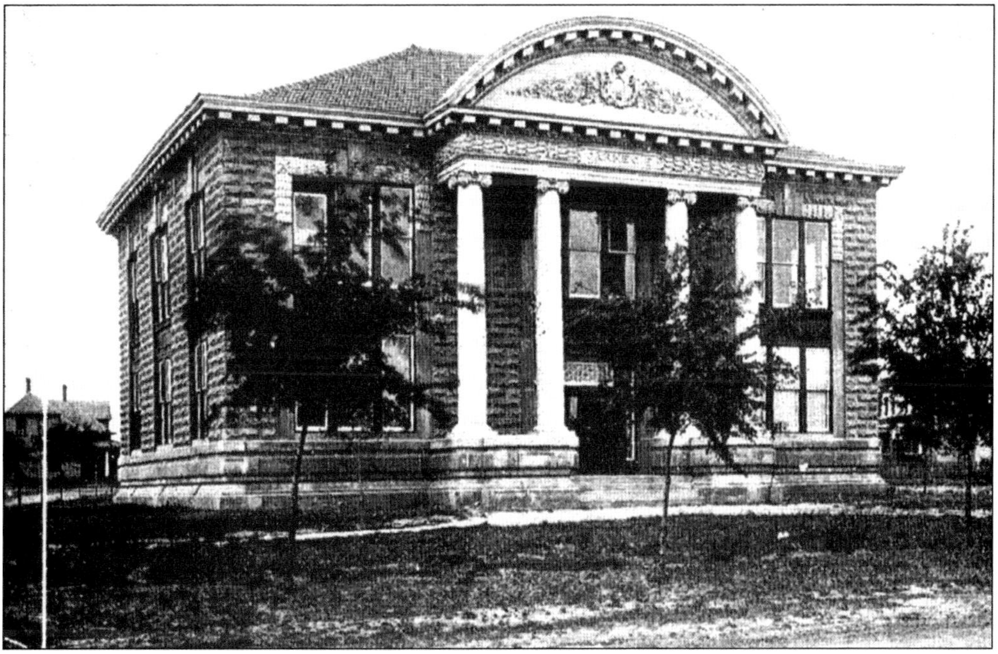

Later in 1906, the Orio Club donated another 350 books and the Sons of Confederate Veterans donated the Masters of Southern Literature, a 30-volume set. The second floor housed Ardmore High School for a time. The building housed the Carnegie and Chickasaw Library System collections. When these two collections divided, the Carnegie collection became Ardmore Public Library. The building now houses the Garden Club. (Courtesy of Sally Gray.)

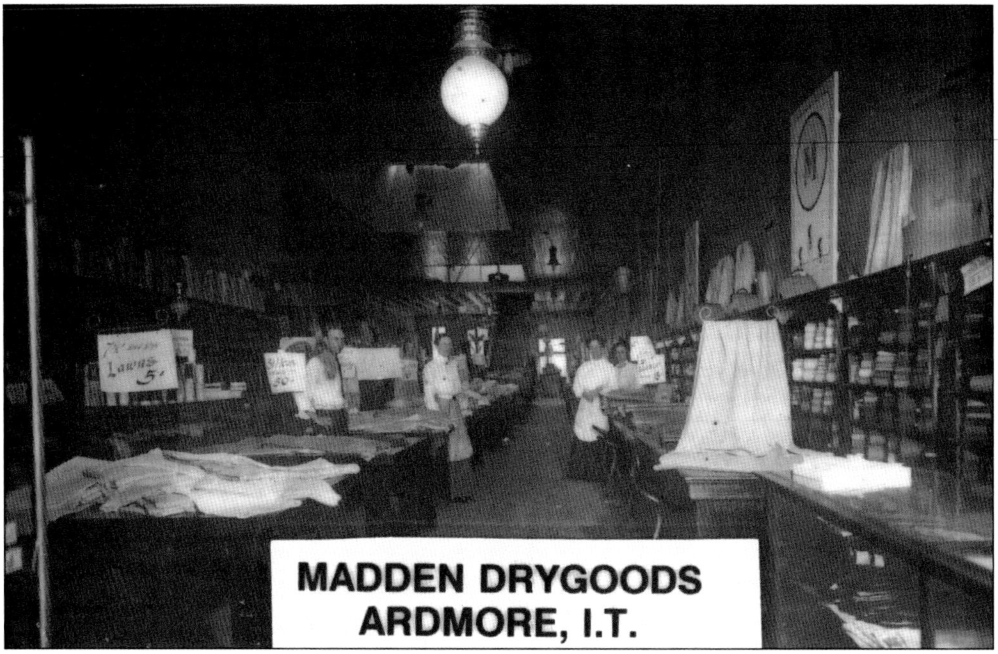

The Madden Store was a dry goods store with merchandise displayed in shelves along the wall and in display cases. Shoppers would stand at the counter and call off needed items, which the shopkeeper would gather up on the counter near the register. The customer took a wooden box or a woven basket into the store to carry out the items purchased. (Courtesy of Greater Southwest Historical Museum.)

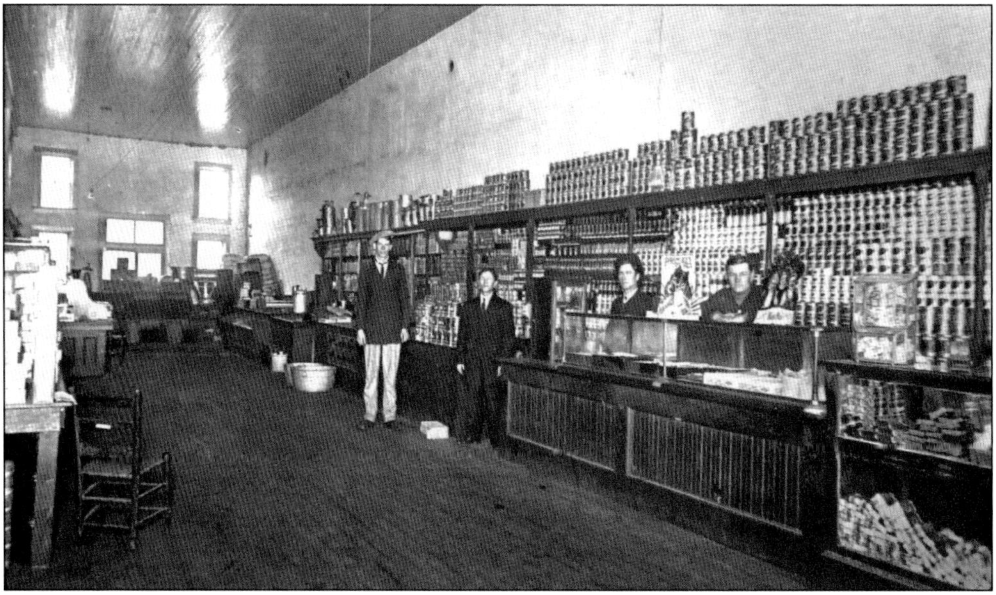

This store may have belonged to the Moore family or to Craddock and Bates, or A. P. Staples, or J. D. Love, or any of dozens of other early grocery merchants. It has the wooden floors so typical of downtown businesses in early Ardmore. The earliest buildings, those that burned so quickly in the great fire of 1895, were made of soft cottonwood lumber. Later buildings had hardwood floors and were constructed with brick and native sandstone. (Courtesy of Sally Gray.)

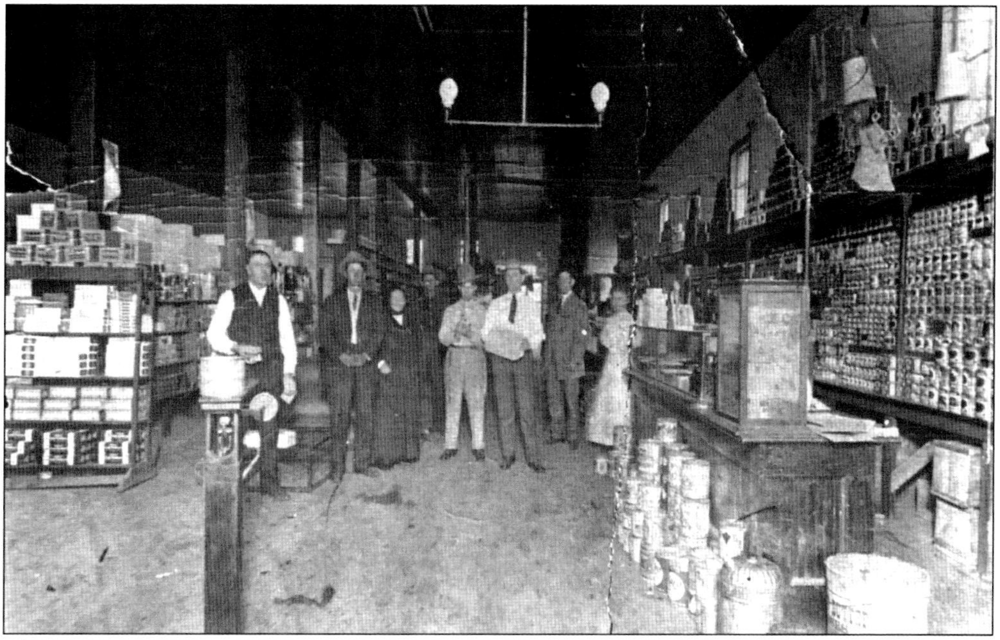

The earliest grocers and merchants such as Zuckerman and Frensley received their goods via wagon from Dennison and Gainesville in Texas. As soon as the railroad tracks were laid, goods came by rail. This mercantile may have belonged to J. Matt Moore, grandfather to Dorn Moore. The Moore family operated grocery stores in the Ardmore area for many decades. (Courtesy of Sally Gray.)

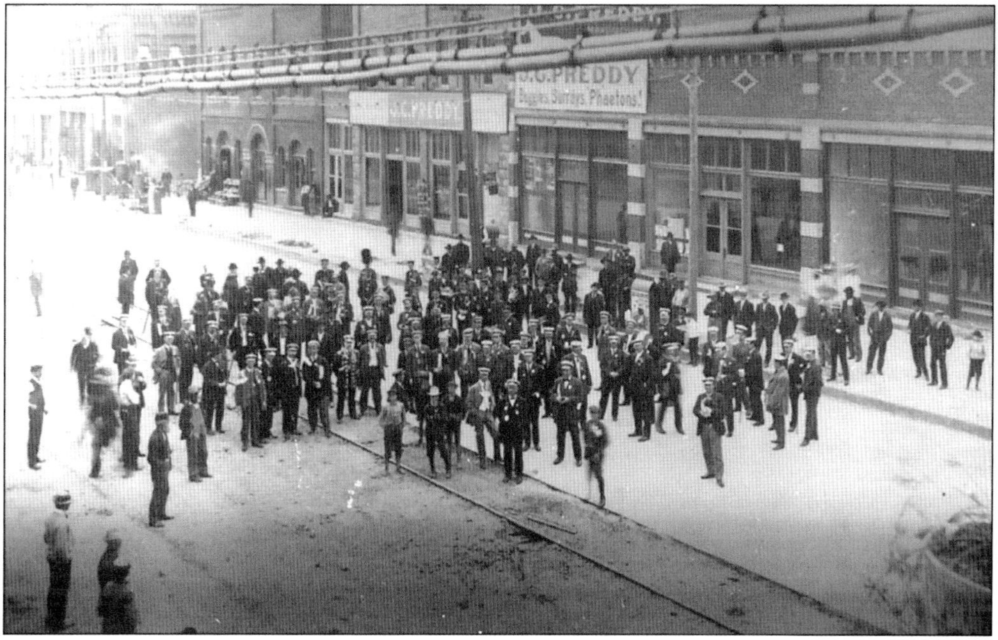

Men in uniform gather in the middle of street over cable car tracks as if they were gathering for a convention group photograph. Since Ardmore was one of the most important cities in Indian Territory and then in the new young state, it is probable that either the fire department or the police department sponsored a convention. (Courtesy of Ardmore Main Street Authority.)

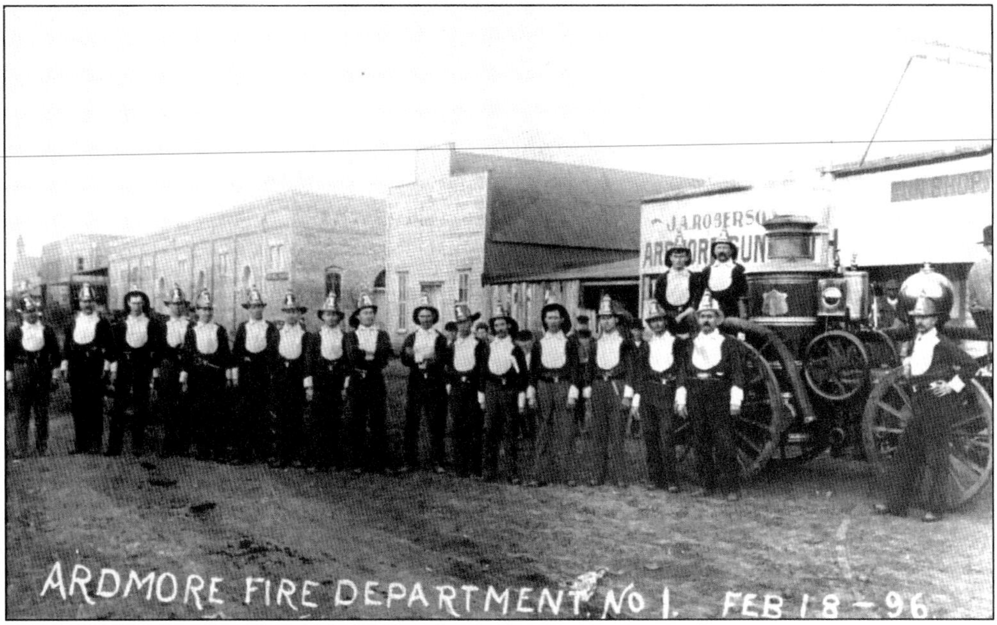

Ardmore organized its fire department in 1896 after the great fire of 1895 and a second fire east of the track in 1896. Although the community had no legal right to set up a fire department, 25 volunteers under Chief J. S. O'Mealy began training. Businessmen put up money for a steamer, which was used until about 1915, when it was placed into storage. (Courtesy of Main Street Authority.)

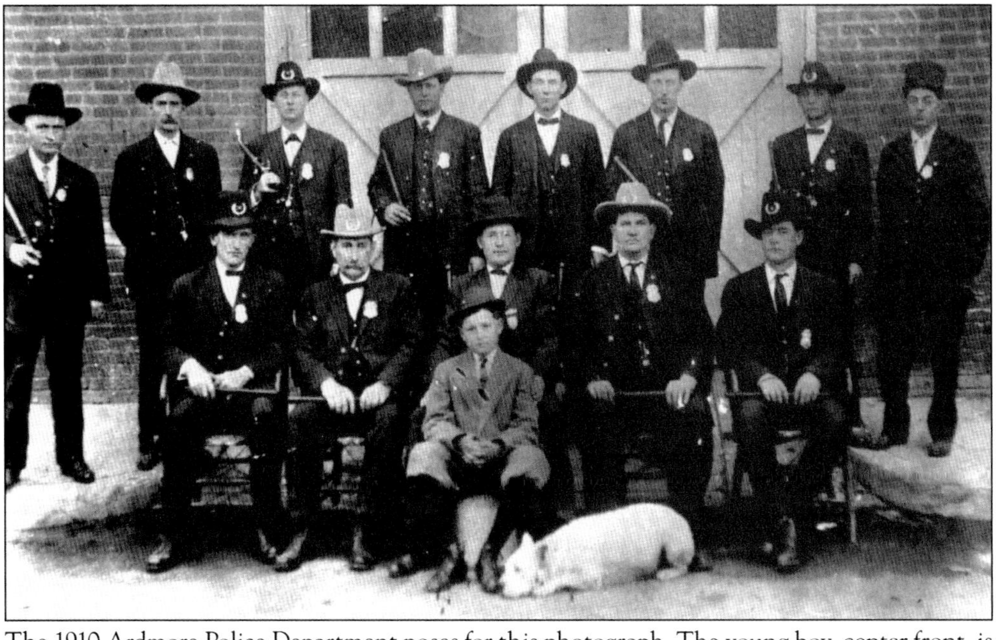

The 1910 Ardmore Police Department poses for this photograph. The young boy, center front, is Raymond Garrett, son of police chief Buck Garrett, seated immediately behind. At Raymond's feet is his dog, Old Nuisance. From left to right are (first row) Fred Emerson, Max Butcher, Buck Garrett, ? Redmon, and ? Lathrop; (second row) ? Roberts, unidentified, Jake Williams, Walter Stroud, Tom Tippett, Tom Carter, unidentified, and Gene Cook. (Courtesy of Sally Gray.)

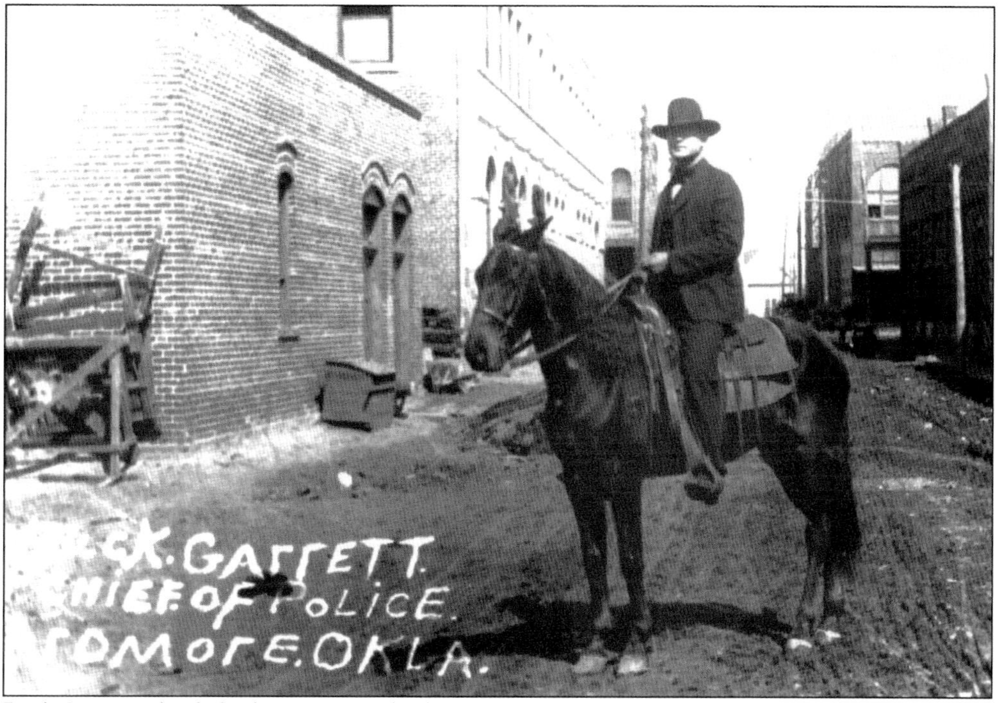

Buck Garrett, chief of police, poses on his horse. Garrett, nephew to Pat Garrett, became Ardmore police chief in 1904. This photograph was taken from the northeast lawn of the Carter County Courthouse looking northward along B Street toward Main Street. In the background, the corner buildings on Main Street were replaced with the Exchange Bank and the First National Bank buildings following the 1915 explosion. (Courtesy of Ardmore Main Street Authority.)

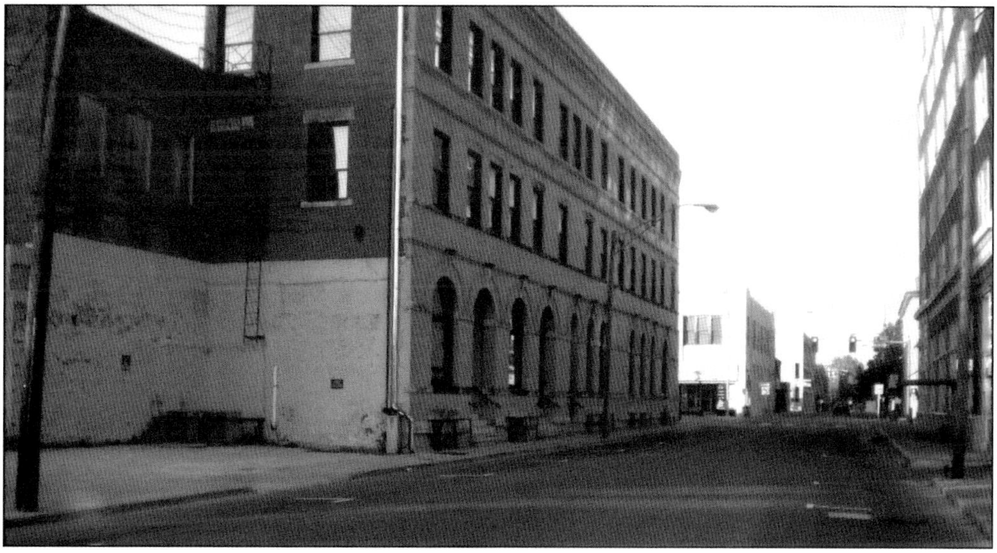

In comparing this current photograph to the picture of Buck Garrett on his horse, it can be seen that the building to the right of Sheriff Garrett is no longer in existence. The other building can be identified by its arched windows. Farther down the street, across Main Street, the building in the first picture has been replaced by the Exchange Bank building, erected after the 1915 explosion. (Author's collection.)

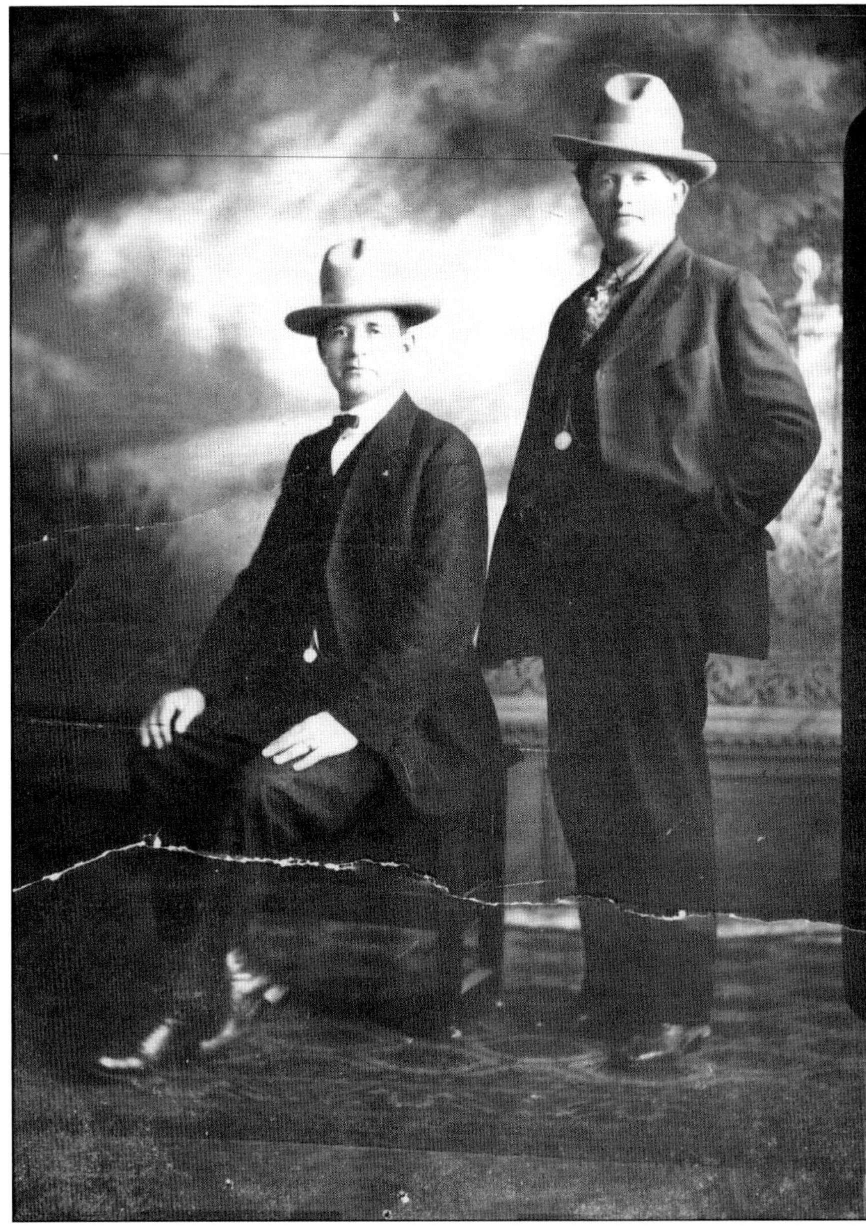

As a deputy United States marshal, Buck Garrett was involved with the apprehension and killing of Bill Dalton in northwest Carter County. He remained a deputy United States marshal from 1894 until 1905. Garrett rarely carried a gun, but he was certainly capable of using one against outlaws when needed. In 1910, he was elected Carter County sheriff, holding the post for five successive terms until 1922 when he was defeated in a hotly contested race. Some believe his defeat was due to his opposition of activities by the Ku Klux Klan in the southern Oklahoma area. Garrett died in 1929 after a stroke. Deputy David Monticello "Bud" Ballew was a gunfighter as well as a lawman. While serving as a deputy for Garrett, Ballew killed at least five men who resisted arrest. He was himself killed in a shootout in Wichita Falls, Texas, on May 5, 1922, when that city's police chief tried to arrest Ballew for disturbing the peace. (Courtesy of Main Street Authority.)

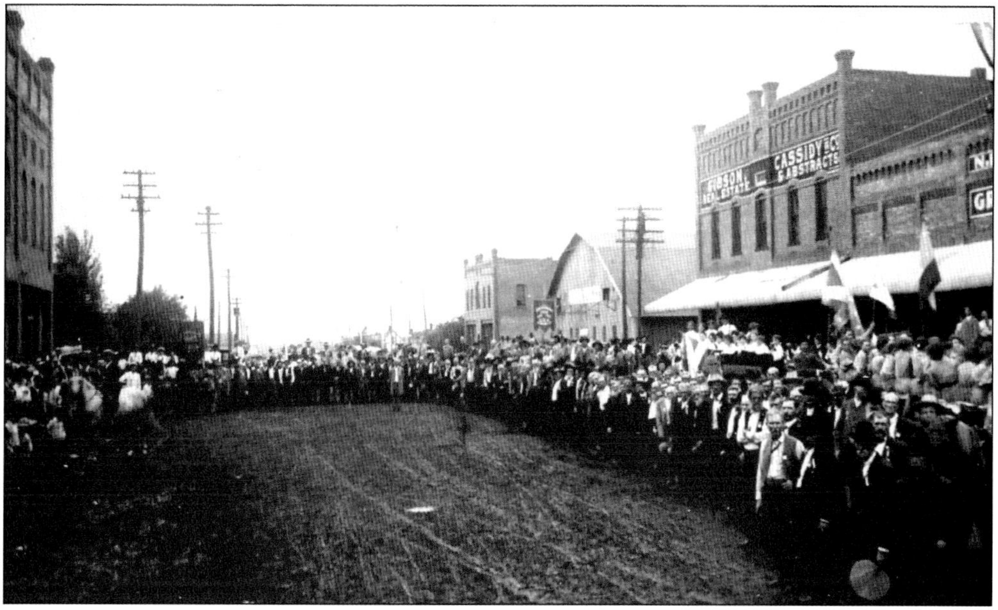

The men posing for the camera in this semicircle appear to be lawmen who have gathered in Ardmore for a convention. With Ardmore being the seat of a federal court, it is likely lawmen did congregate here on a regular basis. The rider of the white horse is probably Buck Garrett. The Royal Roller Rink can be seen on the right with its peaked roof. (Courtesy of Ardmore Main Street Authority.)

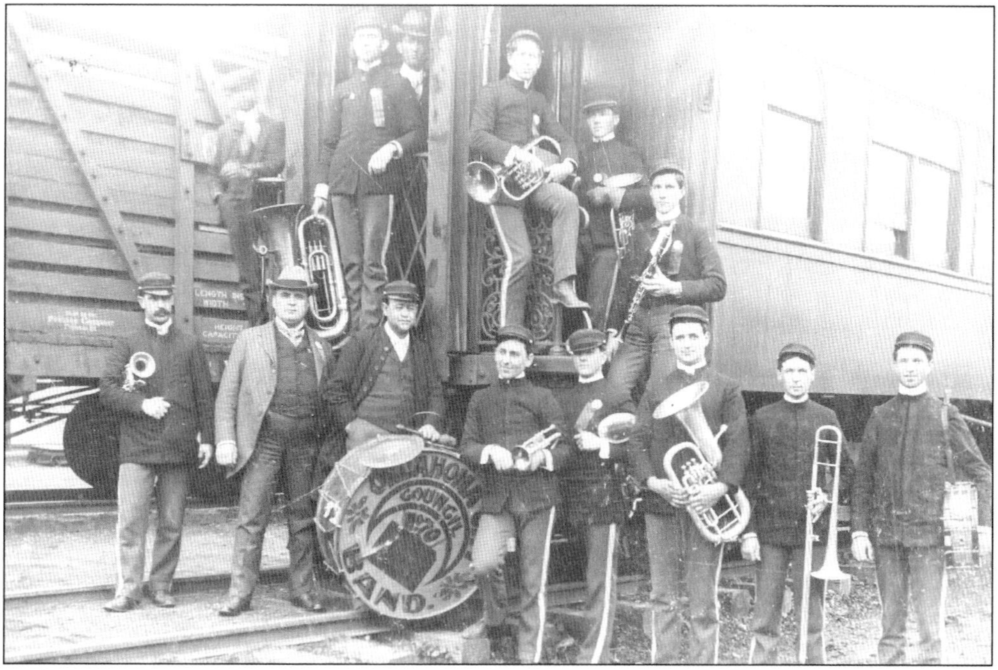

Ardmore has always loved a parade with decorated wagons, elephants, military, law enforcement, and bands. The Oklahoma City Council Band traveled throughout Oklahoma and surrounding states for band competitions. They performed in Ardmore on their way to Dallas. (Courtesy of Sally Gray.)

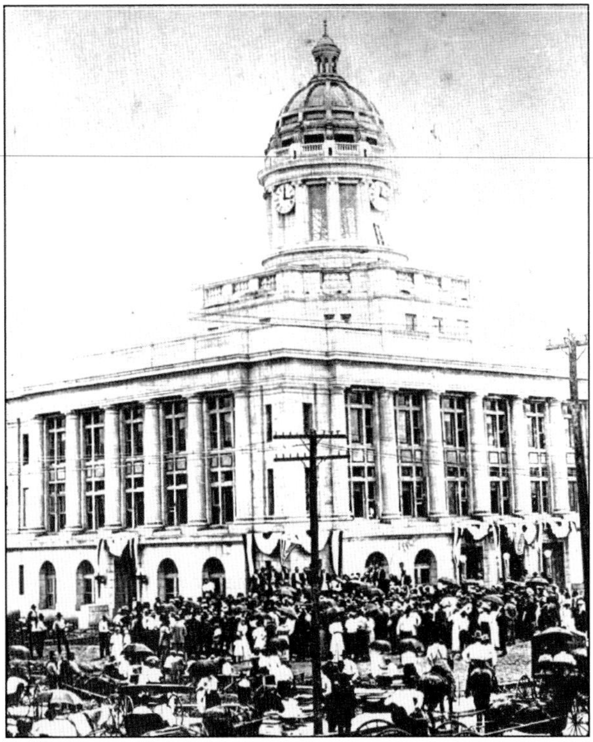

Oklahoma became a state in 1907. The Carter County Courthouse was completed in 1911. The neoclassic style was augmented by Doric columns and an ornate tower and dome. On September 4, 1911, hundreds of people gathered at the festooned granite building to commemorate the laying of the cornerstone. A marker on the lawn states that Lewis Robert Marston laid sidewalks throughout Ardmore, including around the new courthouse. (Courtesy of Sally Gray.)

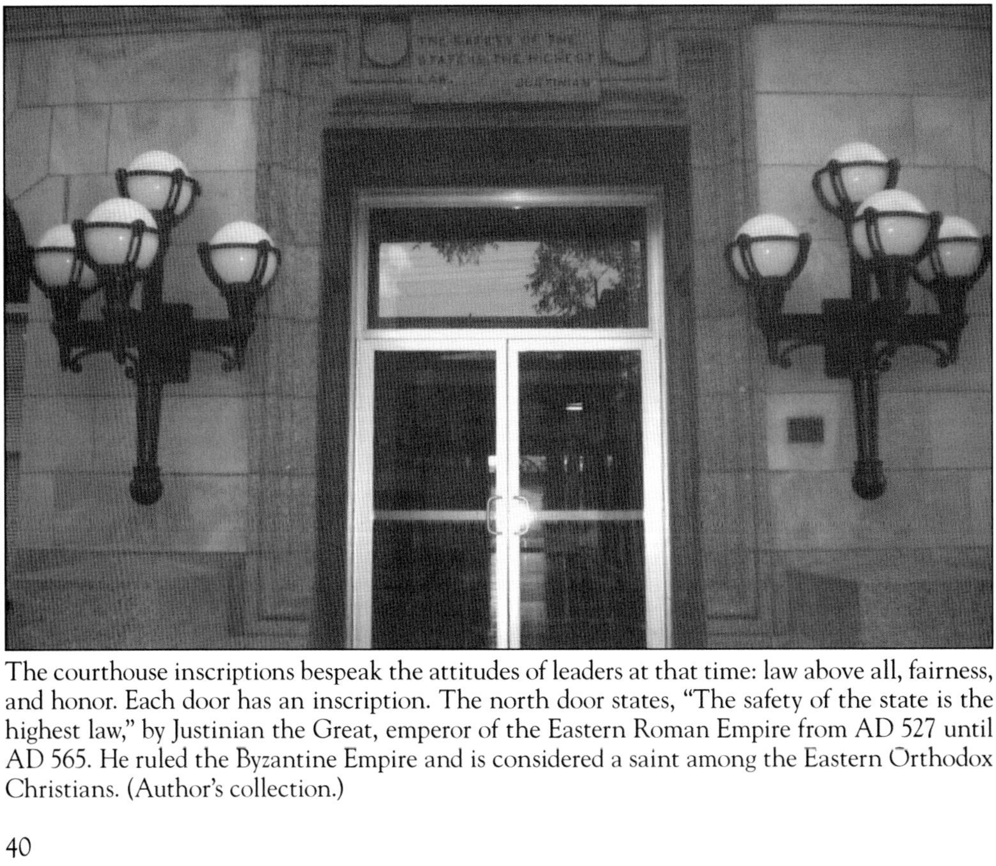

The courthouse inscriptions bespeak the attitudes of leaders at that time: law above all, fairness, and honor. Each door has an inscription. The north door states, "The safety of the state is the highest law," by Justinian the Great, emperor of the Eastern Roman Empire from AD 527 until AD 565. He ruled the Byzantine Empire and is considered a saint among the Eastern Orthodox Christians. (Author's collection.)

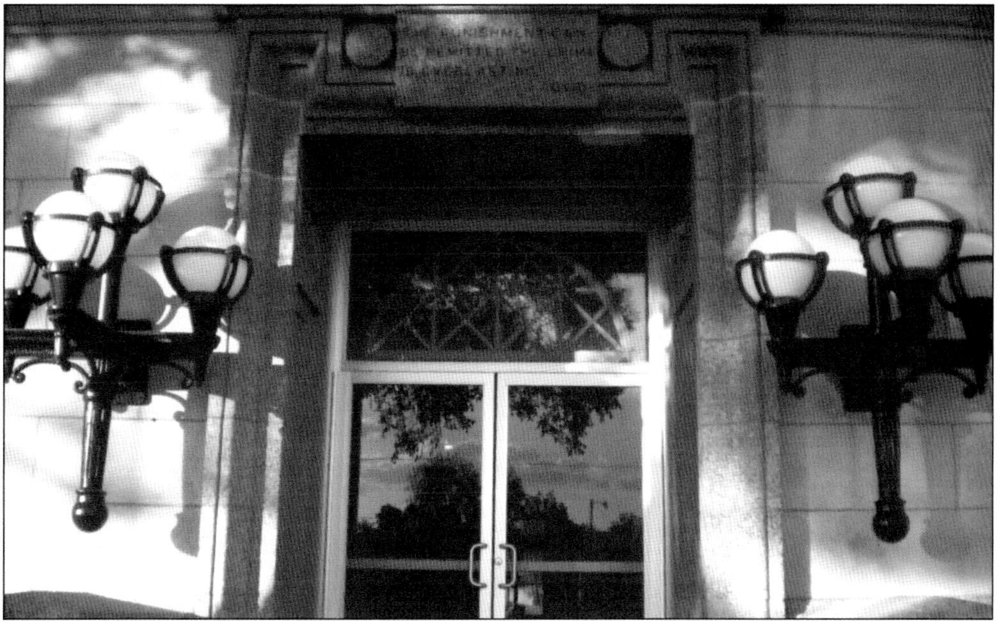

The south inscription reads, "The punishment can be remitted, the crime is everlasting," by Ovid, a Roman poet banished to the Black Sea. He may have known of the planned assassination of Julius Caesar. On the west there were originally three doors. The left inscription, "He who does not prevent a crime when he can encourages it," is by Seneca, a philosopher from the Roman Stoic period. (Author's collection.)

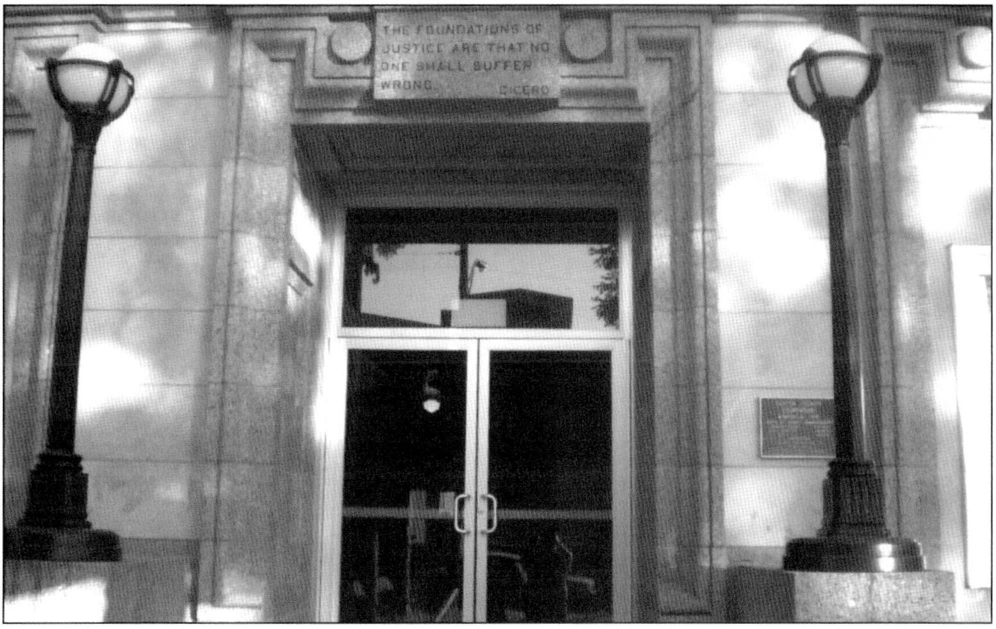

Seneca was banished by one emperor but returned as tutor to Nero. Inscribed over the center door is "The foundations of justice are that no one shall suffer wrong," by Marcus Tullius Cicero, who lived in the last century before Christ. He was a Roman statesman, lawyer, philosopher, and orator who promoted a republican form of government as opposed to the dictatorship of Julius Caesar. (Author's collection.)

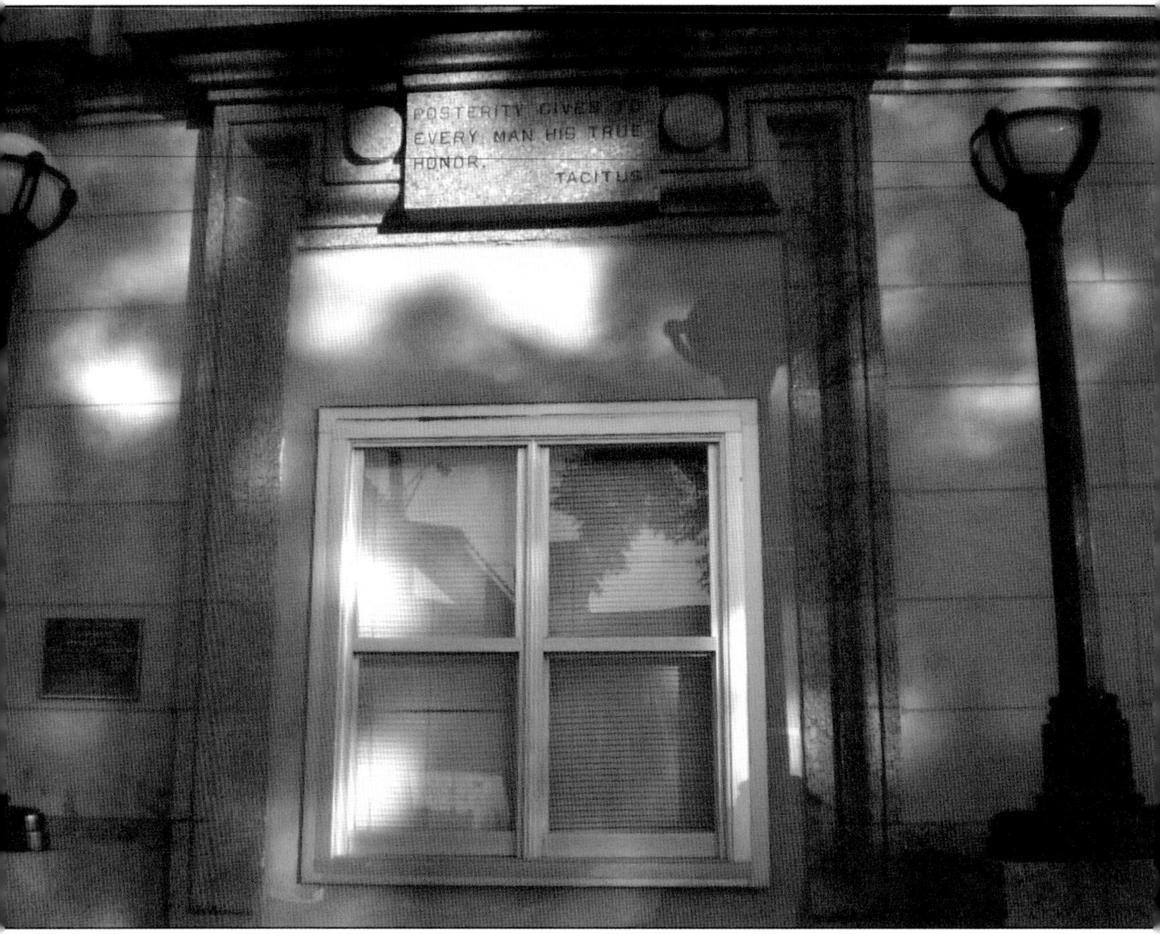

Inside the west entrance is a small room built over the left door. The north wall is black marble with a Latin inscription that translates, "These virtues will be for you, To impose the custom of law, To spare those who have been subjected, And to subdue the haughty," by Virgil, Roman poet and author of the epic poem "Aeneid." After statehood, county officials had to find space in which to carry on the business of the county. They chose the federal courthouse, which had been constructed in 1898 on Main Street. The new county's government soon outgrew the space in the old building. A bond issue of $125,000 was passed by county voters in 1909. Oklahoma City architects Layton, Wemyss, Smith and Hawk drew the plans, and Gill Construction Company brought the building to life. (Author's collection.)

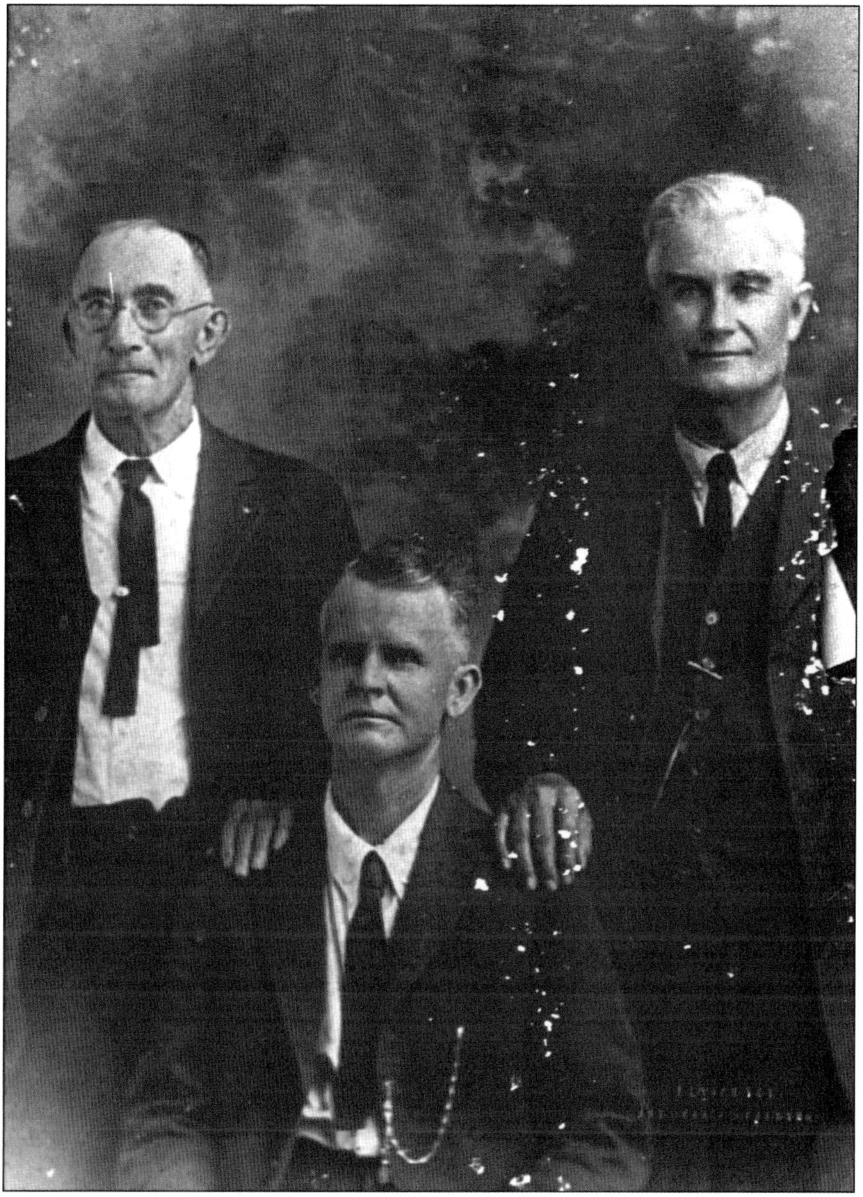

Carter County is divided into three districts under three commissioners. District 1 is basically the northeast part of the county including Springer and the land south of Dickson to State Highway 70. District 2 is the northwest corner from Interstate 35 west and from Healdton north. District 3 is the southeast corner beginning just south of Healdton and including the area south of Ardmore toward Overbrook. These three men were commissioners in 1909. From left to right are Bud Young, District 1, Berwyn, now Gene Autry; George Evans, District 2, Newport; and Joe Taylor, District 3, southwest Carter County. Since the earliest days, one of the major concerns of the commissioners has been the maintenance of county roads. Many of these roads are now blacktopped, but they began as muddy byways that had to be graded often in order to prevent ruts 12 or more inches deep. Building and maintaining bridges also improved transportation. Most important today is that the commissioners maintain the county budget and oversee the smooth operation of county business. (Courtesy of Sally Gray.)

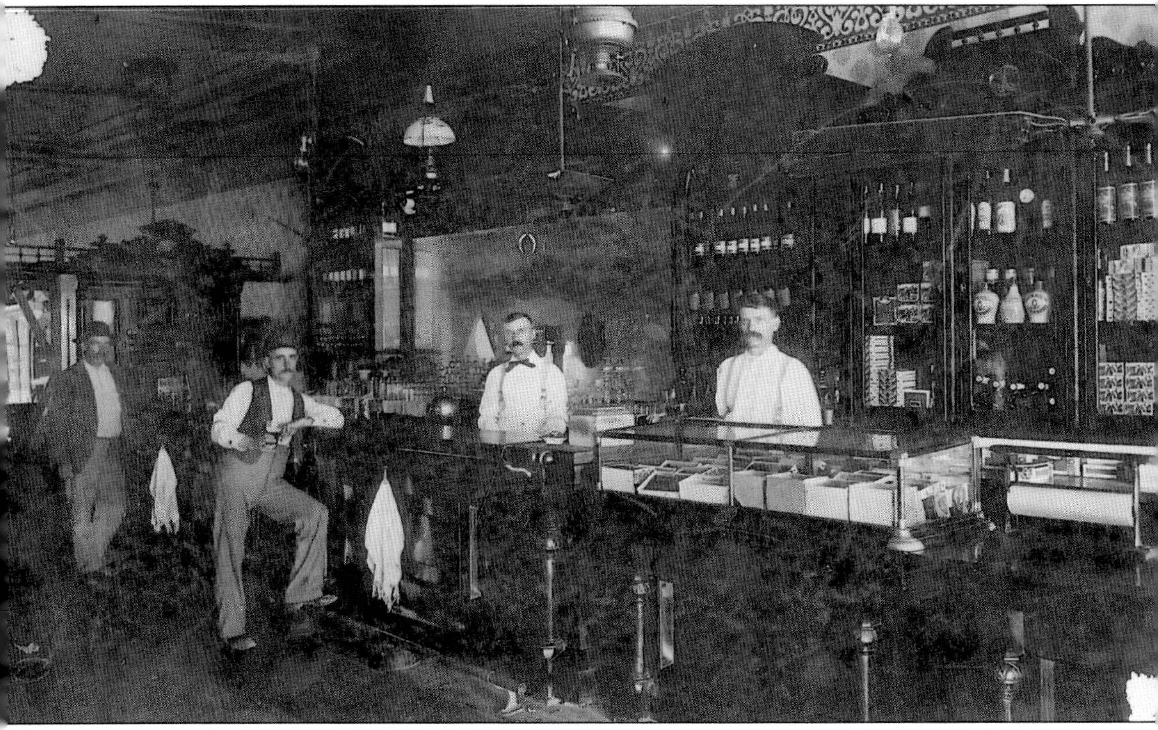

By 1890, three years after the Ardmore station came into existence, there were 10 saloons. Because Ardmore was in the Chickasaw Nation, the saloons could not legally and openly sell alcohol. It was a federal crime to have or sell alcohol inside the Chickasaw Nation, and the crime was usually referred to as "introducing." According to Paul N. Frame's book *A History of Ardmore, Oklahoma, From the Earliest Beginnings to 1907*, saloons stocked such drinks as "oat beer, hop ale, malt mead, malt tonic, Schlitz fizz, hokey pokey, and Pablo." That is not to say that alcohol was not available. Frame also writes, "It was estimated that over two hundred dollars worth of whiskey came into Ardmore every twenty four hours." Out of sight of customers—and the law—saloons carried drinks with more kick. And saloons were not the only source of whiskey. Ardmoreites frequently traveled to Gainesville, Texas, by train and returned with what came to be known as "Gainesville shoes" when a purchase of whiskey was placed in a shoe box and carried home on the evening train. (Courtesy of Sally Gray.)

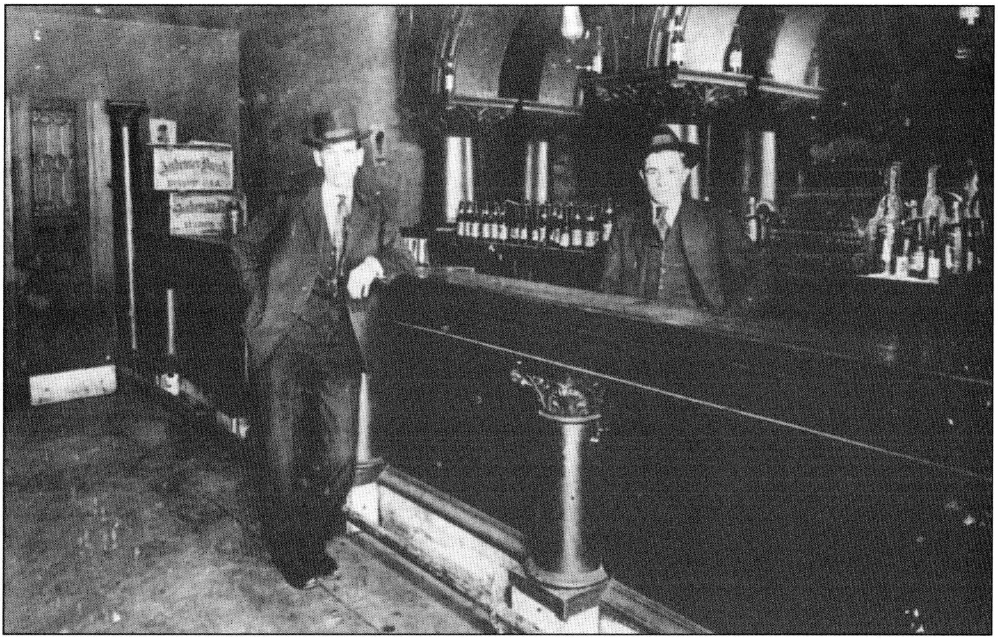

Unidentified gentlemen pose in the famous Dew Drop Inn located in the basement of a drugstore on the northeast corner of Main and Caddo Streets. According to legend, the Dew Drop Inn was connected by tunnel to the California Café to the west and to the Whittington Hotel across Main Street. Guests of the hotel could travel to the bar without being observed or braving the elements. (Courtesy of Sally Gray.)

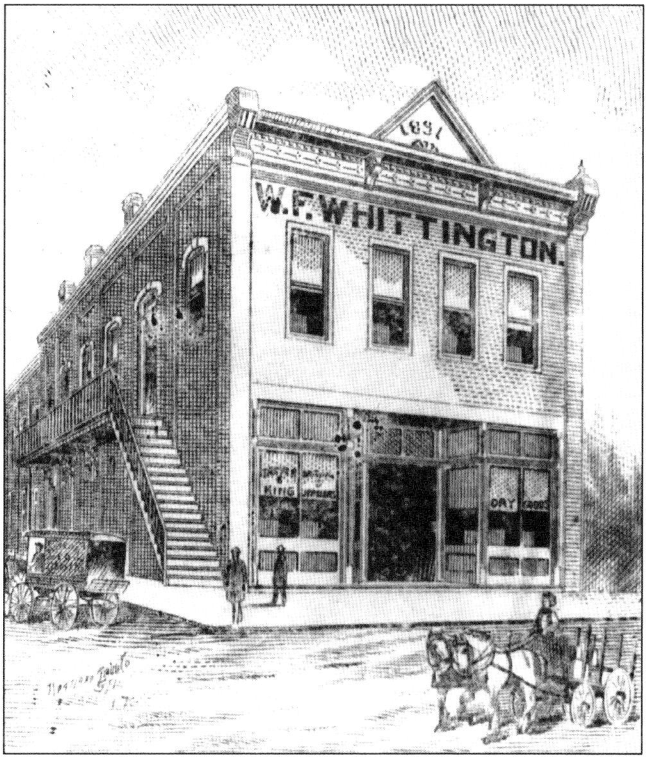

The Whittington Hotel built in 1891 was a wooden structure, probably made of cottonwood, which was a popular building material at that time. It was built by Wiley Frederick (W. F.) Whittington. He had come to Ardmore from Dexter, Texas, and had been a captain in the Confederate army. This first hotel was destroyed in the great fire of 1895. (Courtesy of Ardmore Main Street Authority.)

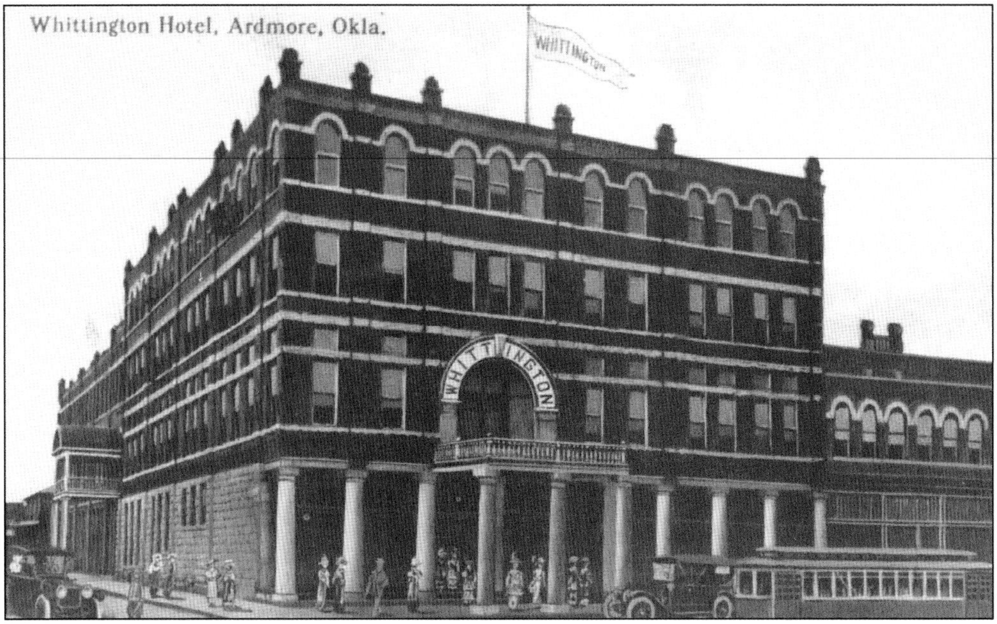

The second Whittington Hotel was rebuilt on the same site at Main Street and Caddo Street. Its 72 rooms were made of brick and sandstone, but it was again destroyed in the 1915 explosion. The next Whittington Hotel was built with brick and boasted the first Otis elevator in Ardmore. After the oil boom, another floor was added to accommodate the businessmen traffic. (Courtesy of Ardmore Main Street Authority.)

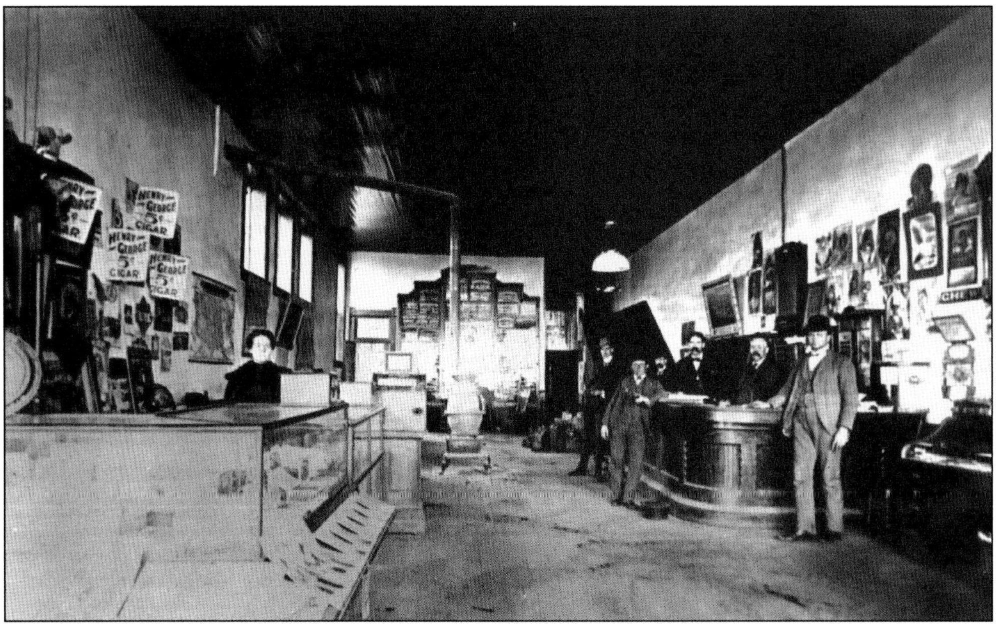

The lobby of the Whittington Hotel was long and narrow. At right is the registration desk with clerk. At left is the cigar counter with female clerk. Several visitors pose, and luggage is stacked, far right back, by the staircase. In the center back is the potbelly stove with flue pipe going up about 10 feet before curving toward the outside wall for ventilation. (Courtesy of the McGalliard Collection, Ardmore Public Library.)

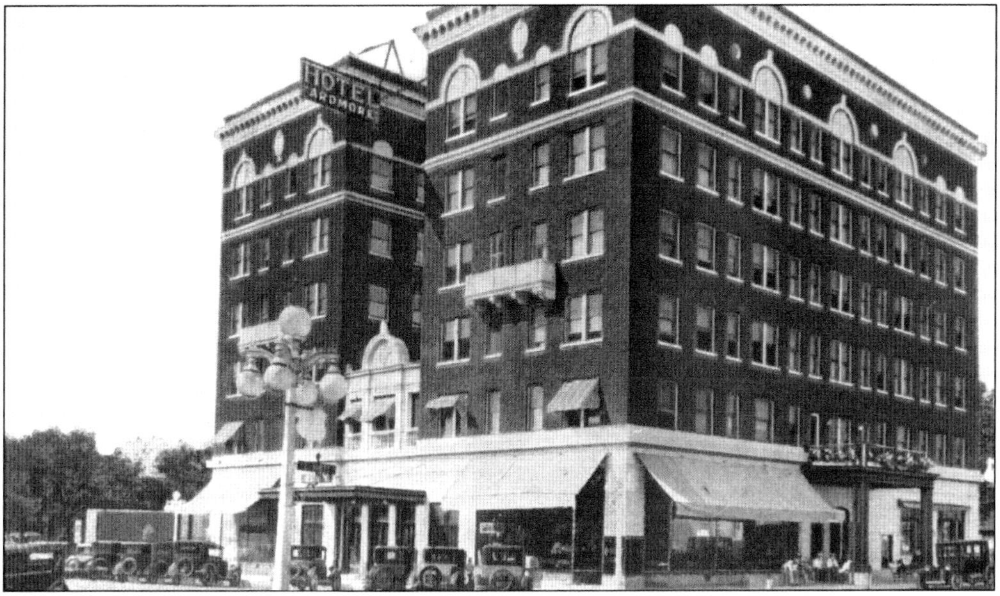

Hotel Ardmore was built between 1916 and 1920 with construction slowed by World War I. The name Hotel Ardmore was purchased from a small hotel on South Washington for $25, and that same small sign was the first one displayed on the new hotel. The Glider Room in the basement was named in 1942 for the glider pilots stationed at the Ardmore Air Base. (Courtesy of Sally Gray.)

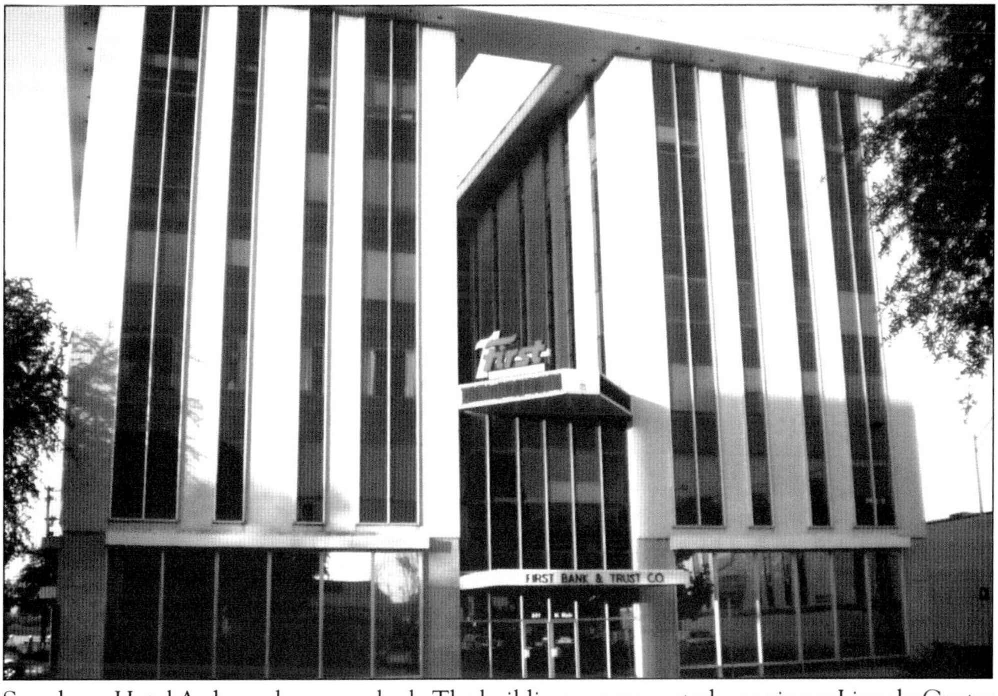

Seen here, Hotel Ardmore has a new look. The building was renovated, opening as Lincoln Center housing Lincoln Bank and numerous offices. Lincoln Financial Corporation was incorporated on December 27, 1955, by John W. Grissom. In December 1999, First Bank and Trust out of Duncan acquired the building. Note the new roofline, with a horizontal crossbar connecting the two sides of the building, and the different window treatment. (Author's collection.)

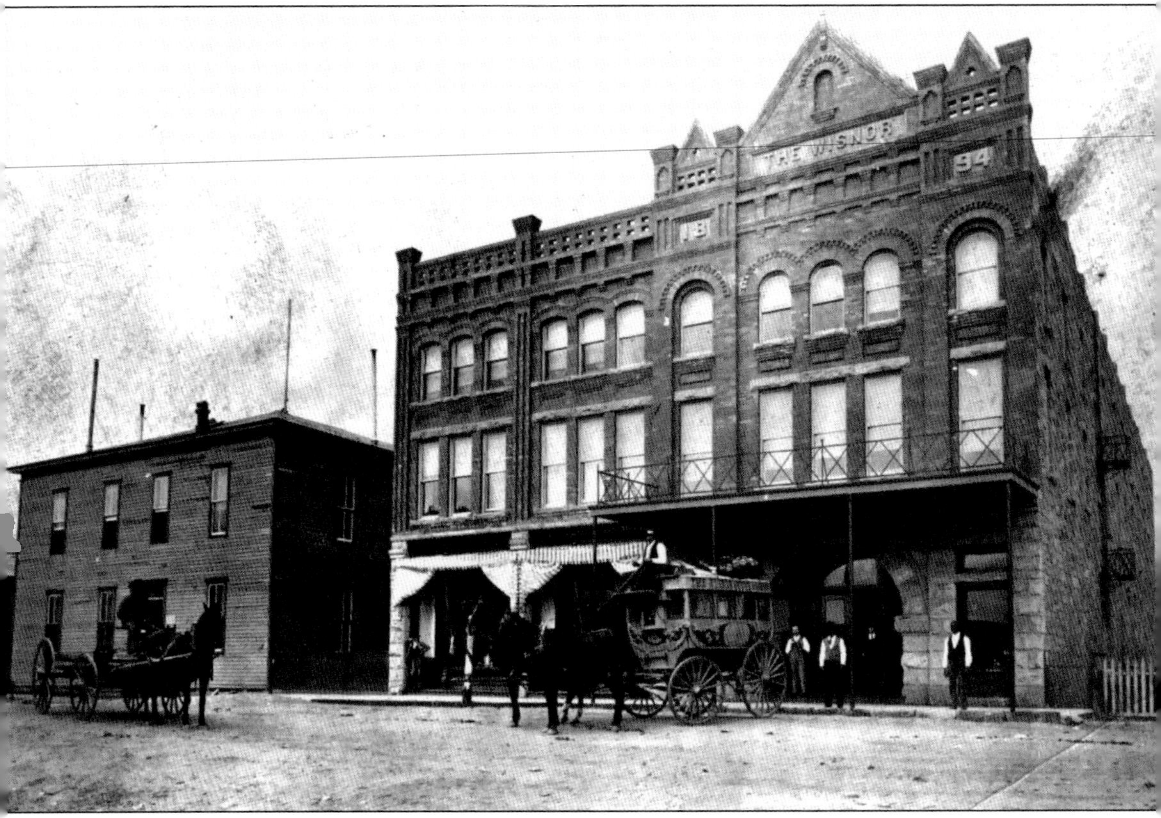

The Wisnor Hotel was located on Springer Street, today named North Washington Street. It was built in 1894 by Charles D. Carter, his mother and partner Serena Guy Carter, and attorney Solomon Jackson. Famous throughout Indian Territory and Oklahoma Territory, the $17,000 building provided bath and plumbing facilities in the rooms. In each room there was a tub and toilet, often without even a curtain to block the view. This building survived the great fire of 1895, but it did burn to the ground in 1899. The building on the left in this photograph is the first federal courthouse. A barbershop and a jewelry store were located on the Wisnor Hotel's first floor. A stagecoach, painted bright red and yellow, shuttled guests between the hotel and the railroad station. It was very stylish to be driven the few blocks from the depot to the hotel in such a fine carriage. Charles D. Carter was elected to represent the brand-new state of Oklahoma from the Fifth Congressional District. (Courtesy of the McGalliard Collection, Ardmore Public Library.)

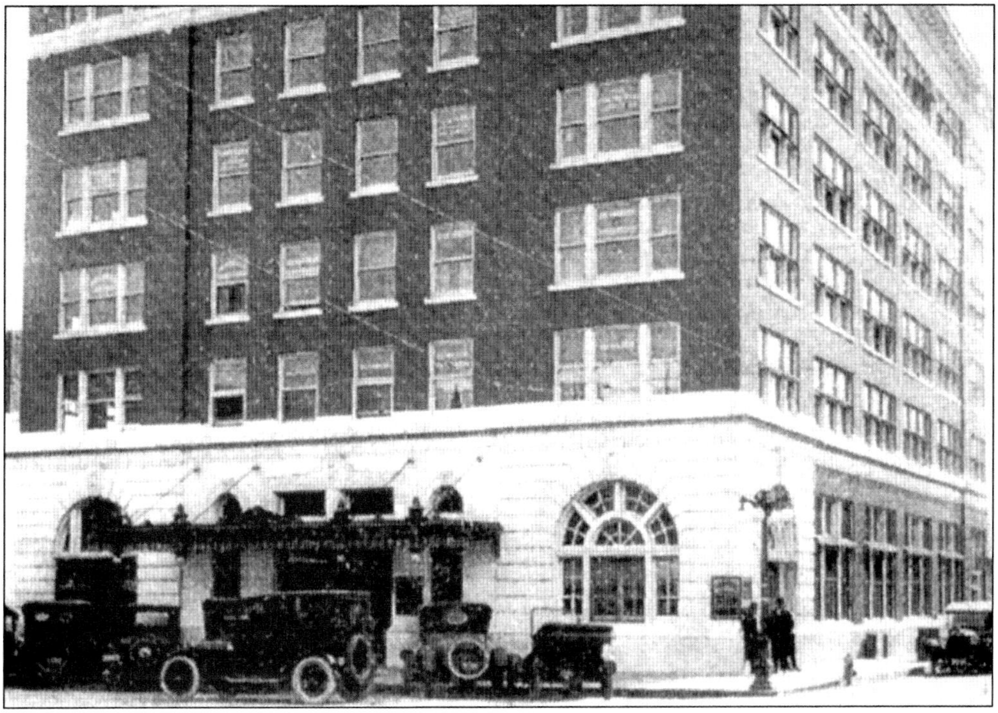

The Simpson Building was originally built in 1916 by B. A. Simpson and Roy M. Johnson. The six-story building has also been known as the Little Building and currently is the Colston Building. It was the birthplace of the Independent Petroleum Association of America (IPAA), founded largely through the efforts of Wirt Franklin, local oil man. Franklin, who protested government oversight, served as the first chief executive. (Courtesy of Sally Gray.)

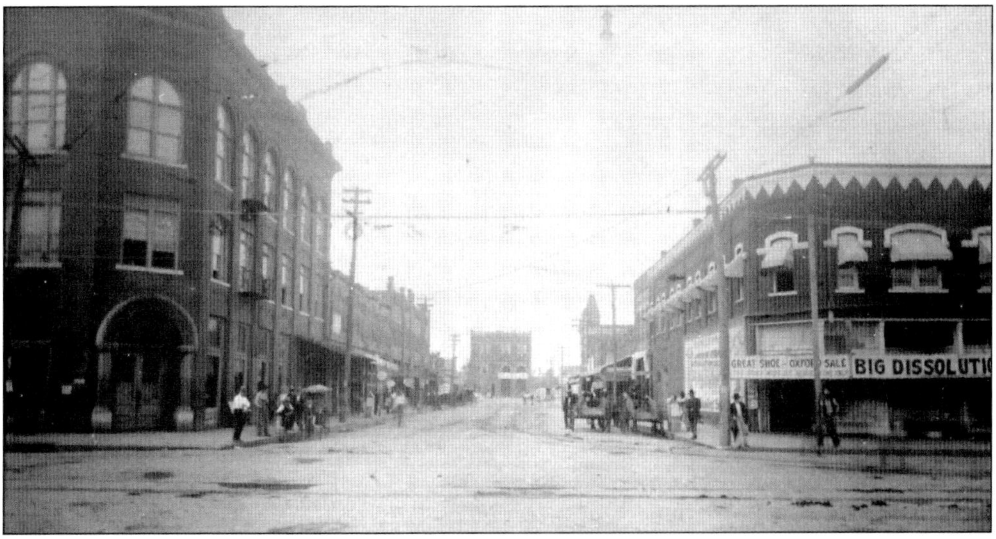

Around the dawn of the 20th century, the building at the northeast corner of Main Street and Washington Street offered a "Big Dissolution Sale." This building was built after the great fire of 1895 and survived the explosion of 1915. In fact, it survived until about the 1960s, when it burned. It has the same beveled front as the Masonic temple, facing toward the intersection. (Courtesy of Ardmore Main Street Authority.)

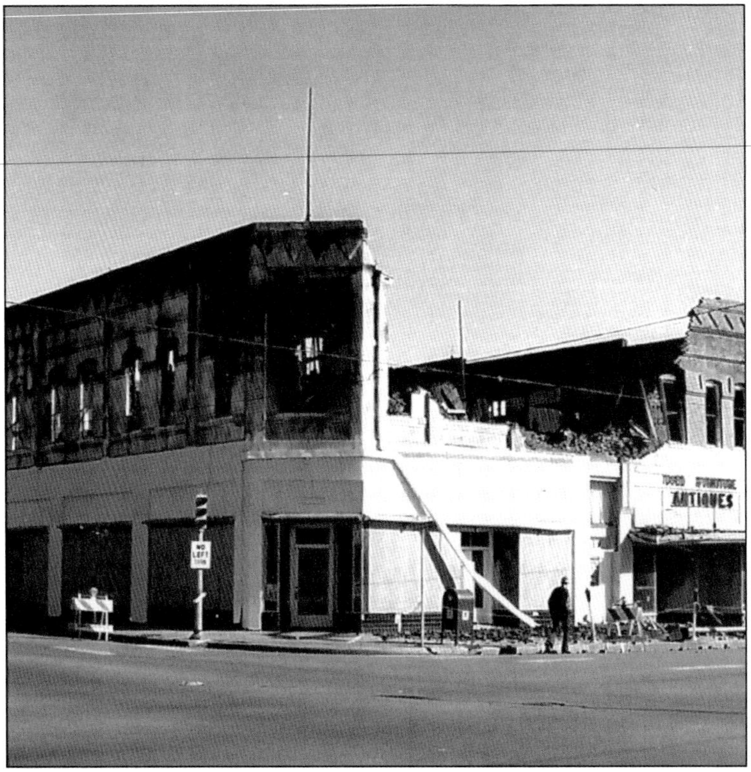

The store building at the northeast corner of Main Street and Washington Street had been a major business in early Ardmore. In later years, it was used for used furniture and antiques. When it burned, it was not replaced but was razed. There is a parking lot there for the benefit of businesses along the first block of North Washington north of Main Street. (Courtesy of Ardmore Main Street Authority.)

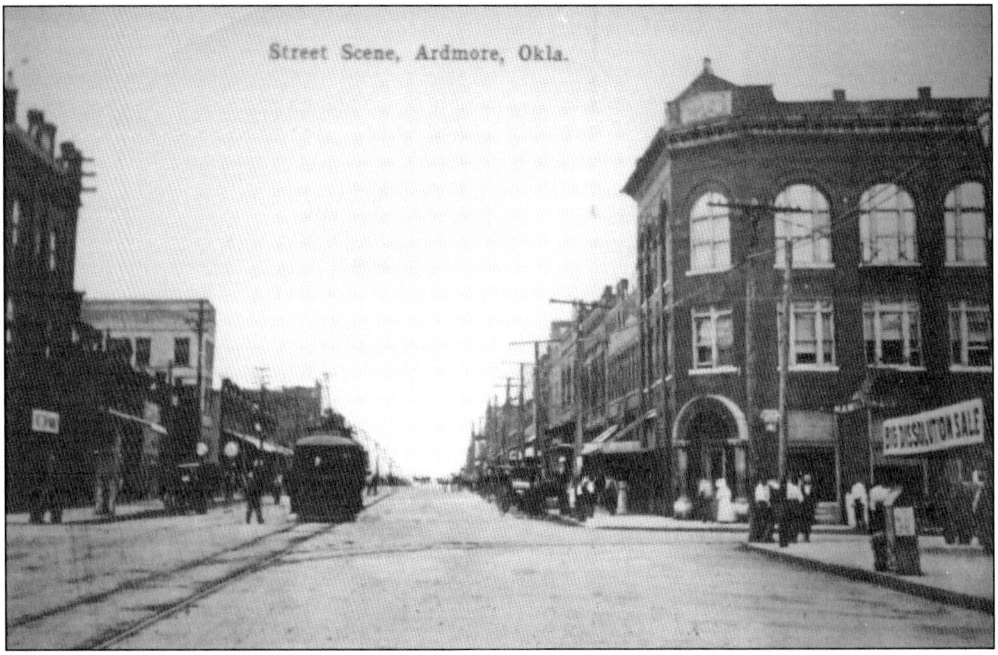

This building was constructed after the great fire of 1895, during which the first Masonic temple was destroyed. It has three stories and is made of brick. It is an imposing building on any day. The cupola was damaged by lightning in later years. After the explosion of 1915, First National Bank moved into the first floor. (Courtesy of Ardmore Main Street Authority.)

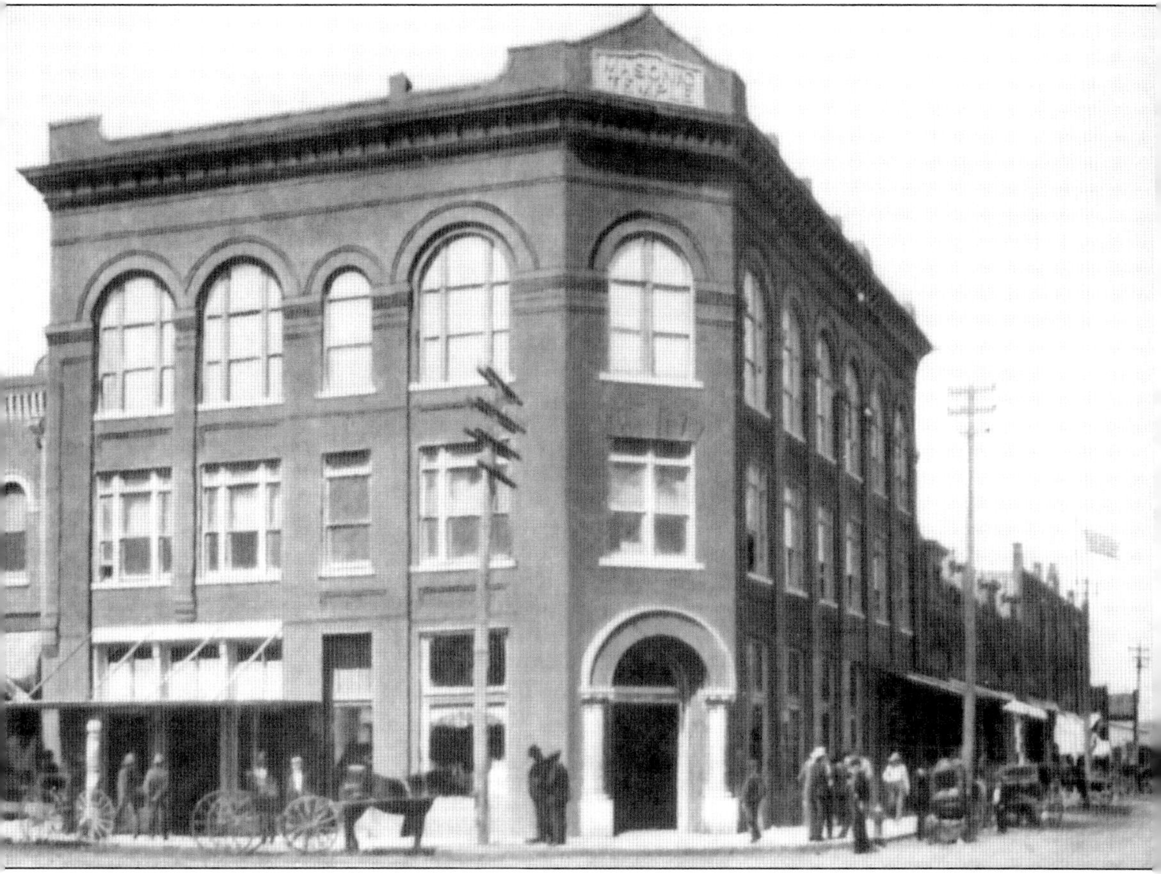

Ardmore has always been on the cutting edge of progress. The beauty of the old buildings on Main Street is a testimony to the advanced planning of the citizens of Ardmore. The Masonic temple served as Mason headquarters; the whole third floor was a ballroom. The building has served as a bank and as a drugstore. For awhile it was unoccupied and fell into disrepair. When the cupola was repaired several years ago, the stone plate bearing the words *Masonic Temple* was not replaced. Today the building is home to the American Law Office. North Washington Street was named Springer Street, and before that, at the time of the great fire in 1895, it was called Court Street. The April 26, 1895, edition of the *Daily Ardmoreite* lists the destroyed businesses along Court Street. (Courtesy of Ardmore Main Street Authority.)

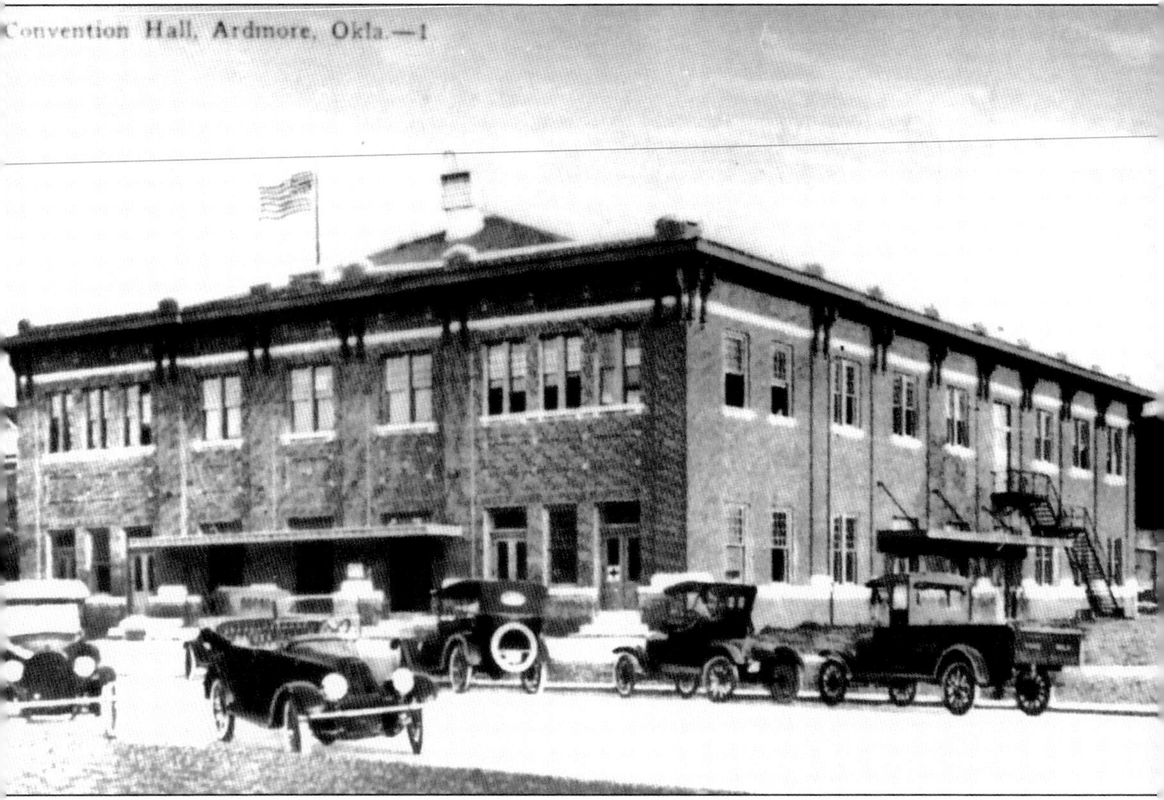

The original convention hall was built in the location where Heritage Hall now stands. When the Ardmore Auditorium was built in 1940 through the Works Progress Administration, part of the south and east walls of the convention hall were incorporated into the new Ardmore Auditorium. At some point the name changed to Civic Auditorium, and in 2000, after much renovation, the name changed to Heritage Hall. (Courtesy of Sally Gray.)

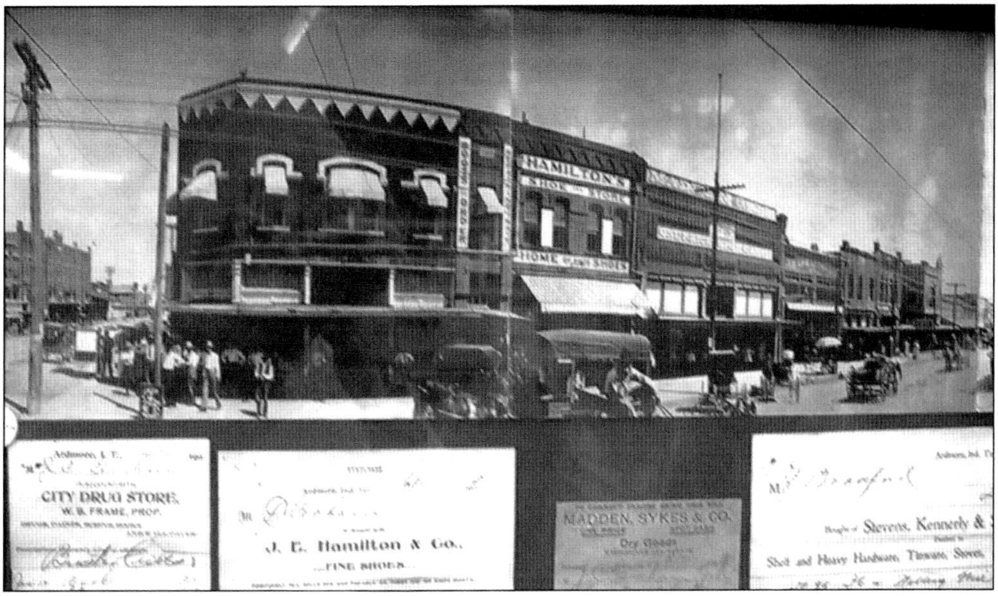

This photograph matches receipts with the Main Street stores. From left to right are a receipt from City Drug, W. B. Frame, proprietor; Ardmore I.T. goes with the large building on the corner; a receipt from J. T. Hamilton and Company offering fine shoes; a receipt for the dry cleaner housed in Madden, Sykes and Company; and a receipt from Stevens, Kennedy, and Spraggins Buggies. (Courtesy of Sally Gray.)

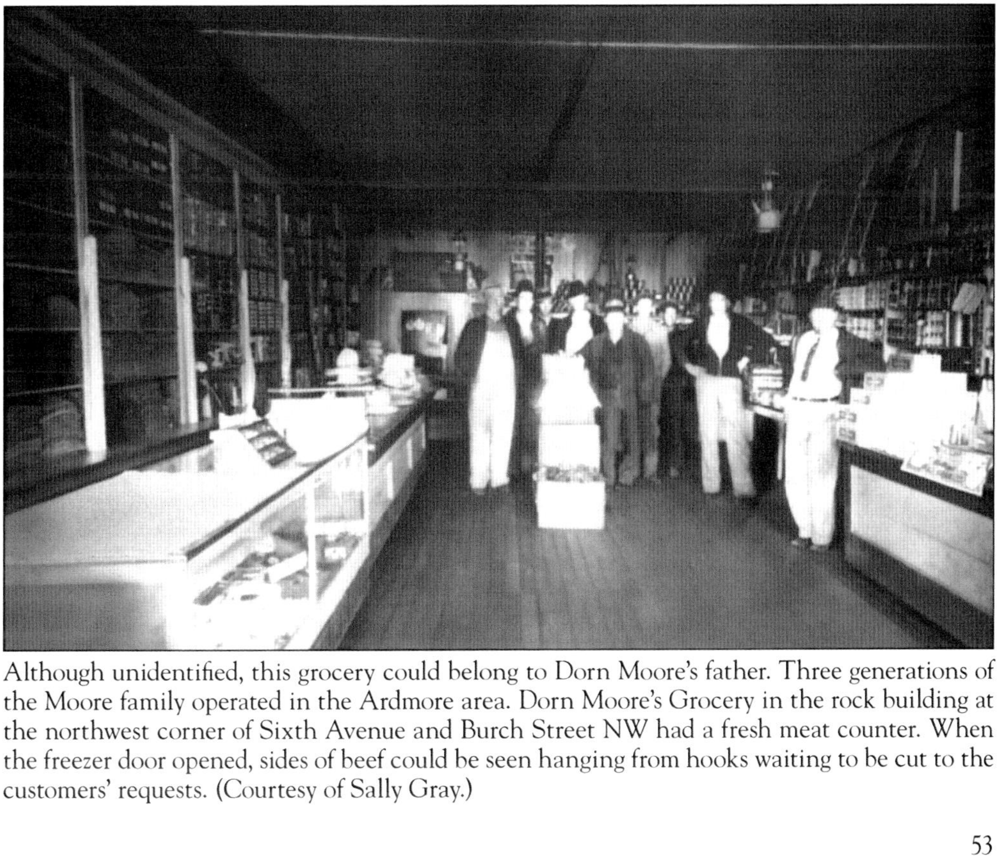

Although unidentified, this grocery could belong to Dorn Moore's father. Three generations of the Moore family operated in the Ardmore area. Dorn Moore's Grocery in the rock building at the northwest corner of Sixth Avenue and Burch Street NW had a fresh meat counter. When the freezer door opened, sides of beef could be seen hanging from hooks waiting to be cut to the customers' requests. (Courtesy of Sally Gray.)

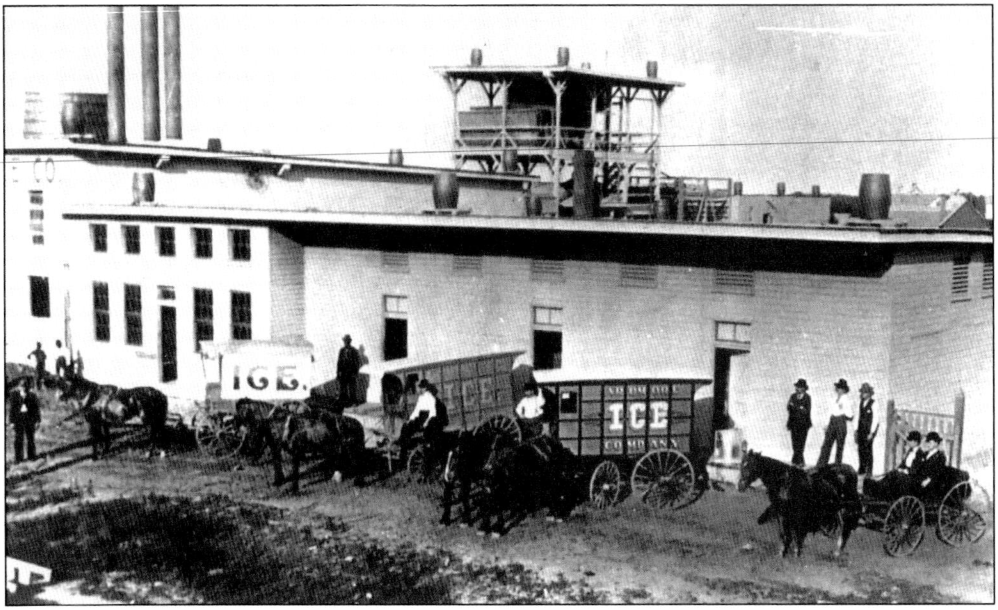

The Ardmore Ice Company at one time trucked in ice, which was unloaded into horse-drawn wagons for home delivery to customers. This photograph was taken about 1910. At some point, the ice plant began making ice. A daily trip to the ice plant was the favorite activity of many children who hoped for a sliver of frozen delight. (Courtesy of Sally Gray.)

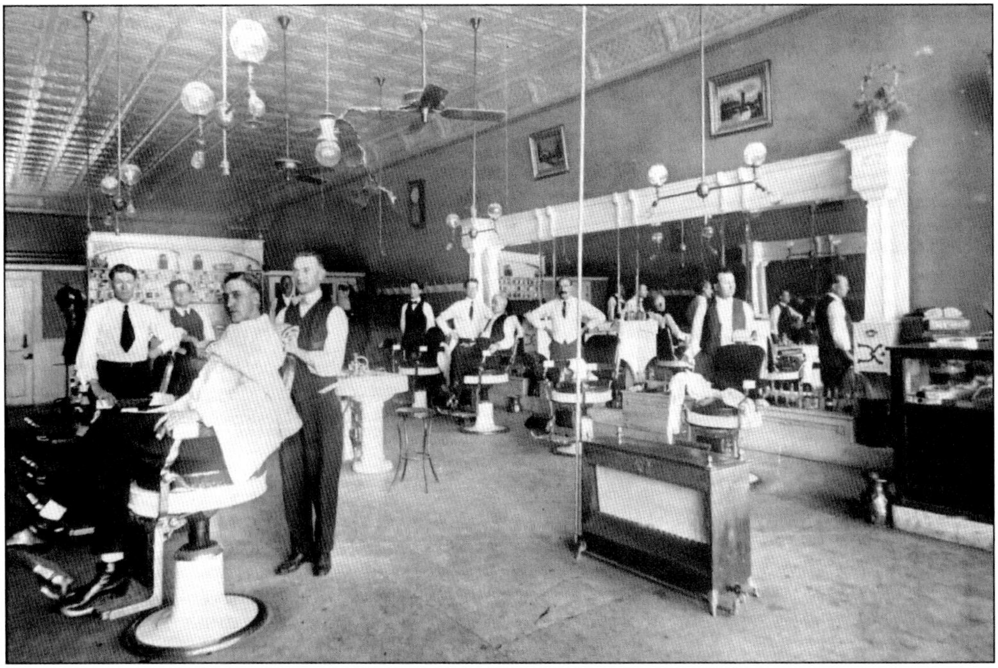

This early-day barbershop has a gas heating stove in the center. Natural gas was piped into Ardmore first from the Wheeler field northeast of the city. W. A. Ledbetter established the Ardmore Heat and Light Company in 1907. This supply of natural gas was used up after three years. Healdton's oil field became the new source of natural gas for Ardmore in 1913. (Courtesy of Sally Gray.)

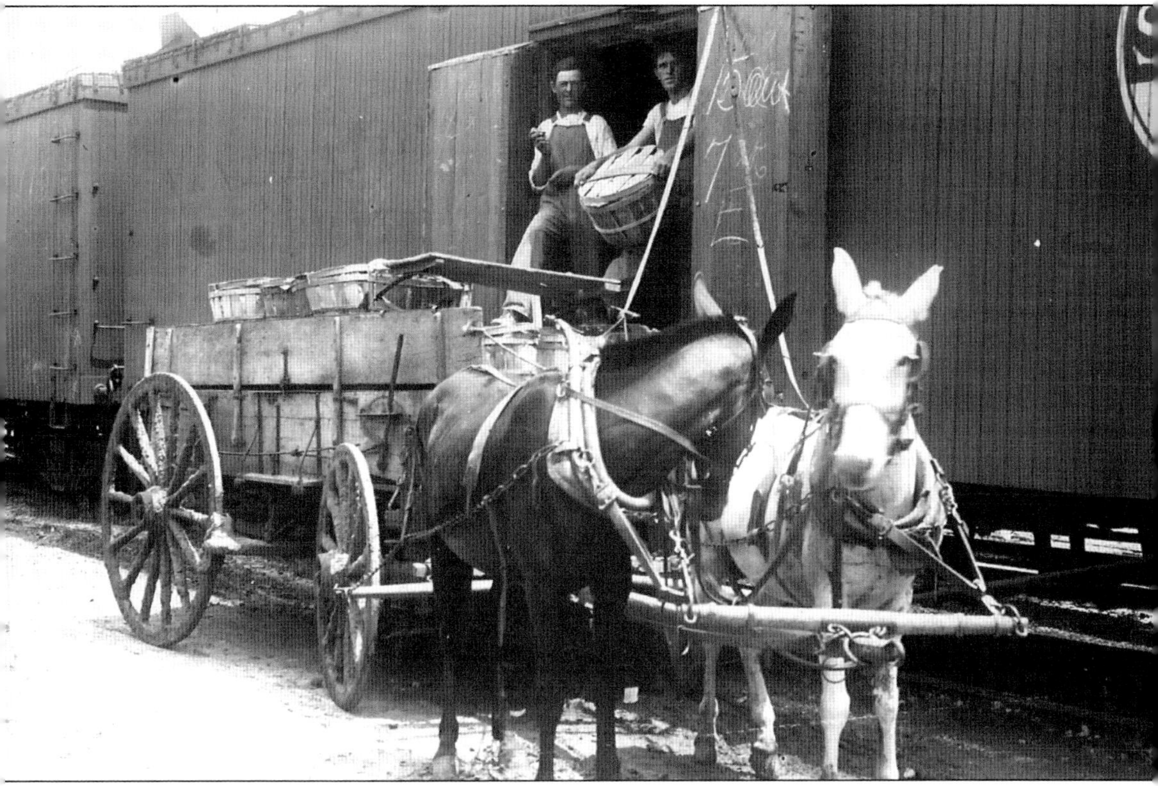

Because of regular shipments of goods into Ardmore on the Santa Fe line, stores were well stocked. People came from almost 100 miles to shop the variety of stores. Supplies were also unloaded directly onto wagons and delivered to nearby farms and ranches or outlying stores. This picture was taken about 1910 and has "Landrum and Team" written on the back. Prior to the railroad, supplies had to be hauled by wagon and horse or mule teams from Gainesville or Dennison, Texas. Roads were not paved, so in the rainy season supplies often took weeks to arrive due to poor road conditions. Fresh meat could not be trusted on a wagon trip, and vegetables often arrived limp and wilted. With the coming of the railroad, grocers could stock seafood, which became quite a treat to the people of Ardmore. Goods such as clothing and furniture could be obtained at a more reasonable rate, and agricultural products, especially cotton, could be sold for higher prices. The railroads brought financial advancement to the area. (Courtesy of the McGalliard Collection, Ardmore Public Library.)

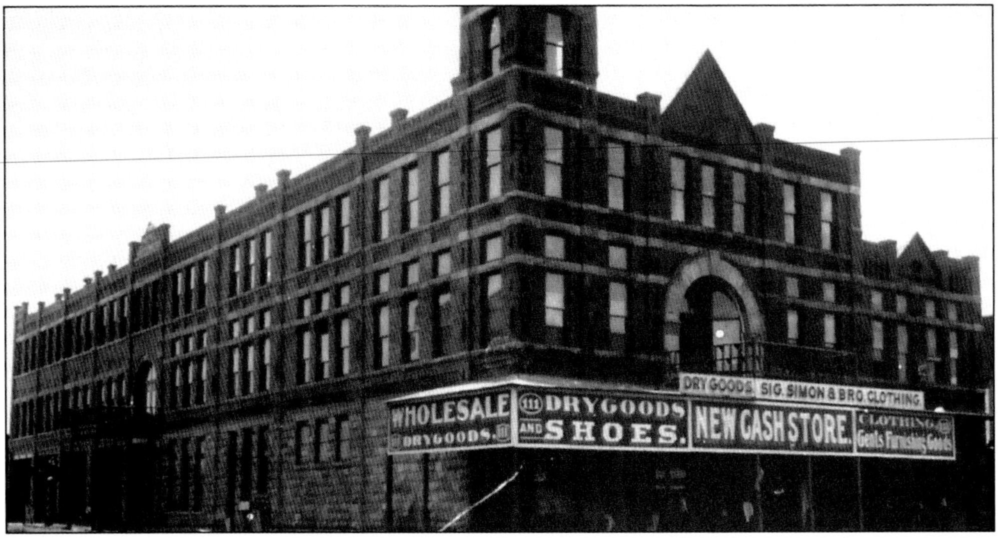

The Cash Store was opened by W. O. Duston and later operated as the Big Cash Store. It was probably damaged or destroyed by the great fire of 1895 because it was rebuilt as the New Cash Store. Each of the early stores had a special hook for customers. One of the most interesting advertisements was for the Cheap Store, first established by John R. Chitwood. According to Paul N. Frame's book *A History of Ardmore, Oklahoma, From the Earliest Beginnings to* 1907, he sold it to Abraham Kloski, who continued the theme and offered "Socks until you can't rest for 5 cents per pair" and "Ladies' Hats, trimmed, 75 cents, latest Parisian Style." Another inviting store was also established by John R. Chitwood, and he called it Cheap John's. Stores were named for their content and also for their structure: the Red Store and the Blue Front. The Iron Store, the largest and best-equipped store in Pickens County, was named for its sheet iron exterior walls. (Courtesy of Sally Gray.)

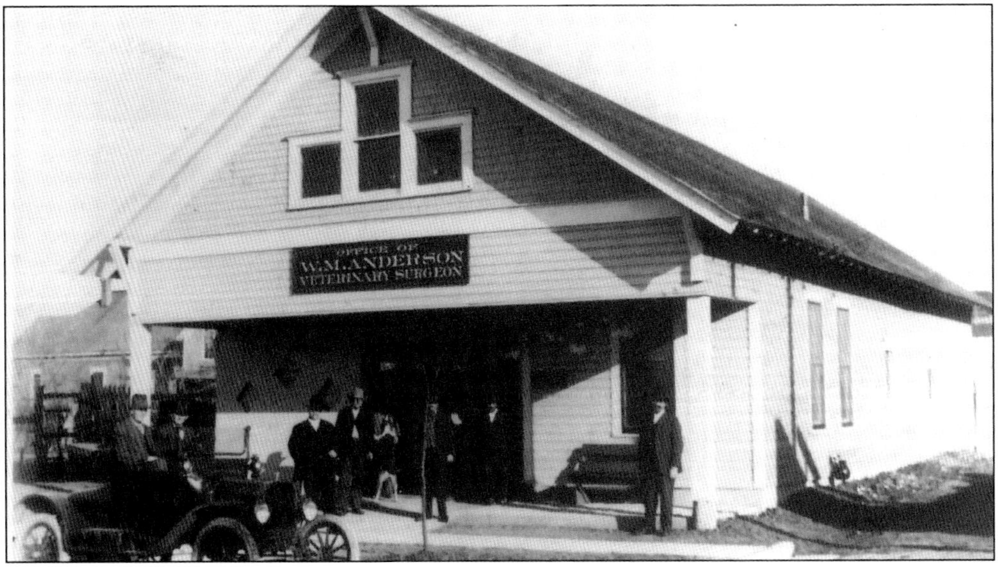

W. M. Anderson opened the first veterinarian hospital in southern Oklahoma. It was located about 8 East Broadway and opened in September 1915, just about the time of the great explosion. Anderson advertised himself as a veterinarian surgeon. His facility was the most modern of any veterinarian hospital between Oklahoma City and Dallas, Texas. (Courtesy of Sally Gray.)

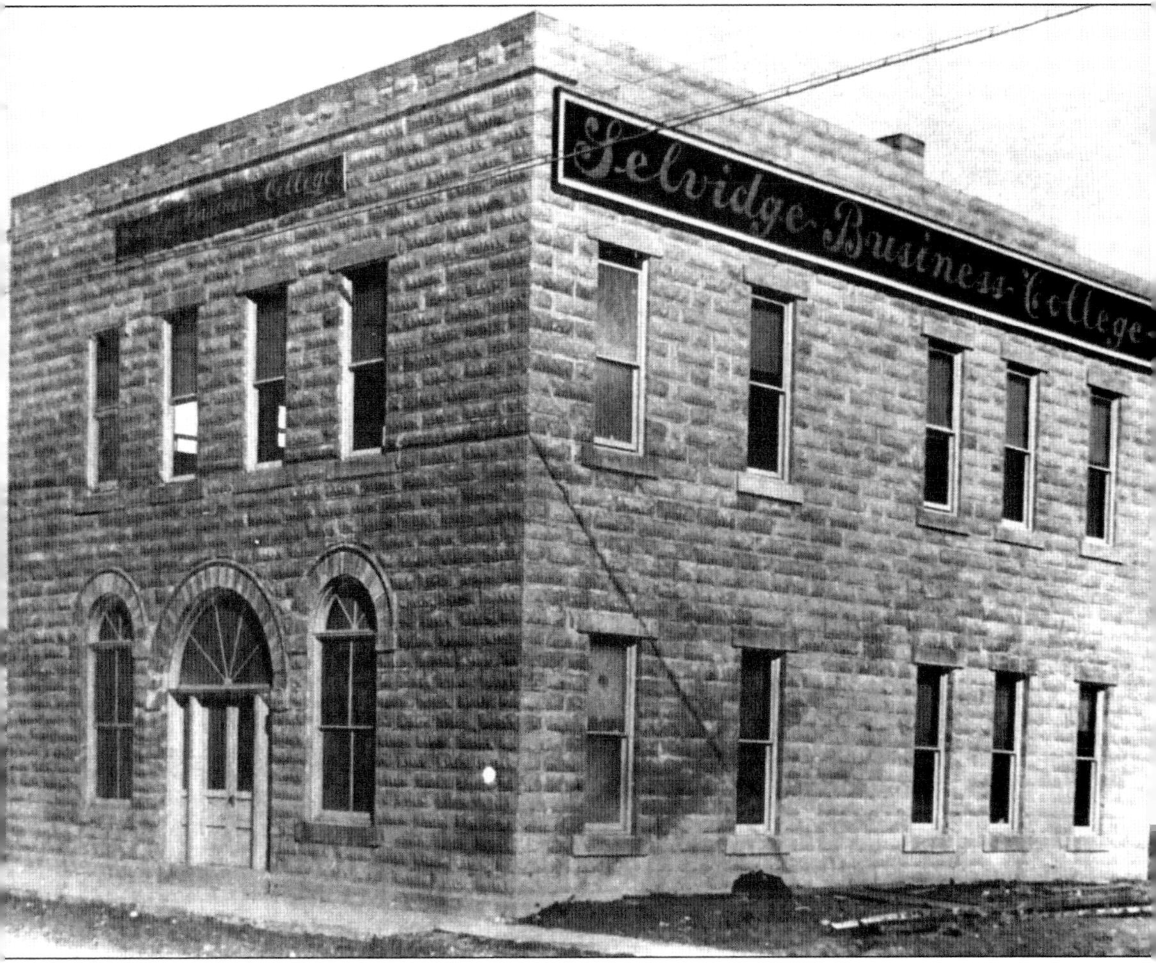

George P. Selvidge opened the Selvidge Business College to train students in bookkeeping, accounting, and stenography. It was preceded by the Indianola Business School between 1894 and 1903. Ardmore Business College followed the Selvidge Business College. Ardmore Business College provided access to business classes for many servicemen returning from World War II. (Courtesy of Sally Gray.)

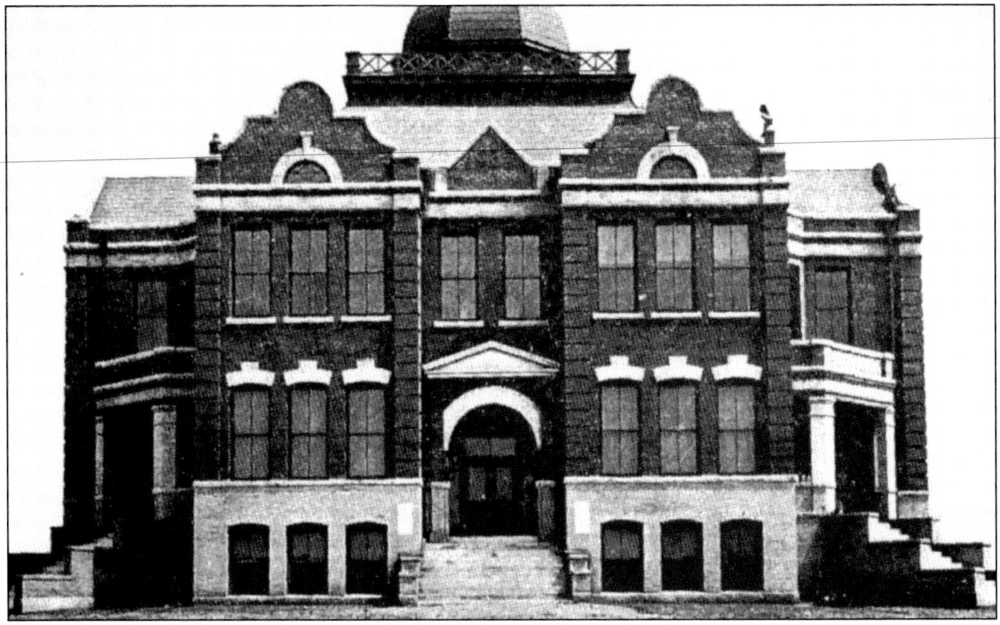

This beautiful old building known as Bloomfield Seminary at Ardmore no longer exists. Built in 1917 when the federal government purchased land two miles north of downtown Ardmore, where Hargrove College had been moved in 1908, this new building housed the Bloomfield Academy for Girls, which had previously operated near Durant. The school was later named Carter Seminary in honor of Charles D. Carter and his family. (Courtesy of Sally Gray.)

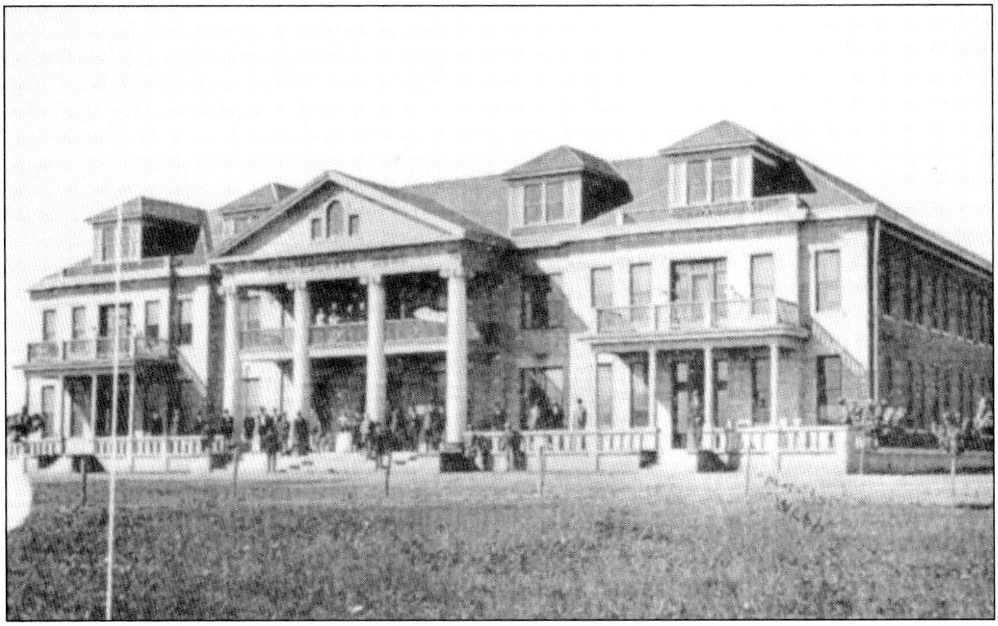

The Oklahoma Confederate Home opened in July 1911 under the superintendency of John L. Galt, the first mayor of Ardmore. The facility was furnished by the Oklahoma chapters of the Daughters of the Confederacy. In order to live in the home, one had to be an Oklahoma resident for two years and have served honorably for the Confederate states, or be the wife or widow of a qualifying soldier. (Courtesy of Ardmore Main Street Authority.)

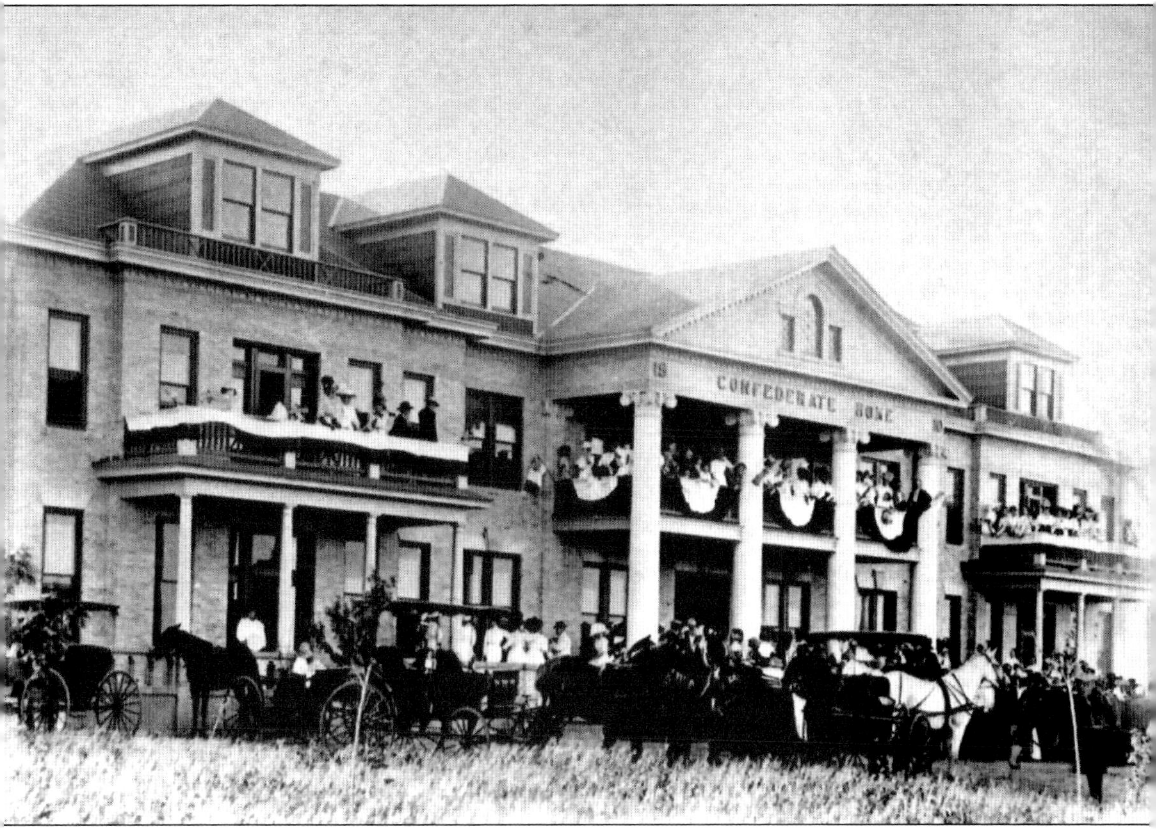

The Oklahoma Confederate Home is decorated with bunting, and apparently a parade is lining up in front. The Confederate veterans held a parade each year for several years complete with military units and marching band. Eighty-five veterans, wives, and widows moved into the facility. The Oklahoma legislature assumed responsibility for maintaining the home for 25 years, or as long as eligible veterans or widows needed care. Two groups persisted on behalf of Confederate veterans in Oklahoma. The Oklahoma Division of the United Confederate Veterans and the Oklahoma Division of the United Daughters of the Confederacy became active in politics. When costs outran the estimate of $25,000, Gov. Lee Cruce agreed to grant an additional $10,000 in state funds in return for deeding the property to the state. (Courtesy of Sally Gray.)

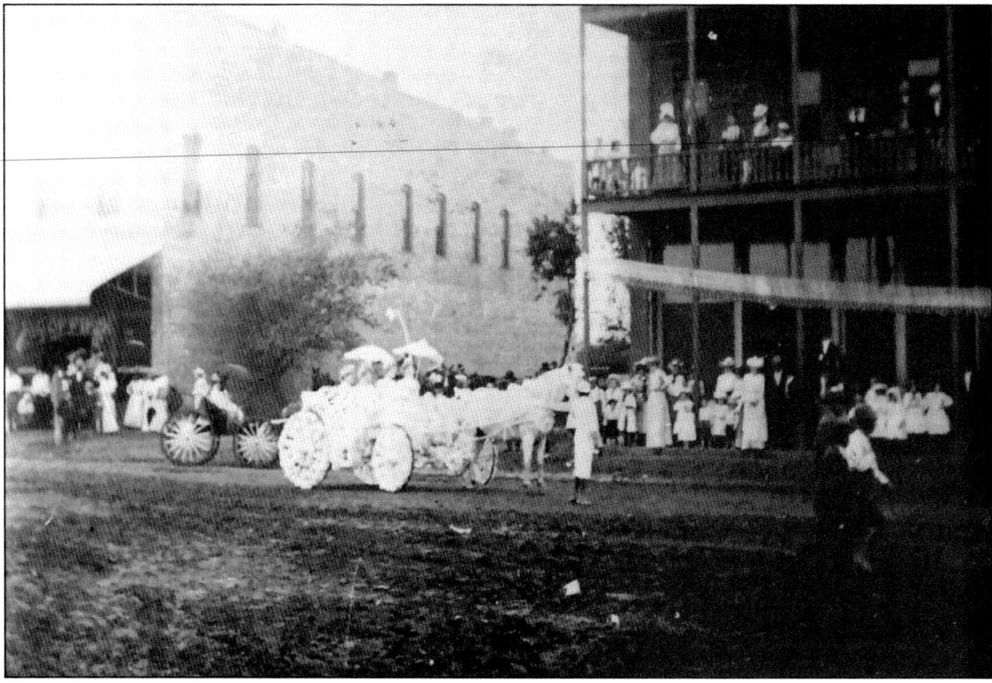

In his research into Ardmore's history, Paul N. Frame found the following reference in an article printed in the *Daily Ardmoreite* on May 30, 1898: "A wagonette, laden with young ladies, flowers, and flags, a truly pretty sight," which followed the veterans' organization in the annual parade. It is likely this photograph captured a moment in such a parade. (Courtesy of Sally Gray.)

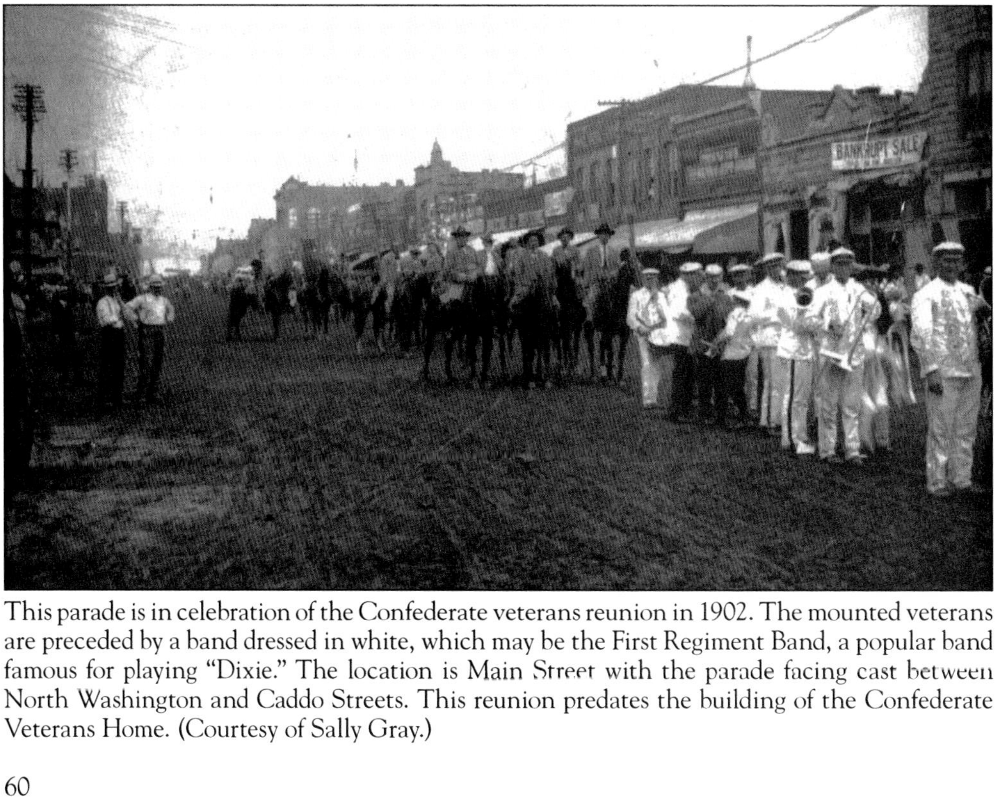

This parade is in celebration of the Confederate veterans reunion in 1902. The mounted veterans are preceded by a band dressed in white, which may be the First Regiment Band, a popular band famous for playing "Dixie." The location is Main Street with the parade facing east between North Washington and Caddo Streets. This reunion predates the building of the Confederate Veterans Home. (Courtesy of Sally Gray.)

Three

Disasters

Ardmore has experienced a number of disasters, including fires, explosions, and several tornadoes. The most devastating events occurred in 1895, 1896, and 1915. The great fire began on the wind-whipped evening of April 19, 1895. Before the flames were finally extinguished, 86 buildings—most of the downtown business district west of the railroad tracks—had been destroyed; but no lives were lost. For several years, city leaders had discussed the possibility of a major fire, but as a community in the Chickasaw Nation, the non citizens had no legal right to levy and collect taxes to maintain government agencies such as police and fire departments. Maybe for that very reason most of the downtown businesses were insured so that rebuilding after the fire commenced almost immediately. Within 12 weeks, almost $200,000 worth of construction had begun.

The closest effort toward establishing authority in the city came from the Ardmore Board of Trade, which was a group of businessmen who agreed to abide by a set of rules the group wrote. The Ardmore Board of Trade did hire a night watchman. Other than that, there was little protection before the city incorporated. In 1896, a second fire destroyed most of the businesses east of the railroad tracks. Unfortunately, many of these businesses were never rebuilt or were moved west of the tracks. Following this second fire, a volunteer fire department was organized, but it lacked vital equipment. One of the first acts of the newly incorporated city in 1898 was to establish a well-equipped fire department and a police department.

The railroad explosion in 1915 again destroyed much of the downtown area, and this time 43 people were killed. Because the fault for the explosion was assessed to the railroad, business owners received compensation for their losses with total payments in excess of $1 million.

In addition, several tornadoes have ripped through Ardmore during the last 100 years; but as with the great disasters, the citizens of Ardmore have rebuilt. That willing spirit, the pioneer spirit, which helped create the town, ensured its survival after each disaster.

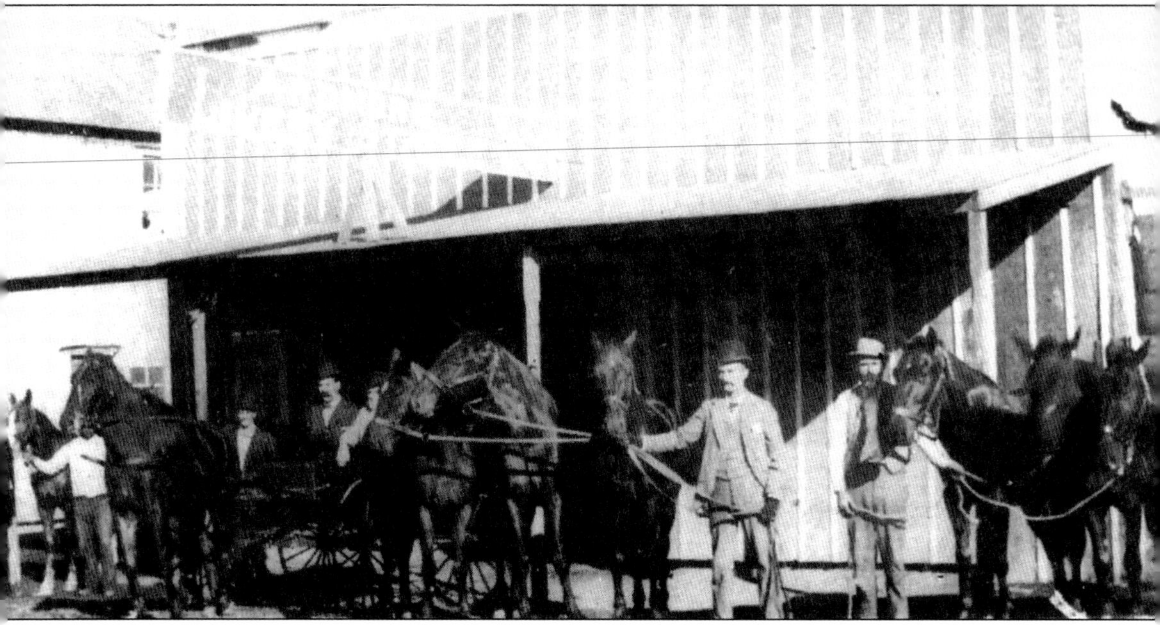

Although the cause was never identified, the great fire began in Harper's Livery Stable on North Caddo Street. High winds caused the fire to spread south, attacking the back walls of businesses on Main Street. It was the Ardmore Board of Trade's night watchman who discovered the flames and alerted the town with several revolver shots, the usual alarm for fire. Scores of people rushed to form bucket brigades, but the wells on Main Street emptied too soon. When it became evident there would be no way to extinguish the flames, store owners tried to save some of their stock by moving it into the street. The fire jumped Main Street and destroyed several businesses on the south side of Main Street as well as buildings south on Mill Street. The *Ardmore State Herald* ran a story the next day stating that "Ardmore has been almost licked clean of buildings." The *Alliance Courier*, the *Wind Bag*, and the *Daily Ardmoreite* were destroyed. The *Daily Ardmoreite* printed its April 26 edition through the *Purcell Register*. (Courtesy of Ardmore Main Street Authority.)

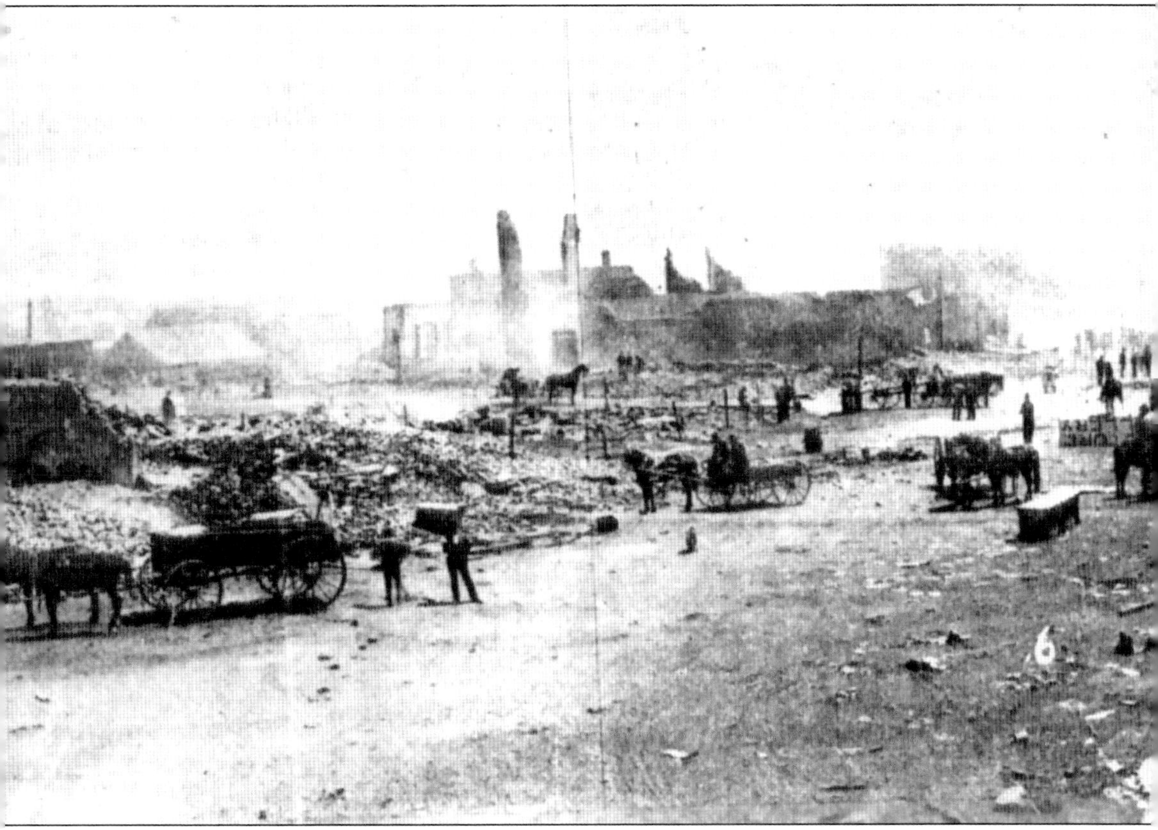

A pall of smoke covered the city as day dawned. Dozens of wagons and teams began the sooty task of removing the blackened devastation. Some of the finest buildings had been destroyed, including the Anderson-Burch Opera House, the Kloski Opera House, and the original Masonic temple. The fire burned south from Harper's Livery, jumped Main Street, and continued down South Caddo Street. The cotton gin exploded, and a supply of ammunition in a hardware store ignited, adding a cacophony of popping sounds. Nearly every doctor office was destroyed, and only two attorneys were able to stay in their offices. All but one newspaper plant was destroyed. The *Daily Ardmoreite* was able to print via the *Purcell Register*. On April 26, the *Daily Ardmoreite* printed a list of buildings and businesses that had been destroyed. The story ended with these words: "The calamity has thoroughly demonstrated the courage and enterprise of our people. They are not the kind to pine over disaster. Great was, great is, and great will Ardmore ever be." (Courtesy of Ardmore Main Street Authority.)

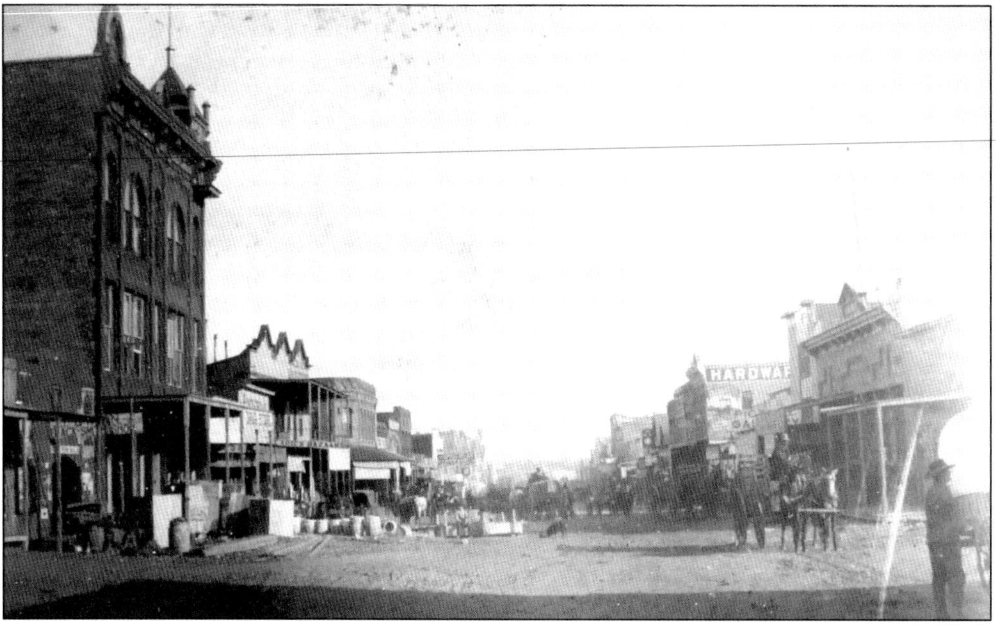

Taken about 1890, this picture shows the buildings that were destroyed in the great fire. Every building on the left and nearly every building on the right side of the street were destroyed. The three-story brick building at left is the T. N. Coleman Drug Store. It is believed that the last of the fire was smothered when this building collapsed. (Courtesy of the McGalliard Collection, Ardmore Public Library.)

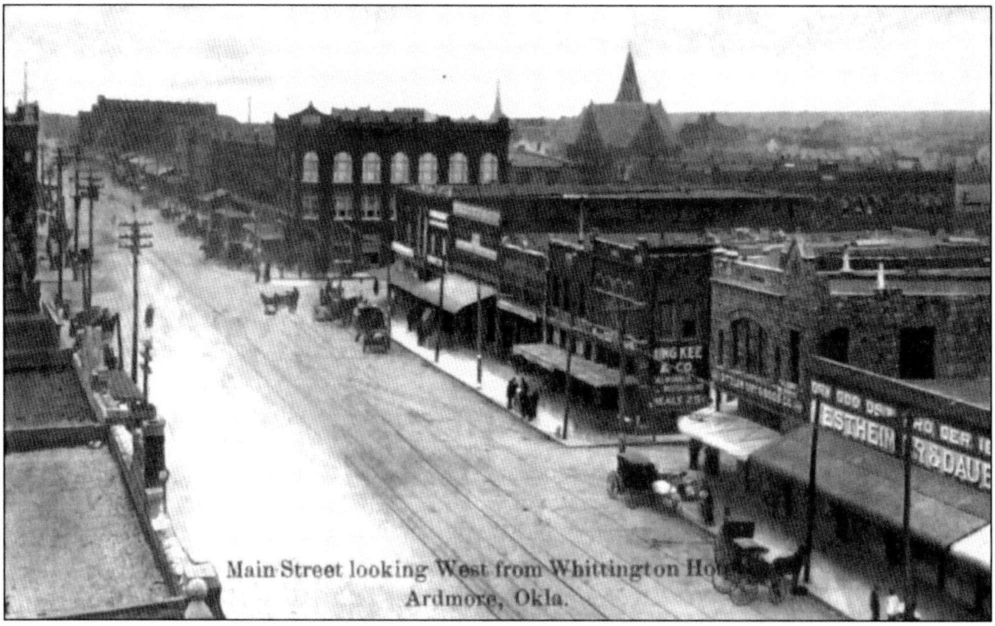

This picture of Main Street, taken from the roof of the Whittington Hotel, was made after the great fire. Washington Street divides upper Main Street west from lower Main Street east. After the fire, lower Main Street was widened 24 feet in an attempt to make it harder for flames to jump across the street. Storefronts were aligned, and there were no longer gaps and spaces between buildings. (Courtesy of Sally Gray.)

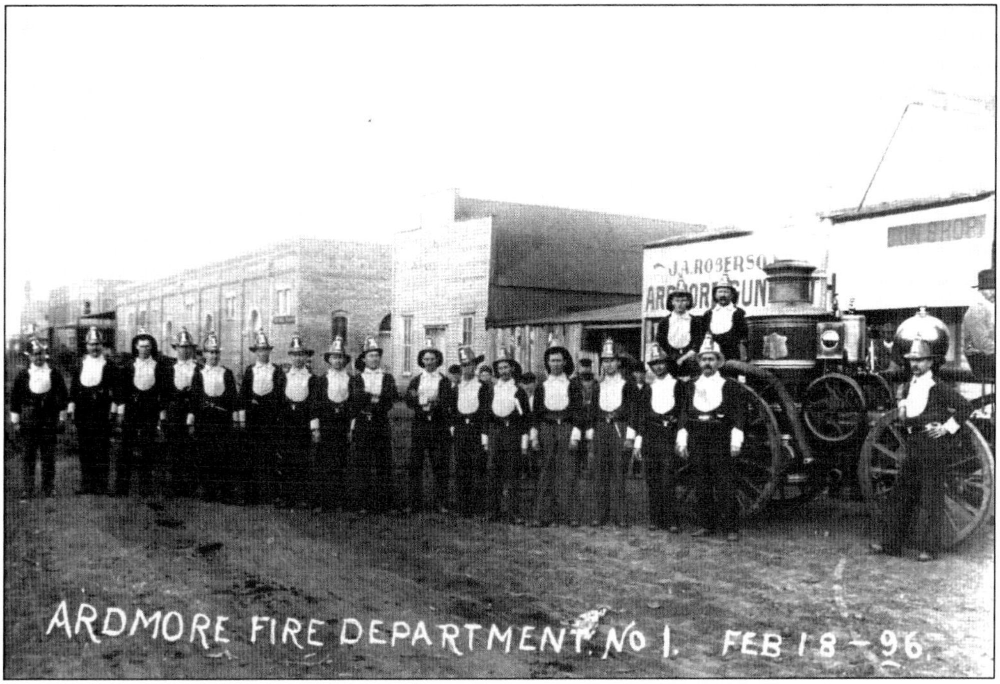

After the fire, the Ardmore Board of Trade helped organize a volunteer fire department in order to satisfy insurance companies, which were threatening to drop coverage of downtown businesses. When the volunteer fire department was organized, John S. O'Mealy became the first fire chief and the 24 charter members also found themselves becoming an elite social club. (Courtesy of the McGalliard Collection, Ardmore Public Library.)

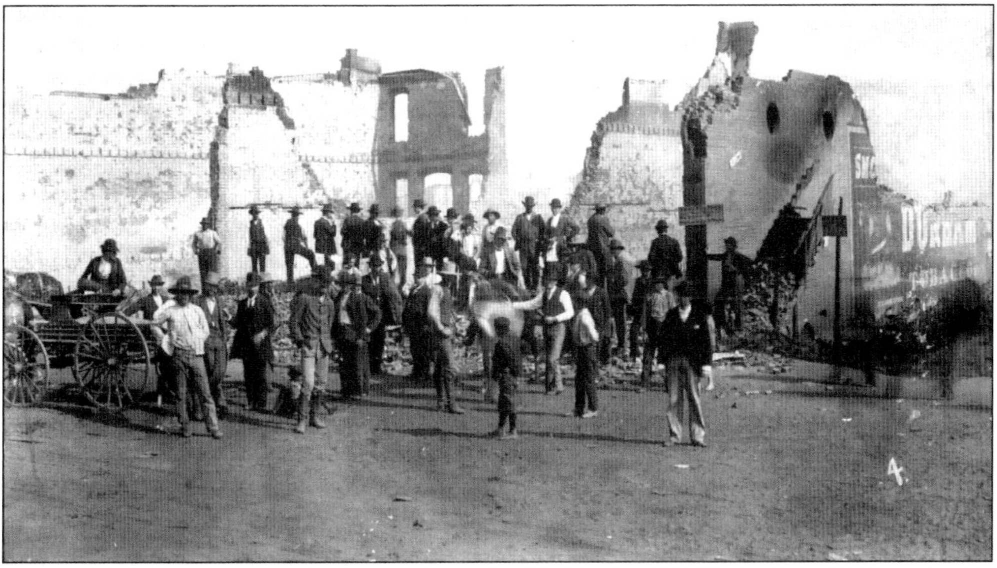

Following a second fire on East Main Street in 1896, the Ardmore Board of Trade raised $1,800 to purchase a fire engine and 600 feet of fire hose. Three large stone-lined cisterns were built on Main Street, which remained in use until 1902. The new buildings erected after the great fire would exist only 20 short years before they would again be destroyed. Here men pose in front of burned-out shells.(Courtesy of the McGalliard Collection, Ardmore Public Library.)

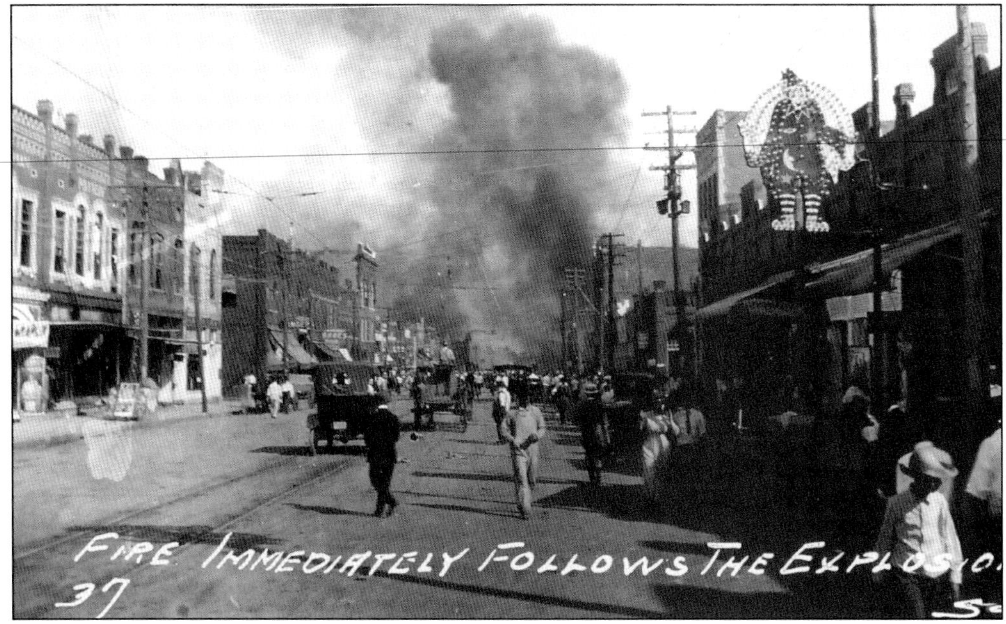

A quick-thinking photographer captured Main Street moments after the explosion. On Saturday, September 25, 1915, a 250-barrel tanker was parked next to the Santa Fe depot waiting removal to the Ardmore Refinery. It was filled with casinghead, a very unstable vapor trapped at the well and added to gasoline to make the mixture more volatile. On Monday, September 27, the tanker was still parked. (Courtesy of the McGalliard Collection, Ardmore Public Library.)

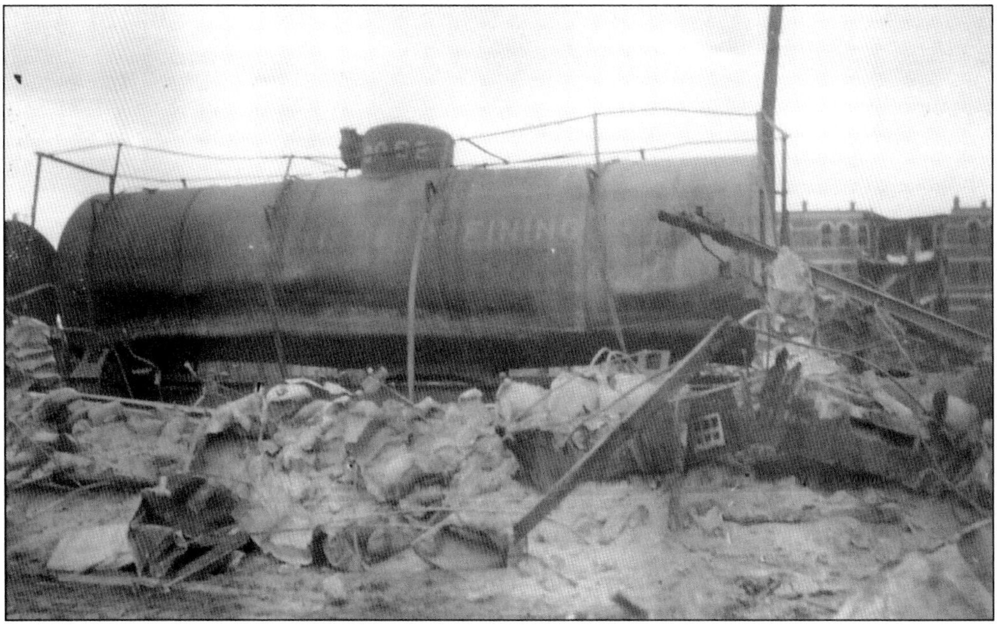

Monday's temperature approached 90 degrees. The unstable casinghead began to seep out of the tanker valves. City commissioner DeWitt went to investigate reported complaints. He could see gasoline mist in the air 80 feet from the tanker. Refinery employee Ira Wood attempted to remove the dome, but pressurized mist shot high into the air. Wood began to run. He did not make it. (Courtesy of the McGalliard Collection, Ardmore Public Library.)

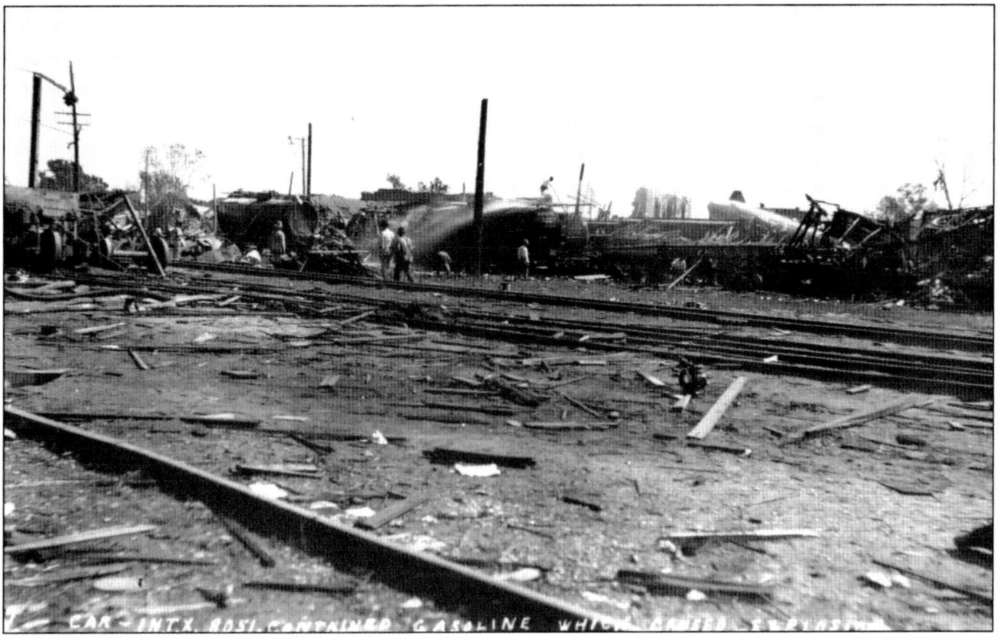

Bits and pieces of the exploded tanker lie amid the debris. Casinghead gas turns to liquid when stored under high pressure, but it must be kept cool or it returns to a vapor. Railroad and refinery officials were aware that fumes were permeating the downtown area, but because of a fire at a nearby asphalt plant, they decided to leave the car parked near the depot. (Courtesy of the McGalliard Collection, Ardmore Public Library.)

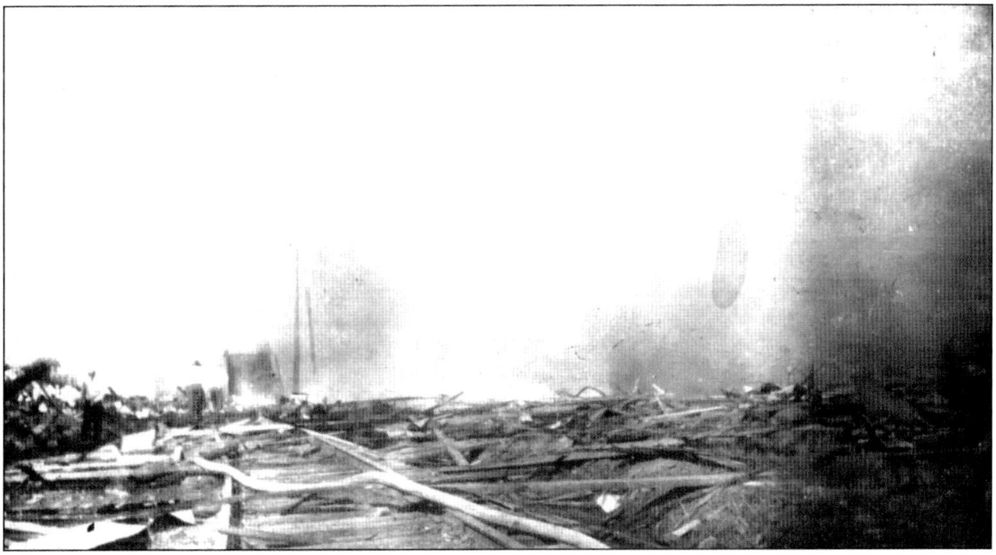

At 2:35 p.m., the mist ignited. The tanker exploded. Following the mist, flames shot 100 feet into the sky and several blocks in all directions. The concussion of the blast from the exploded tanker car simply shattered walls, which fell like dominoes. Immediately there were screams for help, and bystanders quickly began sifting through debris looking for survivors. (Courtesy of the McGalliard Collection, Ardmore Public Library.)

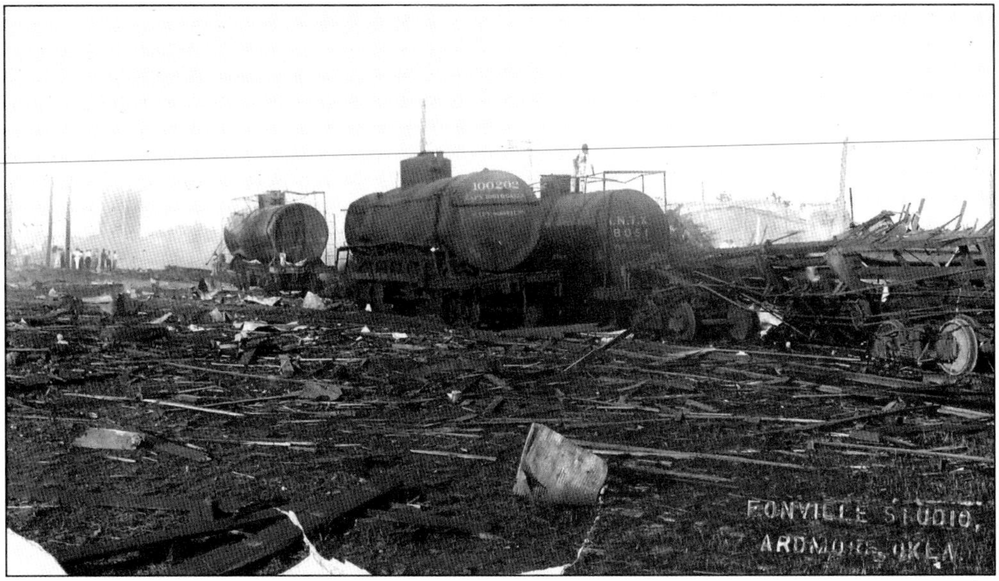

In the immediate area of the explosion, tankers were knocked off the tracks, and even the iron rails were twisted out of place. Debris was flying through the air for hundreds of feet, and the blast itself heavily damaged nearby buildings both east and west of the tracks, but the heaviest business damage was to the west. (Courtesy of the McGalliard Collection, Ardmore Public Library.)

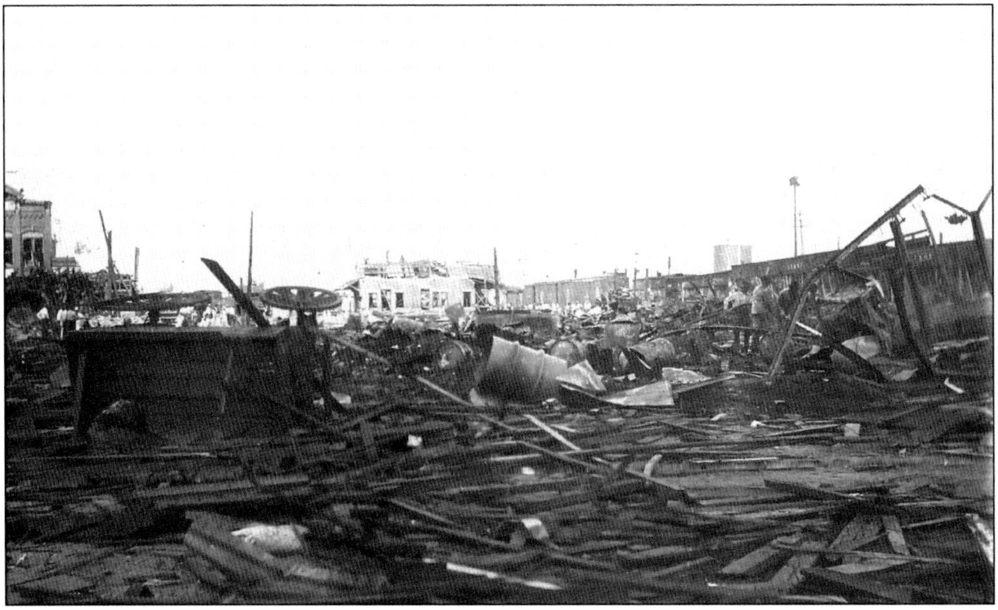

Structures close to the explosion were flattened. Aaron C. Gould, a fruit peddler from Palestine, Texas, along with his wagon and team were literally blown to pieces while crossing the tracks on Main Street. In an interview the next day, the Reverend E. A. Bedichek is reported to have said, "The floors seemed to be rising and the ceiling falling." (Courtesy of the McGalliard Collection, Ardmore Public Library.)

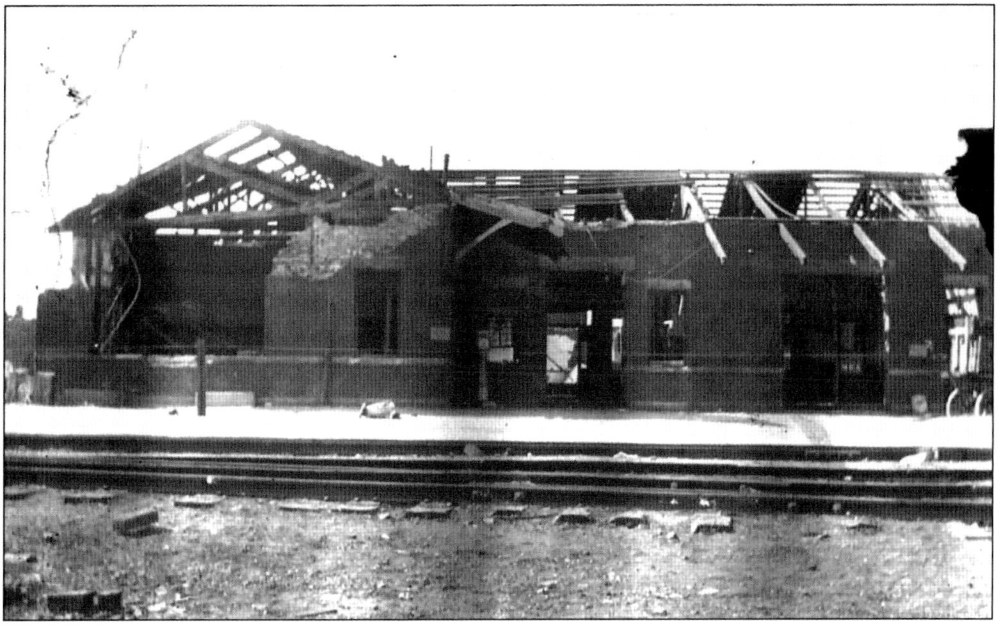

The Ardmore railroad station, which was used by both the Santa Fe Railroad and the Frisco and Rock Island Railroad, was destroyed. Five people were killed in the depot. The Colorado, Rock Island, and Pacific Railroad freight depot and the Santa Fe freight depot burned to the ground after being set on fire by flaming gas thrown from the tanker explosion. (Courtesy of Main Street Authority.)

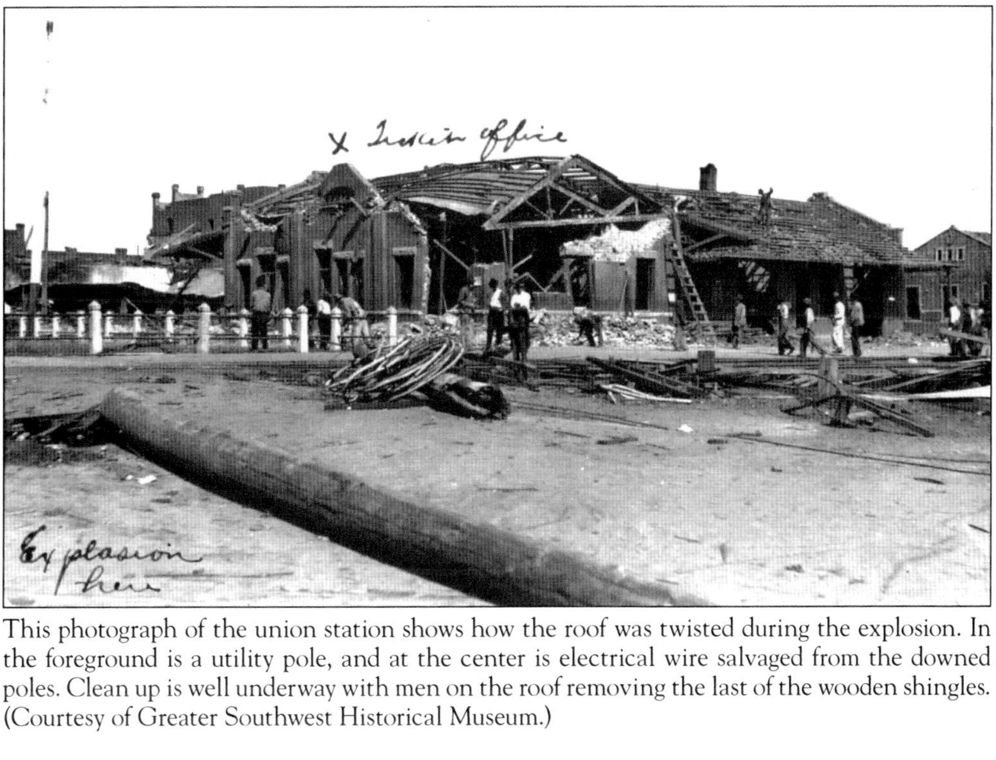

This photograph of the union station shows how the roof was twisted during the explosion. In the foreground is a utility pole, and at the center is electrical wire salvaged from the downed poles. Clean up is well underway with men on the roof removing the last of the wooden shingles. (Courtesy of Greater Southwest Historical Museum.)

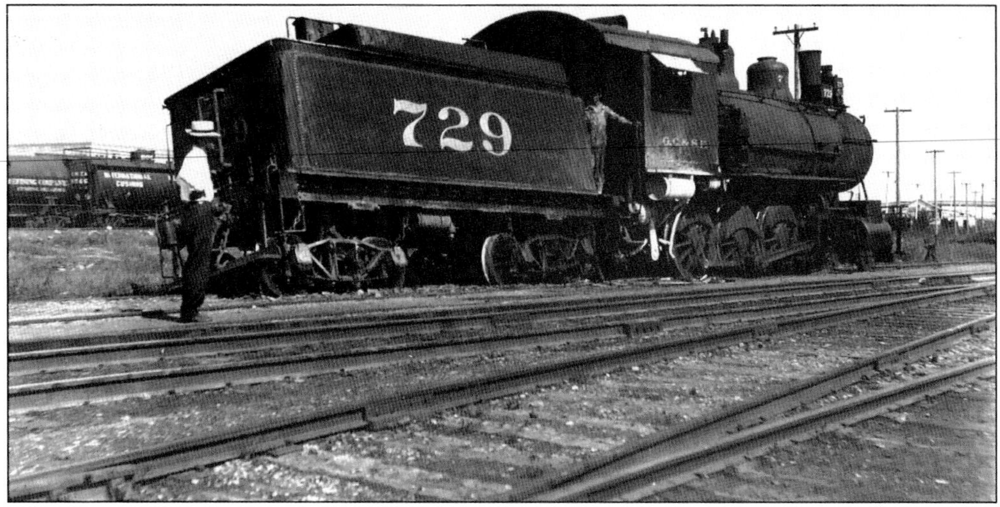

Engine No. 729 was parked on a siding 100 yards to the north of the explosion. The force of the explosion was enough to knock it off its rails. The Colorado, Rock Island, and Pacific Railroad freight depot survived the blast. The DeWitt Cigar factory, which employed 22 girls, was a sturdy rock structure, which survived while buildings on either side were destroyed. (Courtesy of the McGalliard Collection, Ardmore Public Library.)

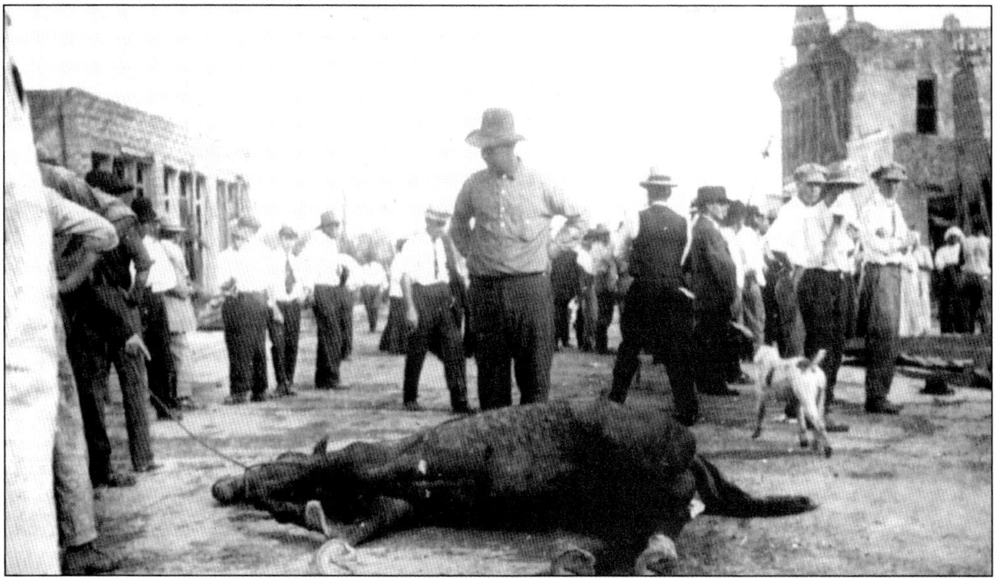

Several horses were killed. One wall collapsed completely, covering a wagon team except for the horses' heads. Houses a half a mile away lost windows and china and crystal in cabinets. Without electricity, there would be no way to continue the rescue effort after dark. Police chief Hutchins declared martial law and called in the militia as the town prepared for the long, dark night ahead. (Courtesy of Greater Southwest Historical Museum.)

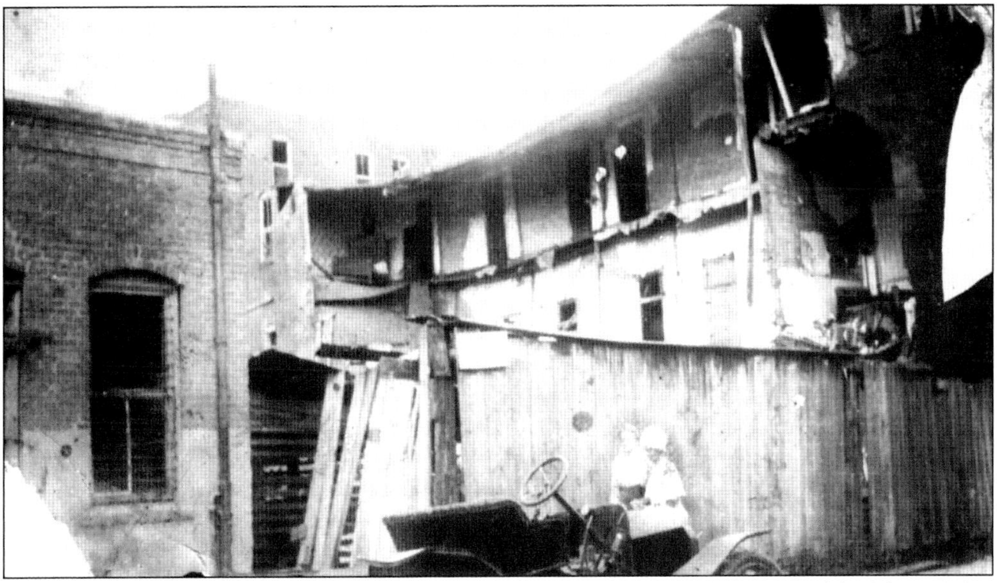

Two women walk past a retaining wall above which looms a severely damaged building. After immediate cleanup efforts cleared city streets, life returned to usual activities amid the continued dismantling of damaged buildings and new construction. This building lost half of the second and third floors. A piece of furniture sits precariously on part of a remaining floor. (Courtesy of Greater Southwest Historical Museum.)

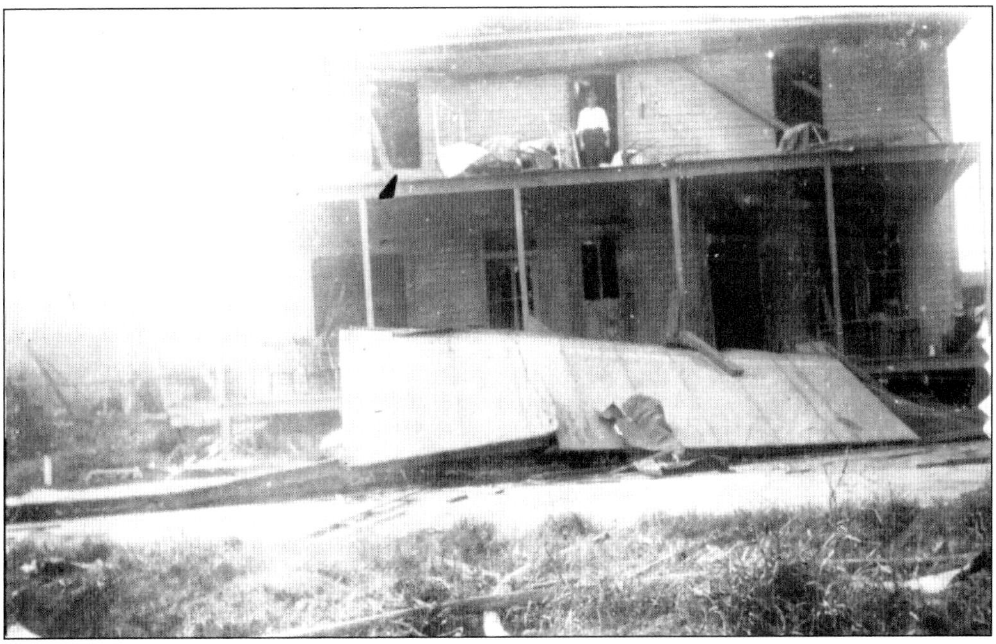

The second-floor roof was torn off this building. Notice the man in the second-story window surveying the damage. The force of the blast snapped numerous utility poles along Main Street. While many buildings collapsed downward, some debris was also scattered throughout the city. One of the most dangerous side effects of the blast was the flying glass and other debris. (Courtesy of Greater Southwest Historical Museum.)

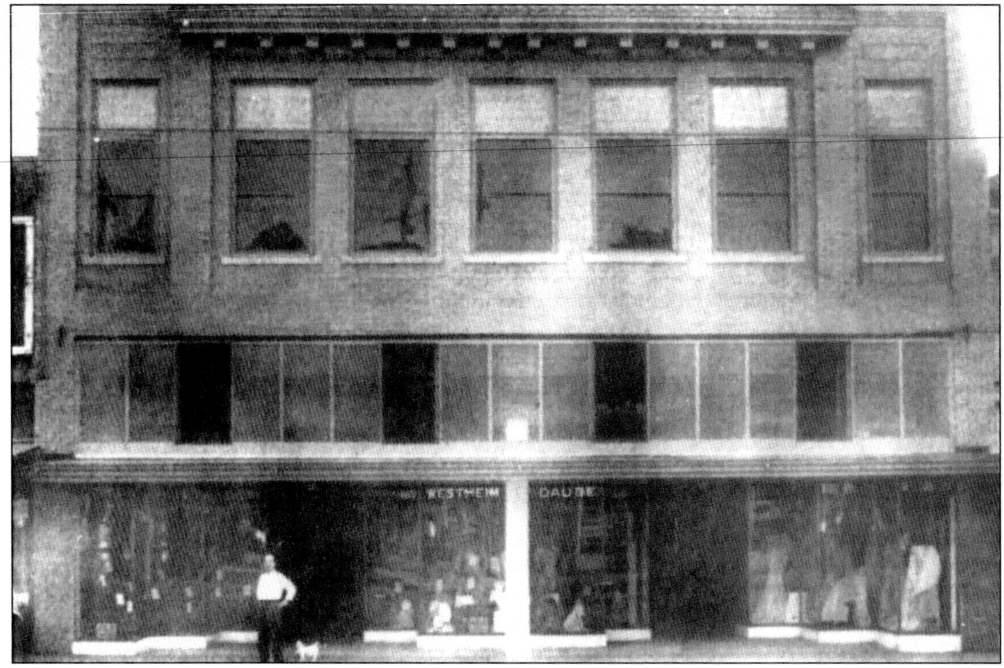

Four blocks away, these curved windows on the first floor of the Westheimer and Daube building survived the 1915 explosion. However, all windows on the second floor were blown out, and windows on the third floor were heavily damaged. Nearly every structure in Ardmore received some damage from cracked windows to total destruction. Two hundred and fifty people were injured, mostly from flying glass. (Courtesy of Ardmore Main Street Authority.)

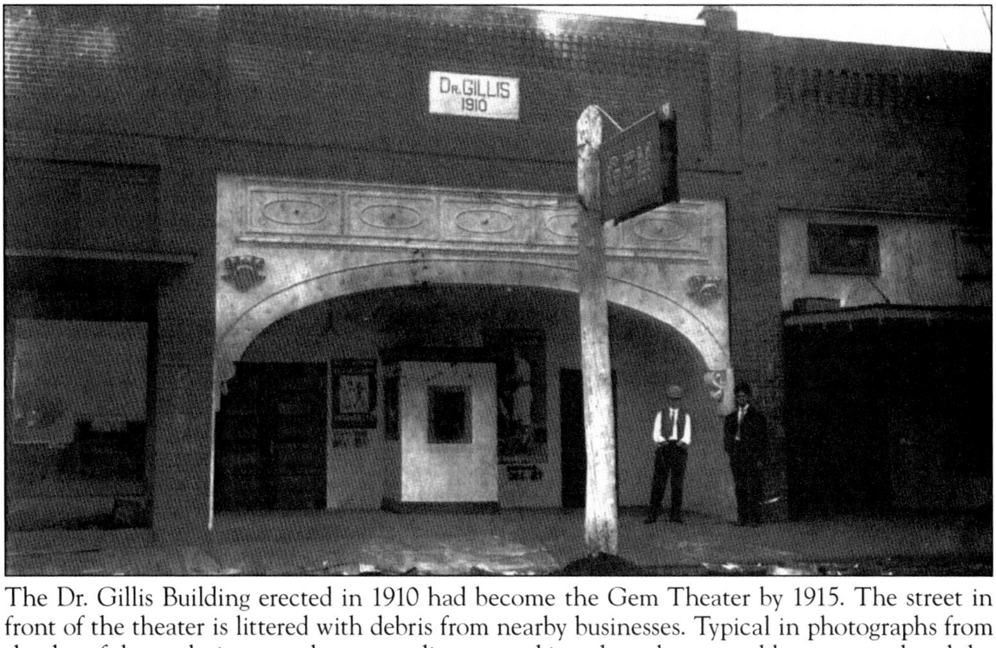

The Dr. Gillis Building erected in 1910 had become the Gem Theater by 1915. The street in front of the theater is littered with debris from nearby businesses. Typical in photographs from the day of the explosion, people are standing around in a daze almost unable to comprehend the gravity of the disaster. The first concerted efforts were to locate survivors and retrieve the dead. (Courtesy of Ardmore Main Street Authority.)

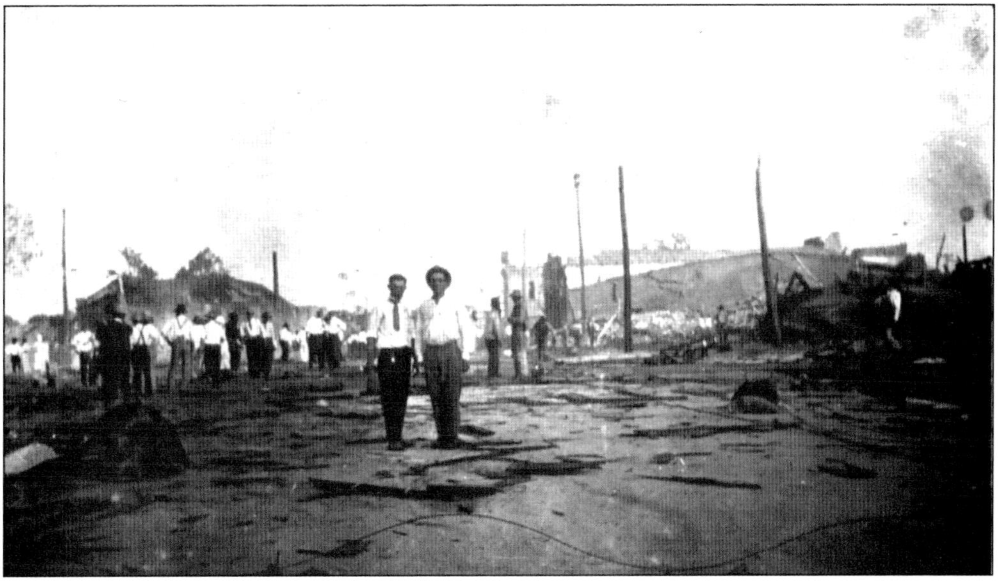

Within minutes people began to congregate in the downtown area. Notice the body language of the bystanders—arms at side in utter disbelief. The devastation was so complete that people hardly knew where to begin the cleanup. Dust from the explosion hung in the air for several days. Notice in the left forefront what appears to be a dead horse. In the background, at right, a roof sags downward. (Courtesy of Greater Southwest Historical Museum.)

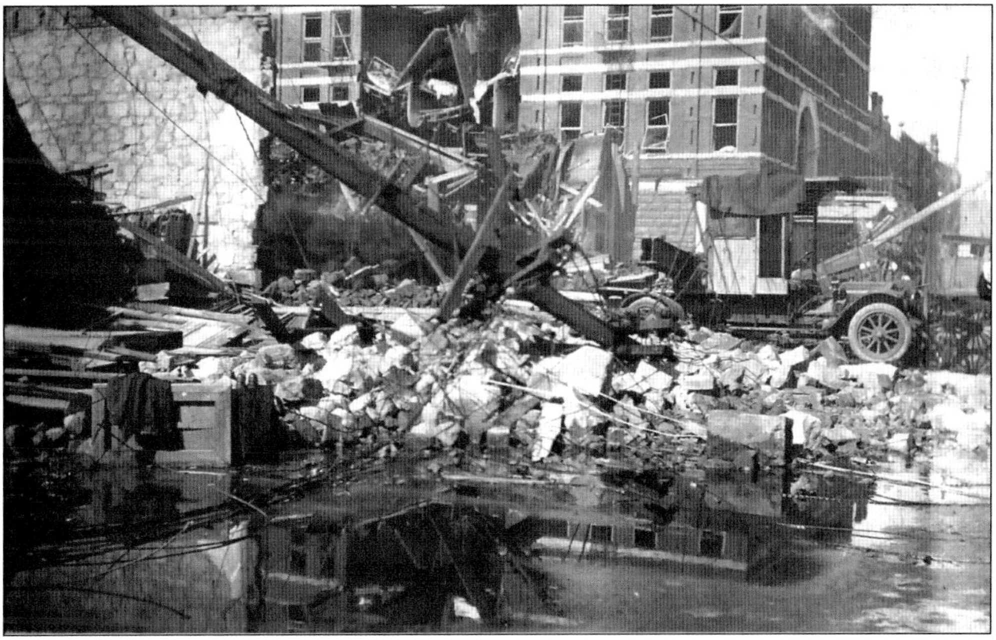

The force of the blast knocked down utility poles such as this one in front of Pennington Grocery. Rock, brick, crates, and merchandise exploded out of the stores onto the street. For 100 feet in all directions from the blast, structures were basically flattened. Ten blocks away, every window in the new high school on North Washington Street was broken. (Courtesy of Ardmore Main Street Authority.)

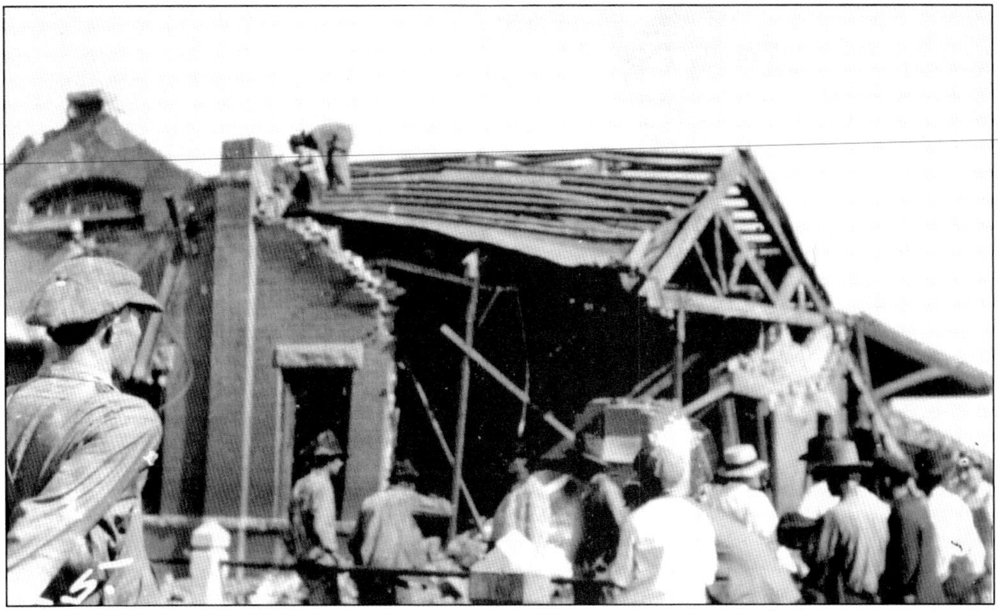

Immediately after the explosion, people began searching for survivors. Both the Santa Fe freight station and the union passenger station were wrecked. At least five were reported dead in the depot. Several horses were killed by the explosion. Most of the injuries came from flying glass and burns. Panic spread when it was rumored that one of the schools had collapsed, killing all the children. (Courtesy of Ardmore Main Street Authority.)

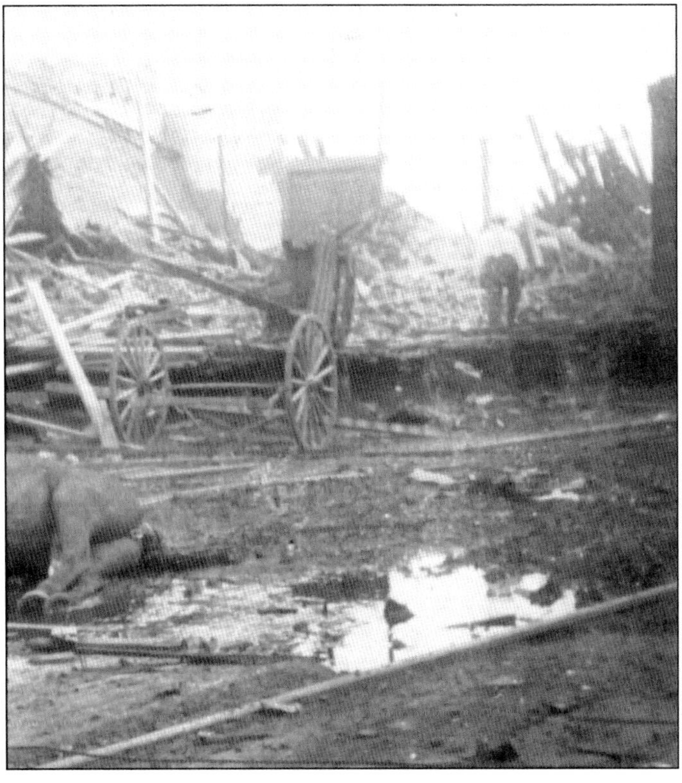

The dead and injured count was difficult to determine because family members took the casualties to private homes after hospitals filled past capacity. Trying to locate and identify the victims was a nightmare. The final official count was 43 dead. More than 250 people were confirmed injured. When the funerals began, it took several days to complete all the burials. (Courtesy of the McGalliard Collection, Ardmore Public Library.)

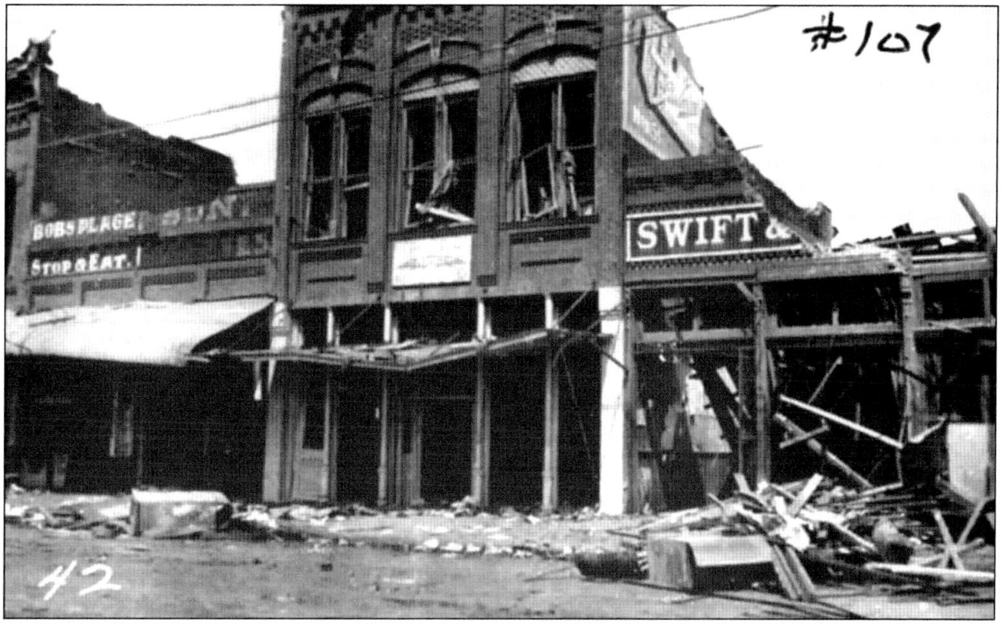

Survivors said the explosion felt like an earthquake. In a pool hall east of Swift's, 13 people were killed. The Ardmoreite building lost doors and windows, and the linotype was damaged. The newspaper still published a Tuesday edition. "The scene beggars description. Almost every family had some member in town somewhere and men and women were frantically searching for missing ones," the *Daily Ardmoreite* reported. (Courtesy of Ardmore Main Street Authority.)

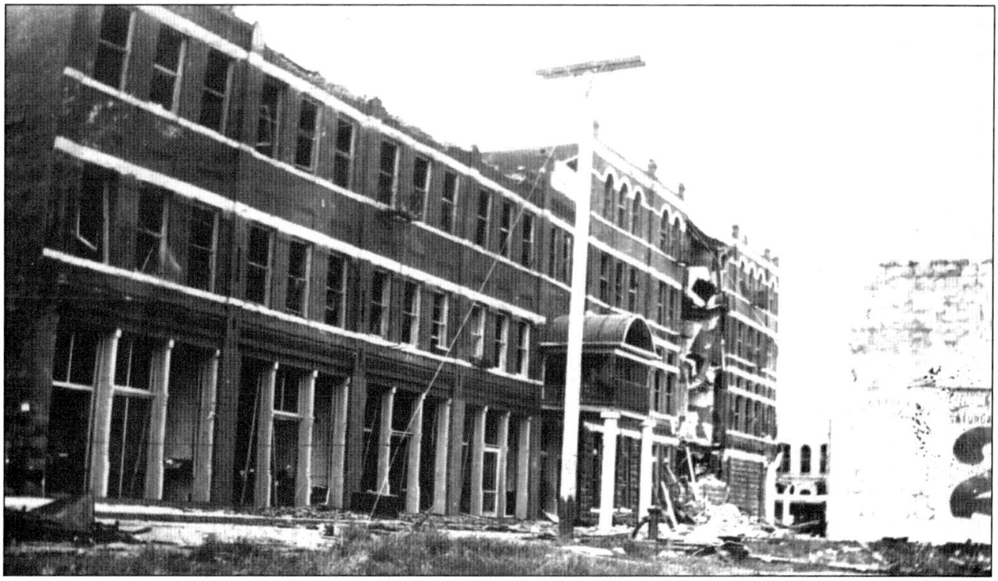
Every window in the east side of the Whittington Hotel disintegrated. About a fourth of the way south along the building, part of the wall gave way from fourth floor to the ground. Floors and ceilings buckled, and wood splintered like matchsticks. This part of the building and Pennington Grocery must have been in a direct line with the explosion. (Courtesy of Greater Southwest Historical Museum.)

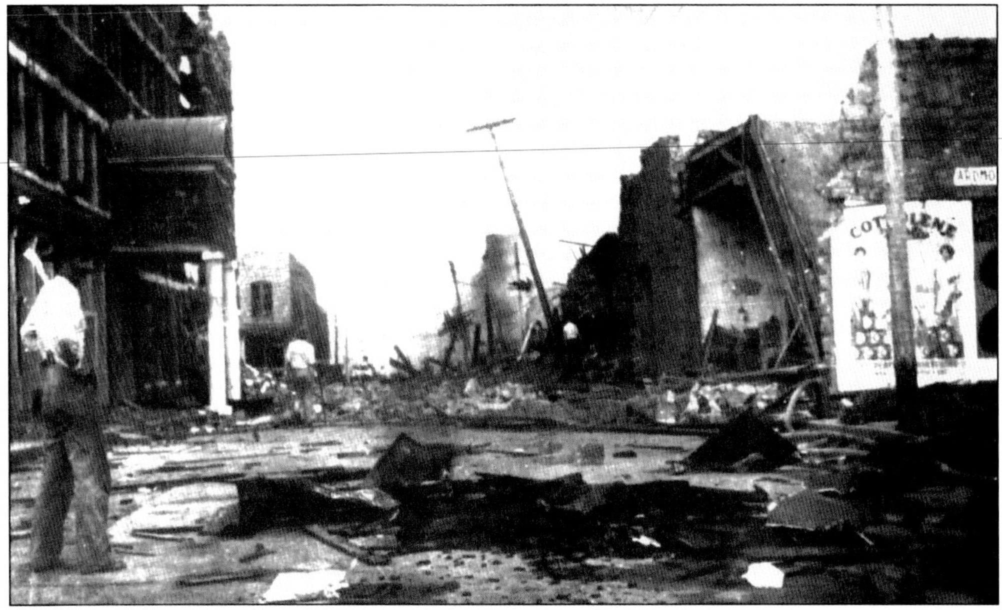

This photograph is of the east side of the Whittington Hotel. Not only did the window glass shatter, but the window frames were also blown out of the wall and doors were blown off hinges. Debris piled as high as 10 feet in several areas. On the right is the heavily damaged Pennington Grocery where six people died. (Courtesy of Greater Southwest Historical Museum.)

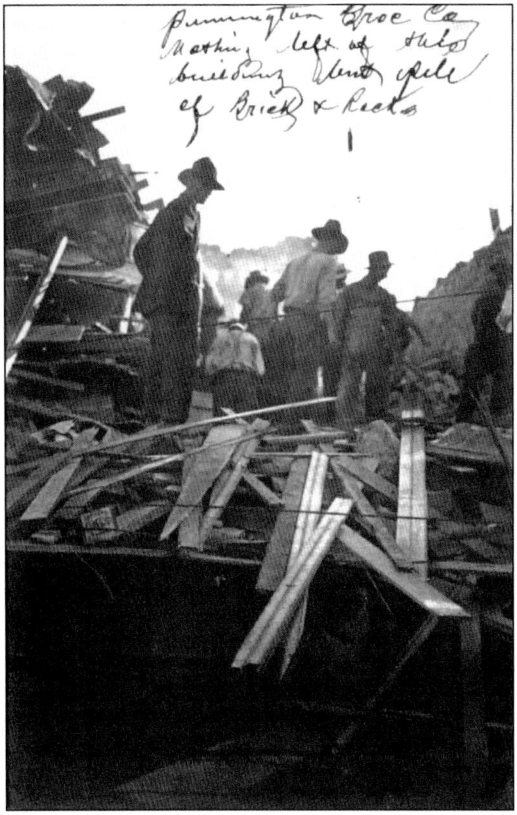

These men are standing on a pile of rubble that had been Pennington Grocery. East of the tracks, Ladd and Davidson's wholesale house was badly damaged and Mrs. Davidson severely injured. The whole downtown area was littered with bits of brick and broken glass; people bloodied from flying glass were in shock. Yet immediately, men began sifting through debris looking for survivors. (Courtesy of Greater Southwest Historical Museum.)

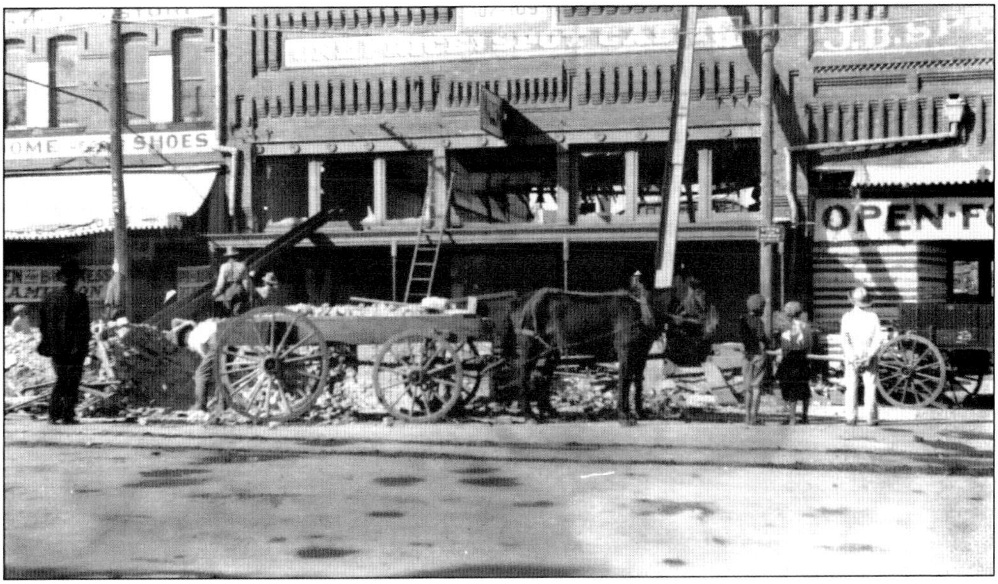

Cleanup from the explosion followed immediately after retrieving the dead. One of the hardest-hit buildings was Madden and Sykes Department Store where the roof collapsed. Even though damaged, J. B. Spraggins harness and buggy store was open for business the next day. A banner was stretched across the front of the store to alert the public. (Courtesy of Greater Southwest Historical Museum.)

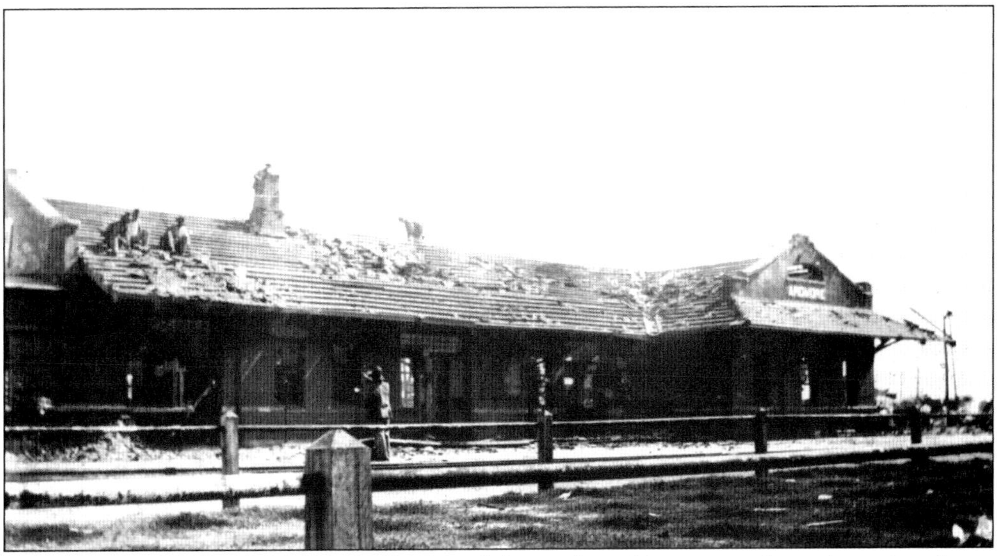

The windows were all blown out and most of the roof was blown away from the union depot, but within a couple of days, men were replacing the heavily damaged roof. One of the biggest problems was hauling away the debris. Tons of brick and stone and pulverized brick had to be shoveled into wagons and hauled away. Much of the lumber was recycled into new buildings. (Courtesy of Greater Southwest Historical Museum.)

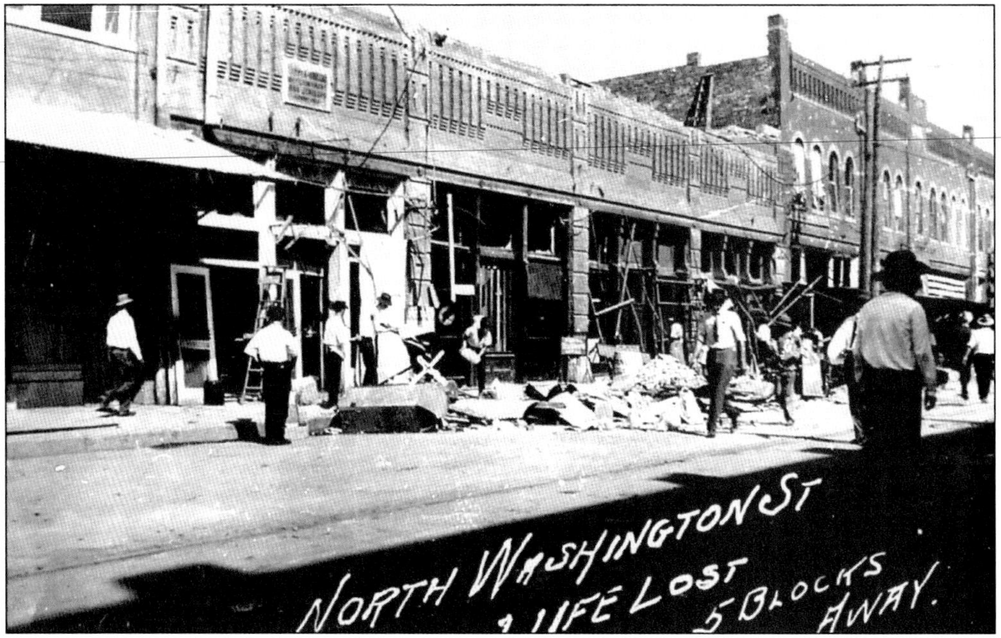

Five blocks away, buildings on North Washington Street were damaged and M. E. Atkins, a drayman, was killed when this wall fell on him and his horse. Twenty-five bodies were recovered on the afternoon of the explosion with another 18 being recovered during the next few days. Newspapers worked frantically to print the names of the dead and wounded so the citizens could find their loved ones. (Courtesy of Ardmore Main Street Authority.)

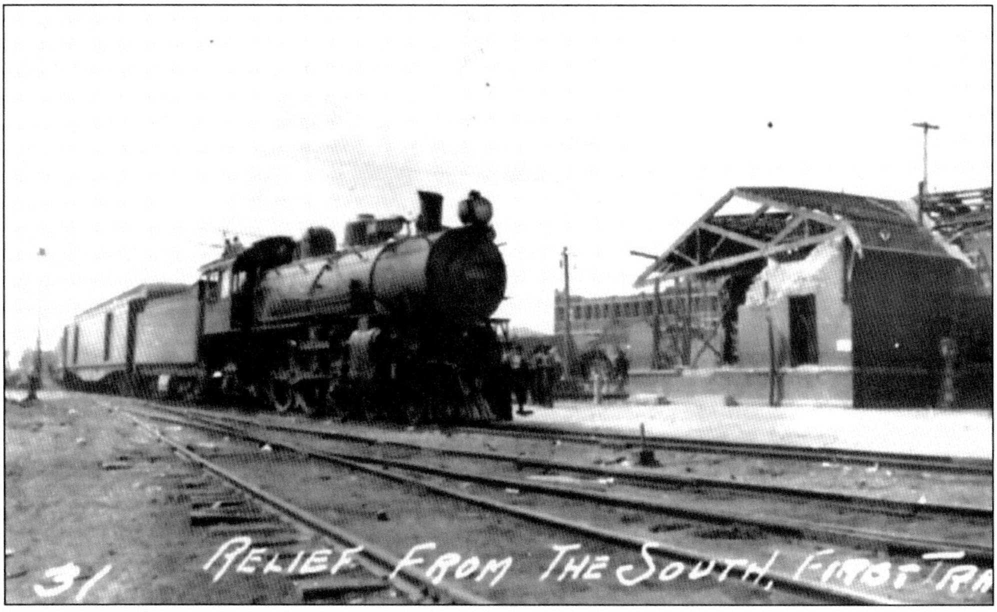

Mercy train No. 1108 brought doctors and nurses into Ardmore from northern Texas. Ardmore's hospital facilities were filled to capacity. Investigation found the Santa Fe Railroad at fault. More than $250,000 was paid in claims. For the second time in 20 years, downtown Ardmore rose like a phoenix, a city reborn from the ashes. This explosion remains the largest oil-related disaster in Oklahoma history. (Courtesy of Ardmore Main Street Authority.)

Four

The Builders

Every community has a group of well-known personages who helped build the fabric of society. For every one of these people, there are 50 to 100 unknowns who have worked faithfully, if on a smaller scale, to improve the community. The early settlers included the intermarried citizens such as the Washington, Fitch, Roff, McLish, and Addington families. Their names come down through history because they were recorded in the annals of the Chickasaw Nation. The intruders such as Zuckerman, Frensley, Munzesheimer, Westheimer, Daube, and Whittington are recorded in history because they brought commerce and built buildings and businesses that carried their names. But without the men who worked for the large ranches as cowhands, the men and women who worked as clerks in the businesses, and the families and small farmers who were the customers, the town of Ardmore would have been only a railroad station. It was the ordinary citizens who came to Indian Territory hoping to find a better life that made Ardmore a city. These are the people who raised chickens and eggs and grew vegetables for the downtown merchants to sell in their stores; the painters and bricklayers; seamstresses and haberdashers; cigar and gun factory employees; and the soda fountain clerk. The ladies and gentlemen who formed social clubs and participated in community projects to improve the cultural climate also helped build Ardmore. It was the everyday citizen who grew the population to 2,500 so that Ardmore could be incorporated as a second-class city. And it was the increase in ordinary citizens that drove the population to 5,000 within a year so that Ardmore became a city of the first class. None of the businesses could have flourished, none of the attorneys or doctors could have sustained their practice but for the general population that came into Ardmore. Just as the *Daily Ardmoreite* summed it up after the great fire in 1895, the people of Ardmore were—and still are—"filled with courage and enterprise."

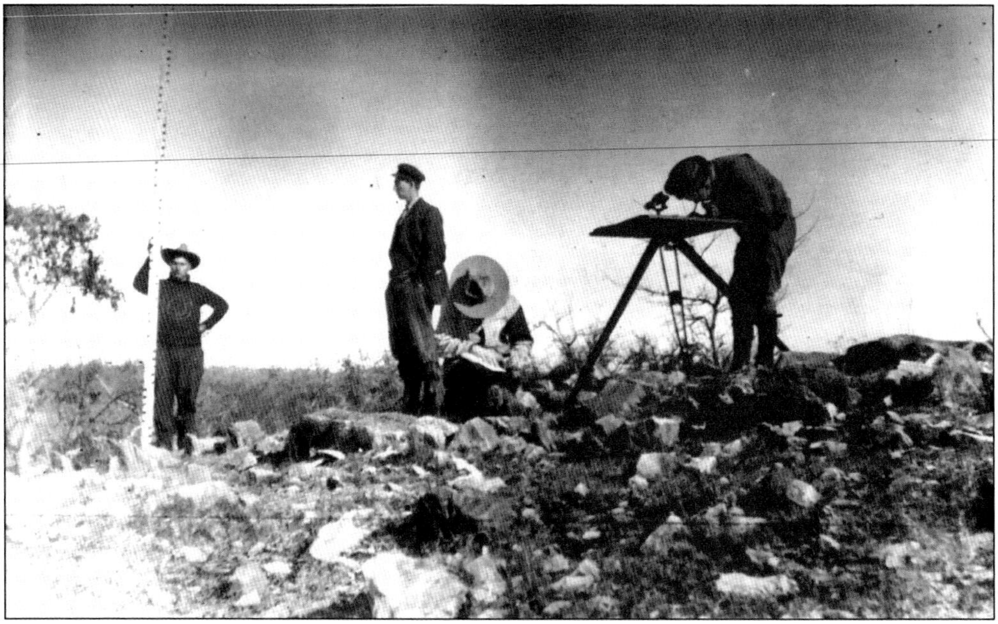

This is the first topographic survey party in the Arbuckle Mountains. They surveyed the initial point from which all property descriptions in Oklahoma emanate, in the Arbuckle Mountains just south of where Fort Arbuckle was located. It marks the intersection of the Indian Meridian, which divides Oklahoma into east and west ranges, and the base line, which divides the state into north and south townships. (Courtesy of Sally Gray.)

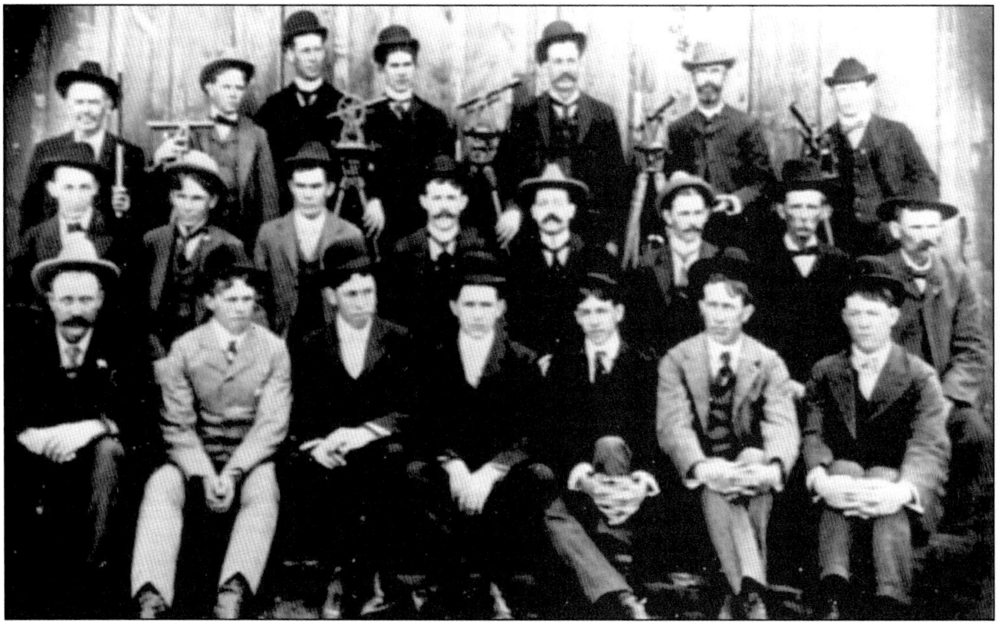

Because tribal lands were communal, neither tribal citizen nor the intruder could own land. The city builders wanted to legally own the town lots on which they had invested to construct businesses. The Dawes Commission's mandate to negotiate with the tribes to allot tribal lands in severalty was a direct result of efforts by businessmen determined to protect their investments. This photograph shows the crew that surveyed Ardmore. (Courtesy of Sally Gray.)

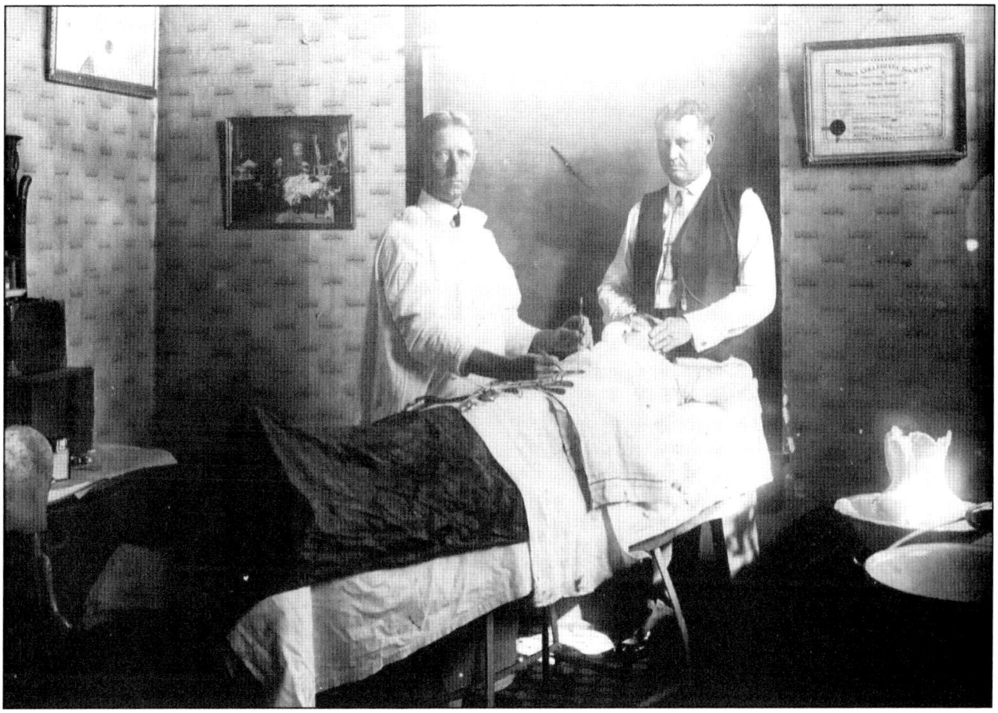

Along with attorneys who came to make their fortunes amid the many land deals that would ultimately arise came the doctors. This photograph from about 1910 shows the doctor and his assistant preparing to operate on a young boy. The diploma on the wall was granted to Brutus C. Rutherford from the Medical Society in Chattanooga, Tennessee. (Courtesy of the McGalliard Collection, Ardmore Public Library.)

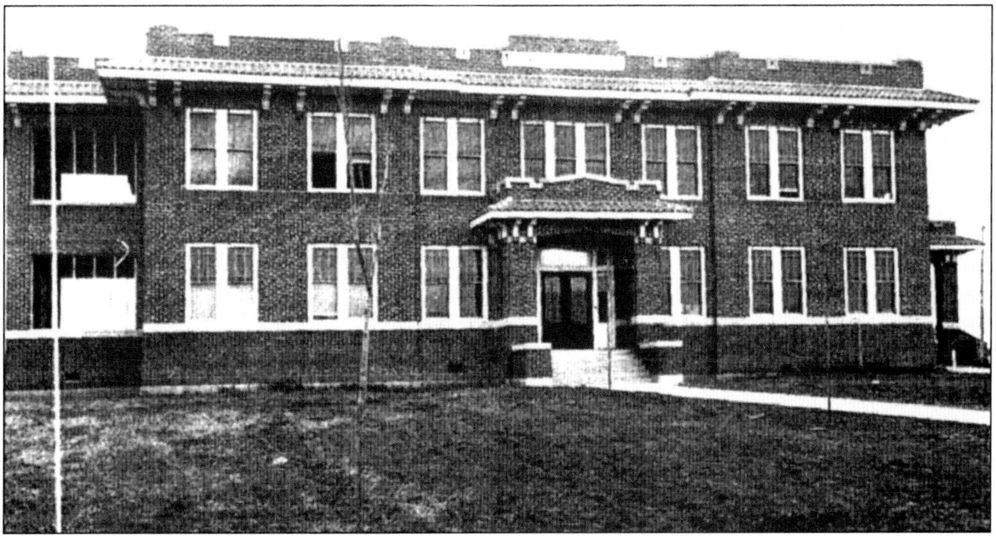

Dr. F. P. von Keller, Dr. Walter Hardy, and several other doctors opened the Ardmore Sanitarium in 1898. The best medical facility between Oklahoma City and Dallas, Texas, the hospital operated on the second floor above Ramsey Drug until 1911. Dr. von Keller, who held degrees from the University of Heidelberg and Rush Medical College, Chicago, built this hospital in 1917 at Twelfth Street and K Street NW. (Courtesy of Sally Gray.)

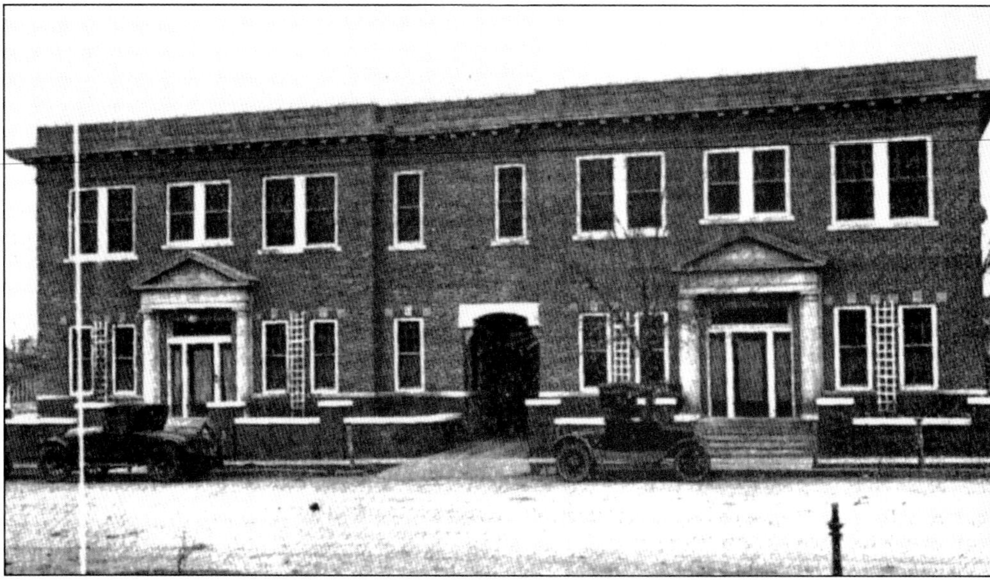

Hardy Sanitarium was built in 1911 on the southwest corner of First Street and B Street SW. Dr. Walter Hardy received his training at Missouri Medical College. He arrived in Ardmore in the 1890s, opening his practice in the second story of a drugstore. He spearheaded organization of the Ardmore Sanitarium in 1898. It advertised "Medical and Surgical cases treated at reasonable terms. Trained nurses in attendance." (Courtesy of Sally Gray.)

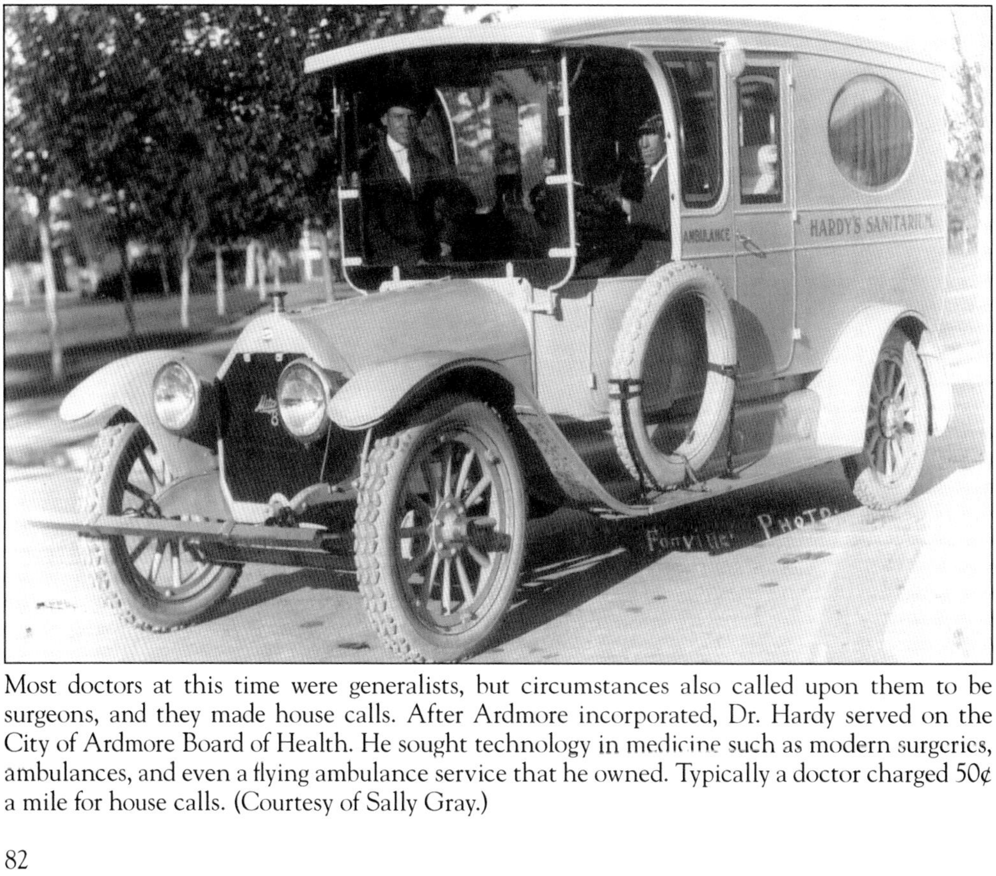

Most doctors at this time were generalists, but circumstances also called upon them to be surgeons, and they made house calls. After Ardmore incorporated, Dr. Hardy served on the City of Ardmore Board of Health. He sought technology in medicine such as modern surgeries, ambulances, and even a flying ambulance service that he owned. Typically a doctor charged 50¢ a mile for house calls. (Courtesy of Sally Gray.)

Before Ardmore incorporated, churches were building and strengthening the fabric of society. Prior to 1887, circuit-riding preachers brought the word to southern Pickens County. By 1888, a 12-member Methodist congregation met as the Broadway Methodist Church with Pastor Lewis H. Stuckey as the first full-time minister. The church built three structures on Broadway before building this sanctuary on West Main Street. (Courtesy of Greater Southwest Historical Museum.)

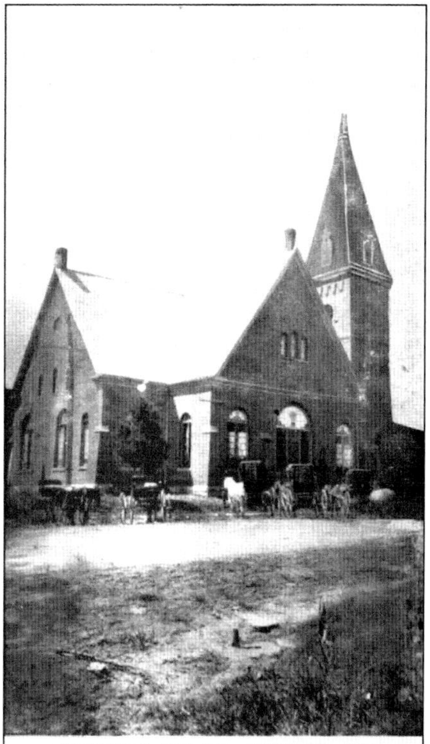

METHODIST CHURCH, ARDMORE, OKLA.

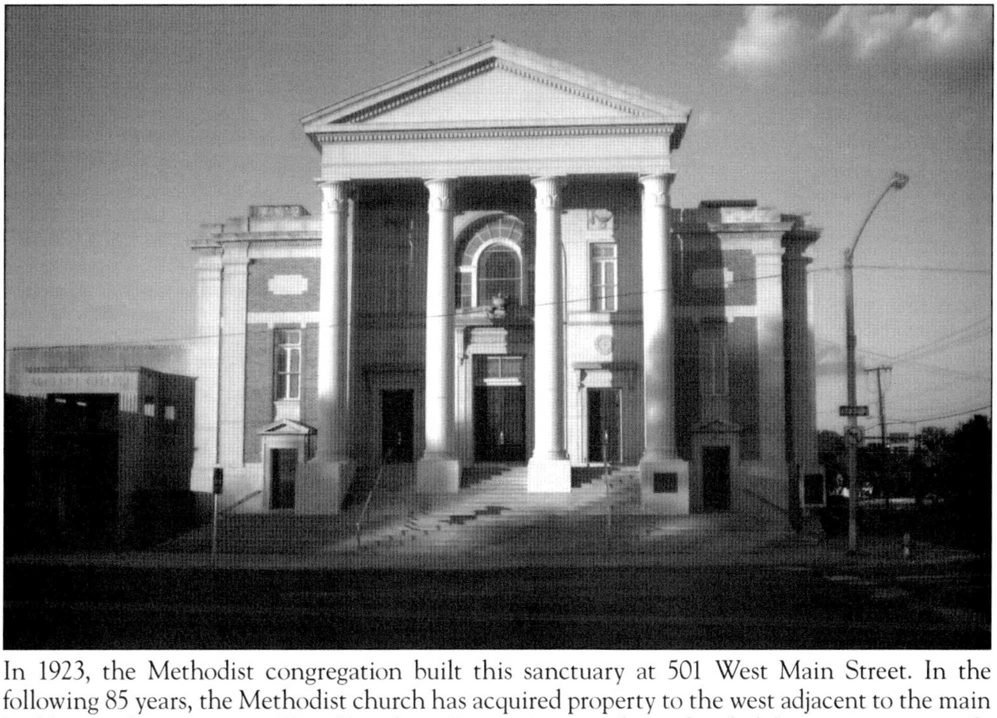

In 1923, the Methodist congregation built this sanctuary at 501 West Main Street. In the following 85 years, the Methodist church has acquired property to the west adjacent to the main building and north across West Broadway Street. A magnificent family life center was recently completed. Today church property covers more than three city blocks. (Author's collection.)

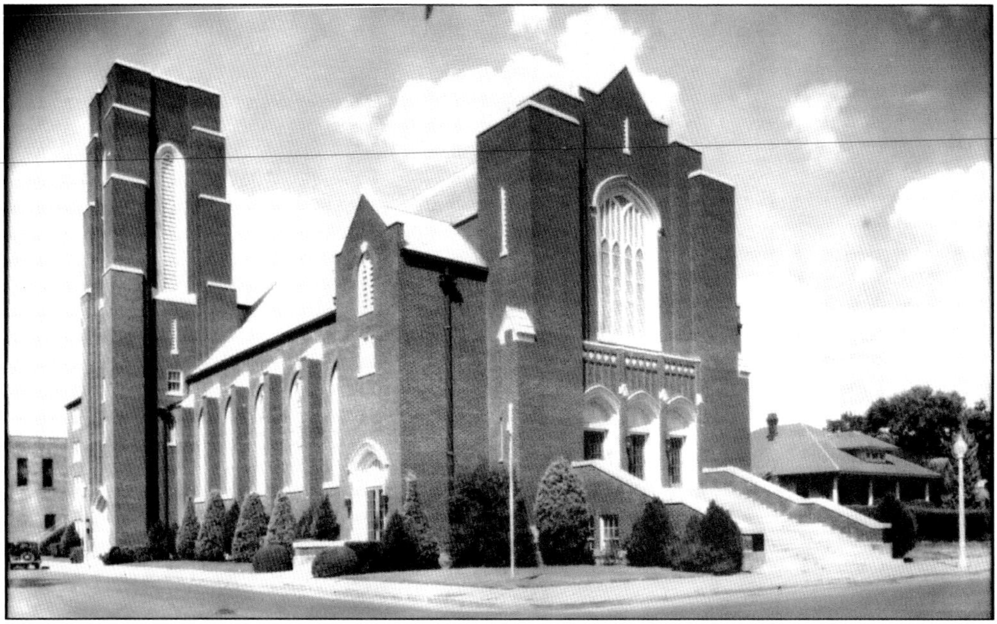

The Baptists also organized a church on Broadway in 1888 under Pastor J. P. Masters. In 1900, the congregation split into two groups known as Central Baptists and First Baptists. In 1907, the two churches recombined, holding services in the larger Central Baptist building under the name Broadway Baptist Church. The current sanctuary located at First Street and C Street SW was built in 1927. (Courtesy of Greater Southwest Historical Museum.)

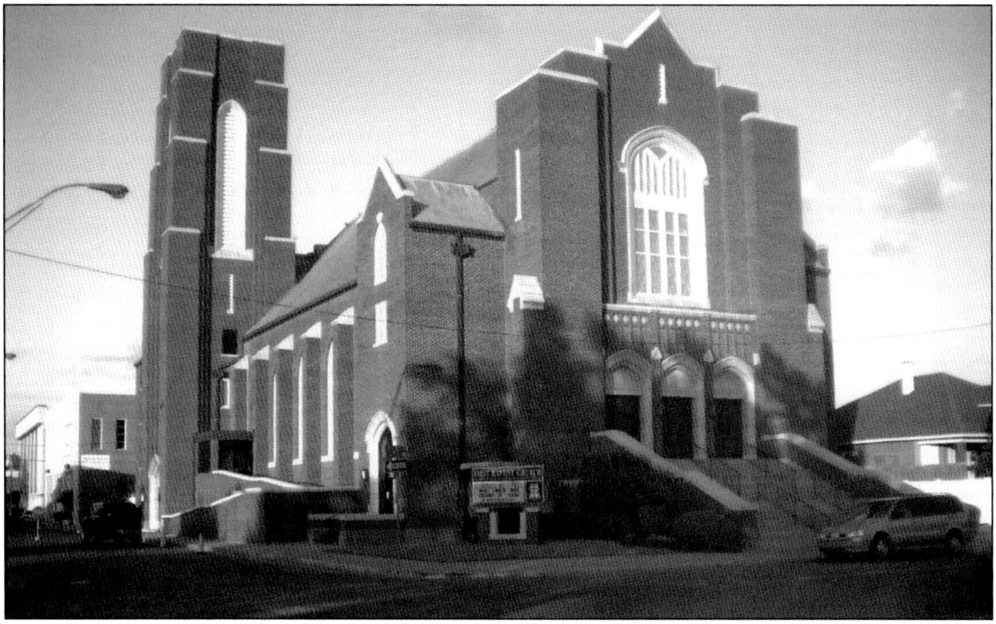

The total membership of First Baptist Church exceeds 4,000. To the west of the main building, Brady Chapel, the adult annex, the children's building, and the fellowship hall have been joined together. One block north on Main Street is the youth building. In the former Craddock Funeral Home is special ministries. A missionary house and Loaves and Fishes sit on a whole city block, which also provides parking. (Author's collection.)

St. Mary's Catholic Church opened in this frame structure in 1901. At far left, behind the church, is the new brick, three-story Third Ward School, Lincoln, which was built in 1903. After the frame church was replaced by the current sanctuary, the church built an addition to the north, which was a Catholic school, then Oak Hall Episcopal School, and Take II Alternative School. (Courtesy of Sally Gray.)

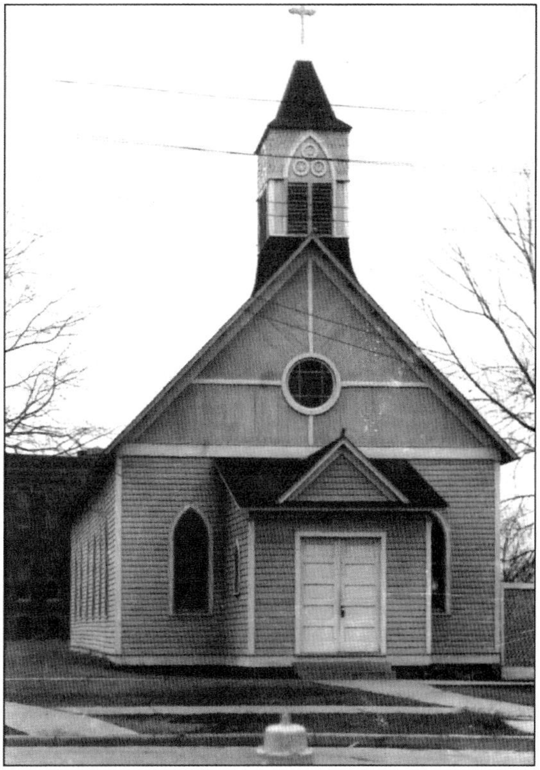

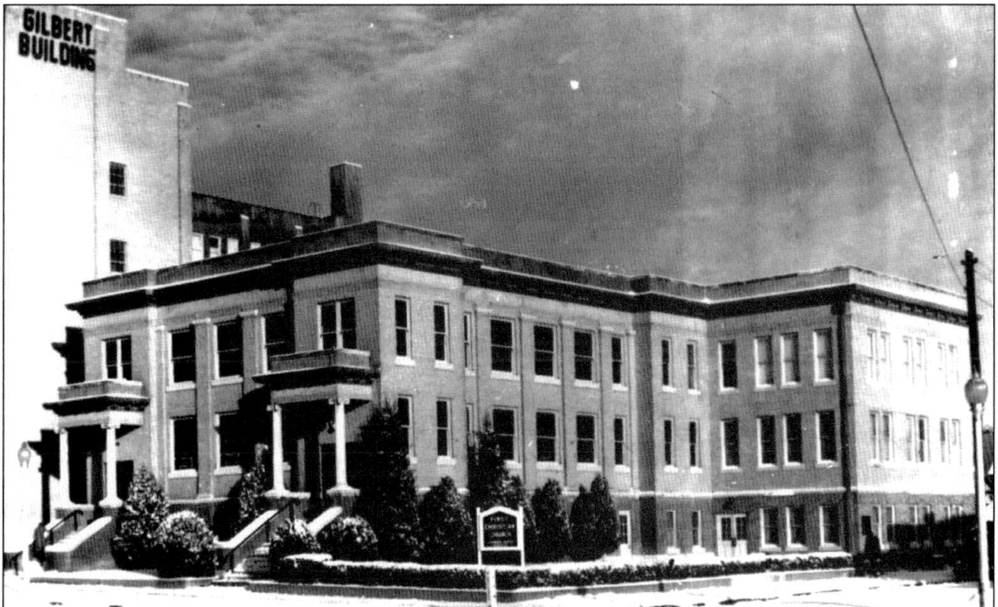

Also in 1888, the Christian church held services on West Broadway under elder A. J. Farthing, who had come to Ardmore from Gainesville, Texas. These first meetings were held in a tent before the congregation moved into a frame building north of the present church. In 1913, the First Christian Church built this sanctuary on the corner of Broadway and A Street NW. (Courtesy of Greater Southwest Historical Museum.)

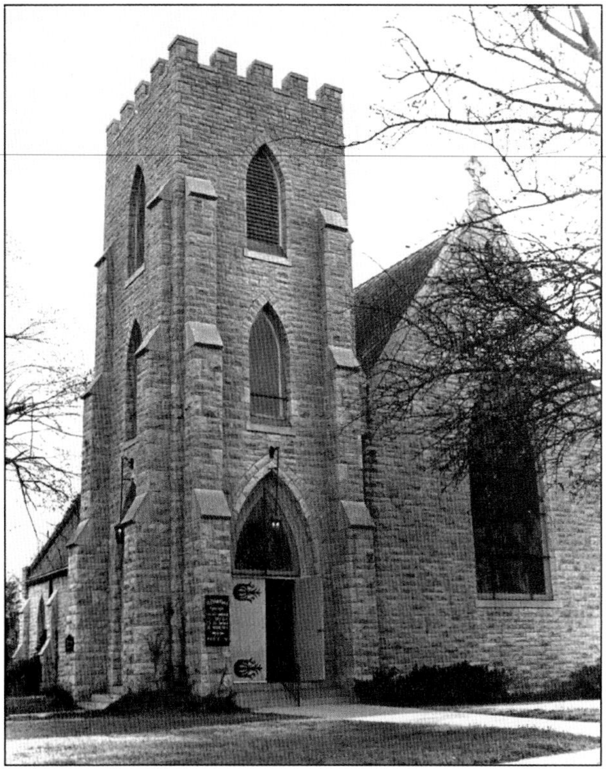

St. Phillips Episcopal Church began in a small wooden structure. This rock building celebrated its first service on Christmas Eve 1927. The first congregation gathered in 1893 to establish the church. Also in 1893, the First Church of Christ, Christian Science, and Carter Avenue Methodist Church were established. In 1898, Temple Emeth was established by the Jewish community. (Courtesy of Sally Gray.)

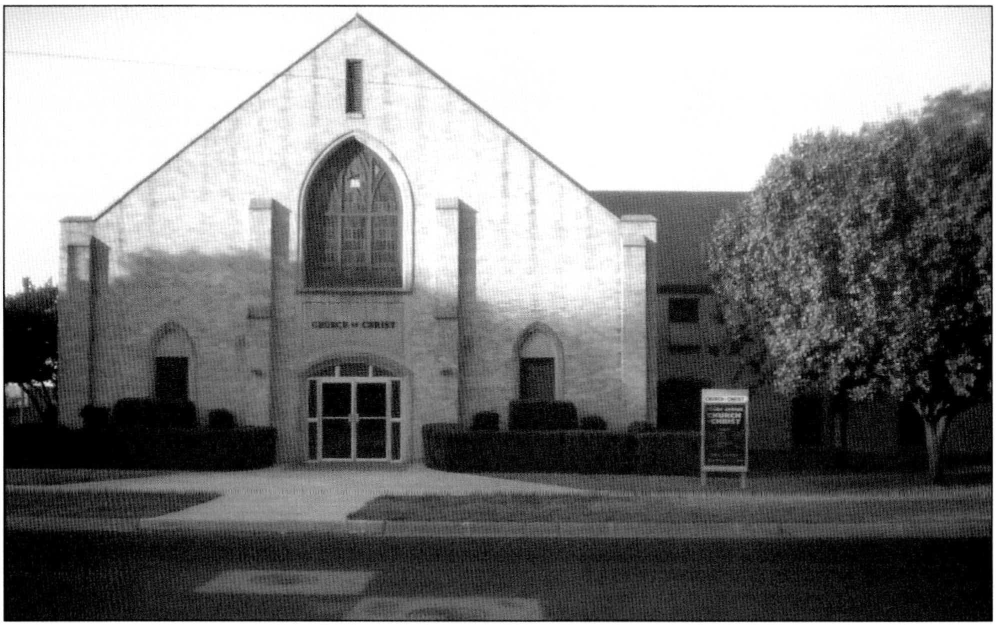

The Central Park Church of Christ is one of six churches established within a block of Central Park representing five different Christian denominations and a Jewish synagogue. Ardmore's early population was clearly religious, and that may have accounted for the consistent expansion of businesses and population. Except for Temple Emeth, each of the downtown churches continues to thrive and expand in the downtown area. (Author's collection.)

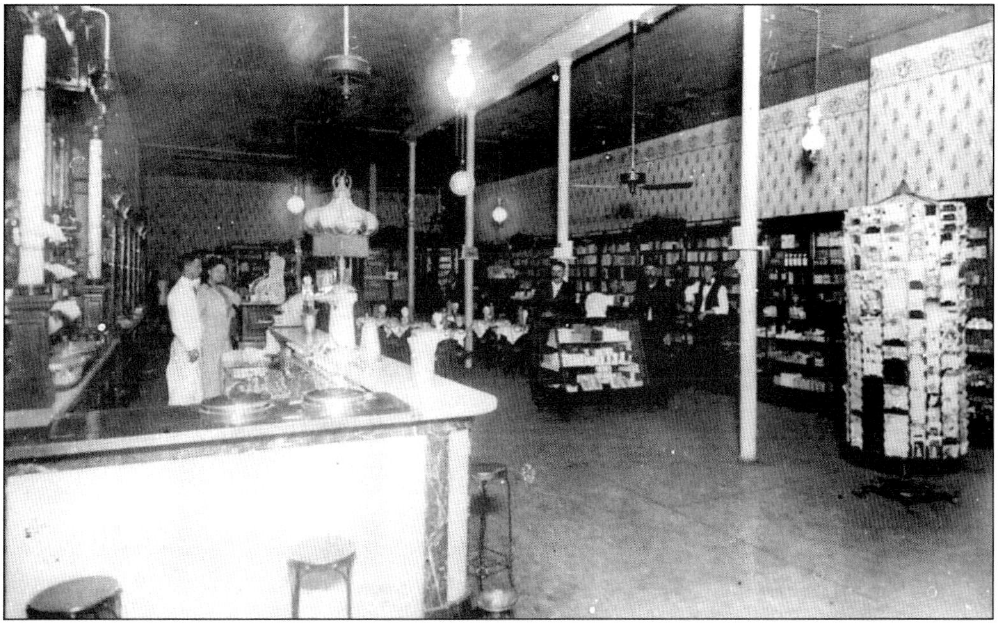

Early-day drugstores, such as this one, typically had a soda fountain at which customers could sip a cool, carbonated beverage or enjoy a scoop of ice cream. Drugstores became the favorite haunt of particular groups as Reaves Drug was a meeting place for teenagers for several decades. Notice the greeting card rack and a spittoon at the base of the fountain. (Courtesy of Ardmore Main Street Authority.)

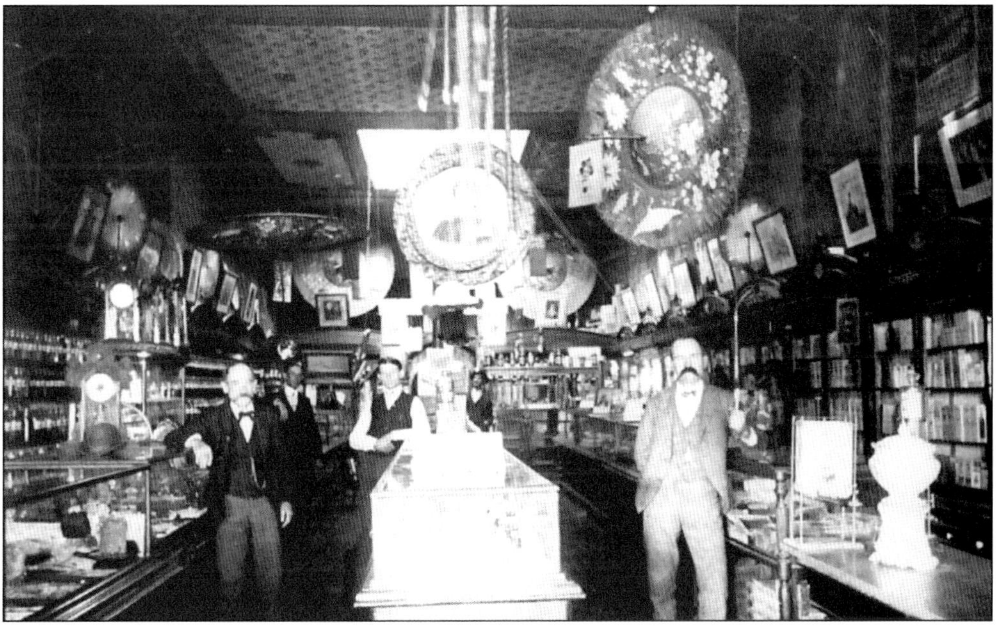

This store was a forerunner of the modern variety store. Merchandise, still behind the counter, is not easily accessible to the customer. Notice the glass display cases at left. Hats hang from the ceiling, and pictures hang above merchandise on the right wall. Typically early stores were very long, as much as 100 feet, and narrow. Stools for the soda fountain are at right. (Courtesy of Sally Gray.)

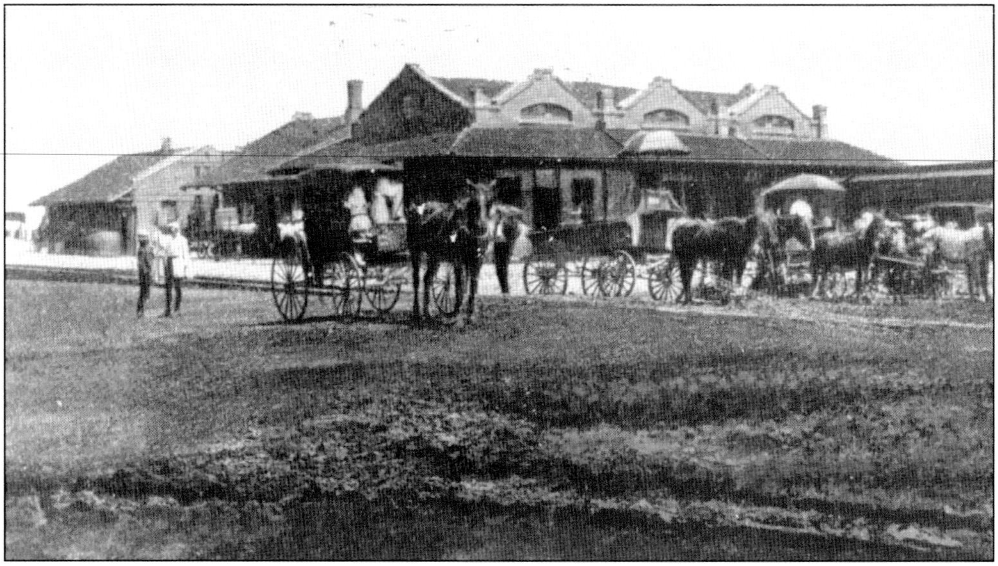

This early photograph of the Ardmore station shows wagons parked beside the rails waiting for the train to bring supplies. Draymen, or deliverymen, unloaded goods and took them to outlying farms, ranches, and rural stores. As many as five different rail companies brought business to the Ardmore station on multiple sets of tracks. (Courtesy of Ardmore Main Street Authority.)

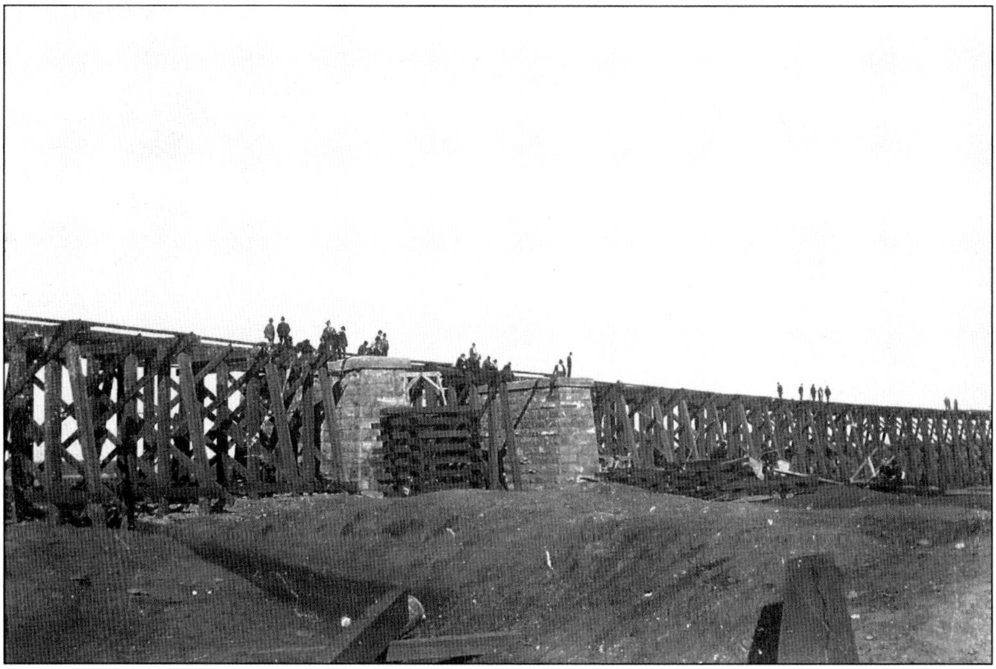

Ardmore was built as a railroad station, and its early history is closely aligned with railroad growth. This photograph dated about 1900 shows men working on a railroad bridge near Ardmore, Indian Territory. The rock supports in the center help carry the weight of the trellis bridge as well as create an underpass for wagon road traffic. (Courtesy of the McGalliard Collection, Ardmore Public Library.)

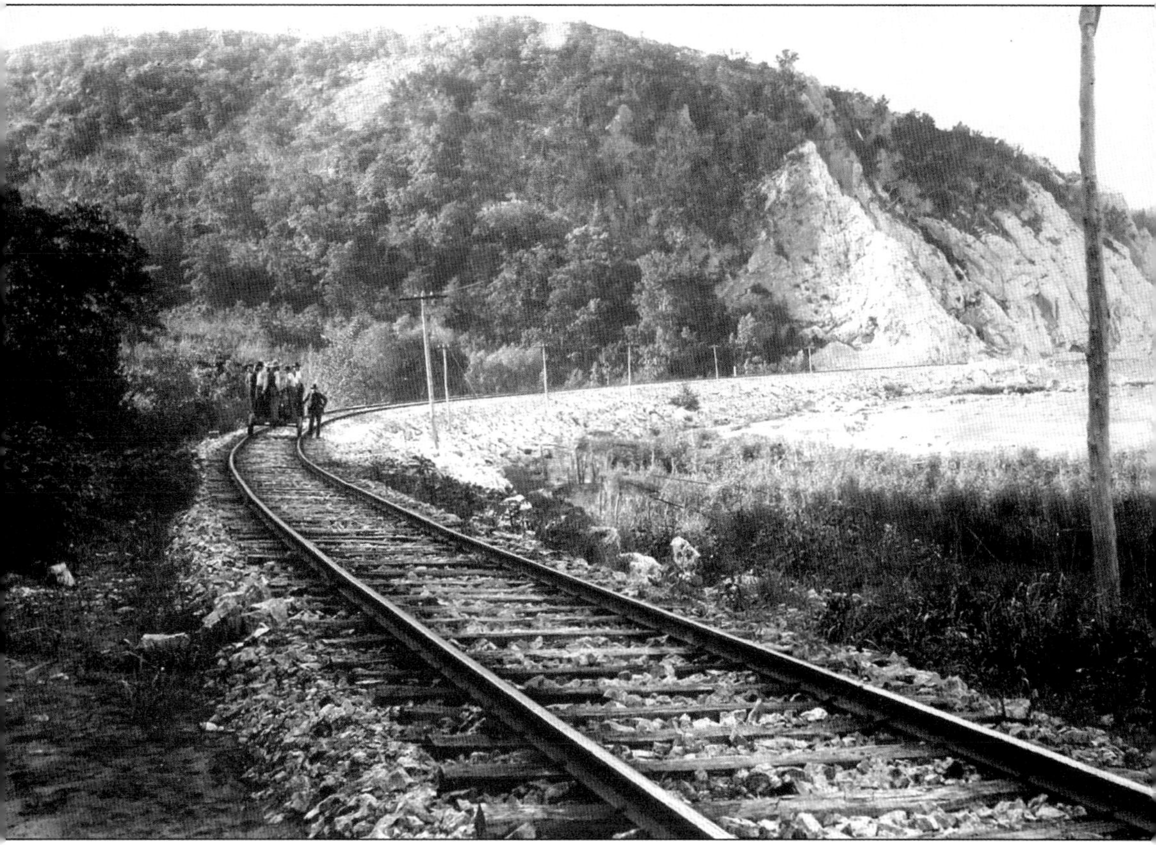

Railroad building did not stop in Ardmore but pressed on northward. The next stop was Berwyn (now Gene Autry), and then the rails pushed farther north. Here the tracks curve to take the path of least resistance at the base of a mountain in the Arbuckles. Crews did have to blast their way through the rock, however, in order to lay track. On the right of this photograph can be seen an area where rock was blasted away in order to lay track. A railroad crew using a handcar is moving up track through the Arbuckle Mountains. After Berwyn, the next station planned by the Pennsylvania Railroad owners was Wynnewood and after that Wayne and Paoli. (Courtesy of the McGalliard Collection, Ardmore Public Library.)

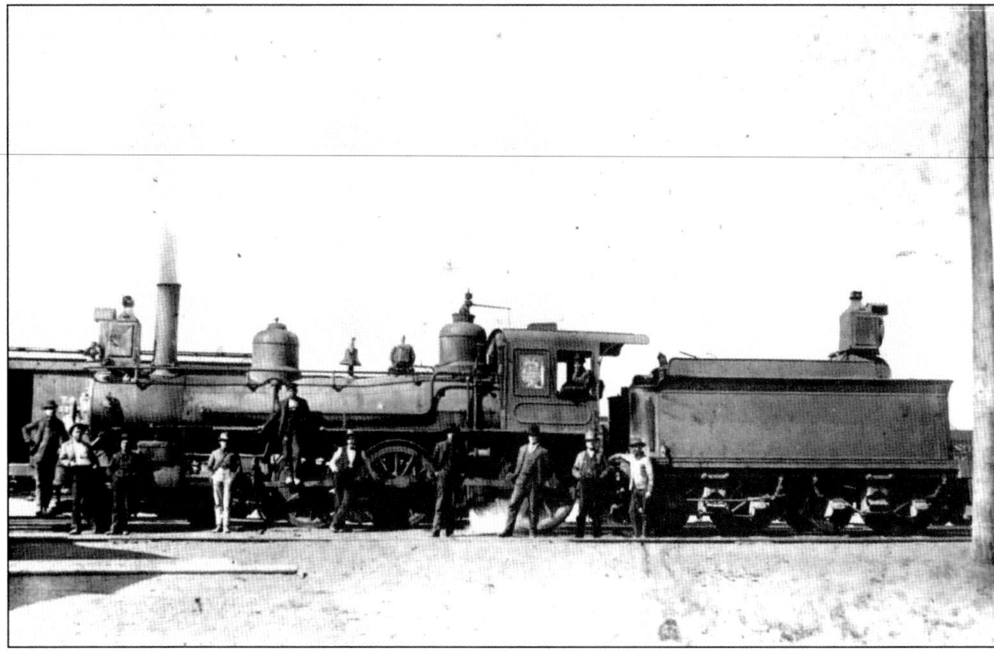

This engine is a new coal-powered engine. Ten railroad employees pose with the engineer in the cab. Additional track lines were constructed through Ardmore, and several railroad companies did business in the city, including the Santa Fe, Union, Rock Island, and Oklahoma, New Mexico and Pacific. (Courtesy of the McGalliard Collection, Ardmore Public Library.)

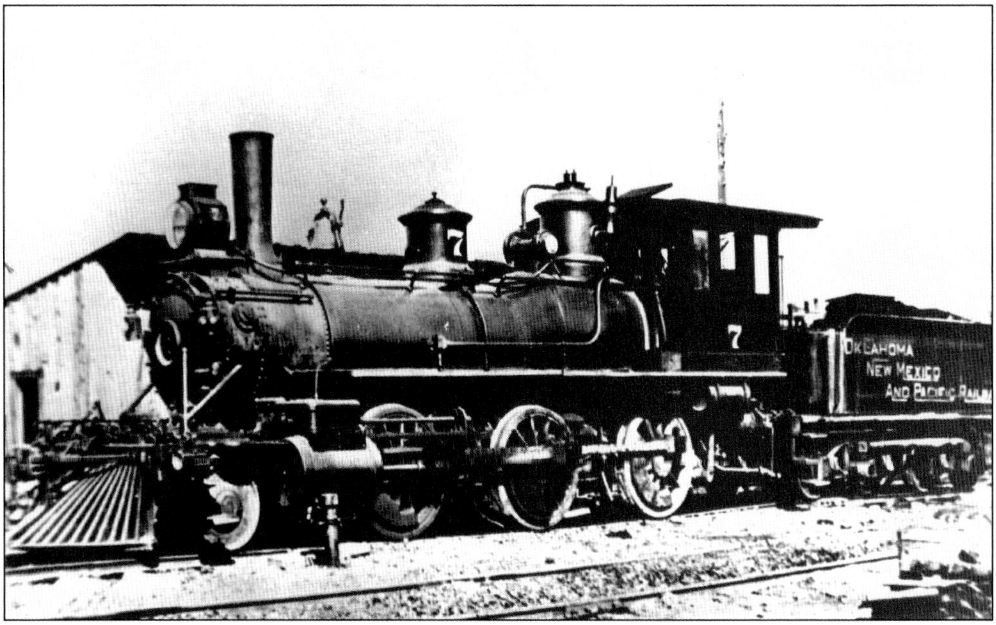

Engine No. 7 was part of the Oklahoma, New Mexico and Pacific Railroad. Its usual route was between Ardmore and Ringling on the special spur paid for by the "bonus" fund-raisers. This photograph was taken about 1915. (Courtesy of the McGalliard Collection, Ardmore Public Library.)

"A Battery of Heavy Artillery" included pictures of local leaders on a poster offered for sale in the community effort to raise enough money for the Ringling spur. The small city of Ringling was the winter quarters of the John Ringling Circus. John Ringling and his partner, Jake Hamon, asked Ardmore to build a spur from Ardmore to Ringling. (Courtesy of Ardmore Main Street Authority.)

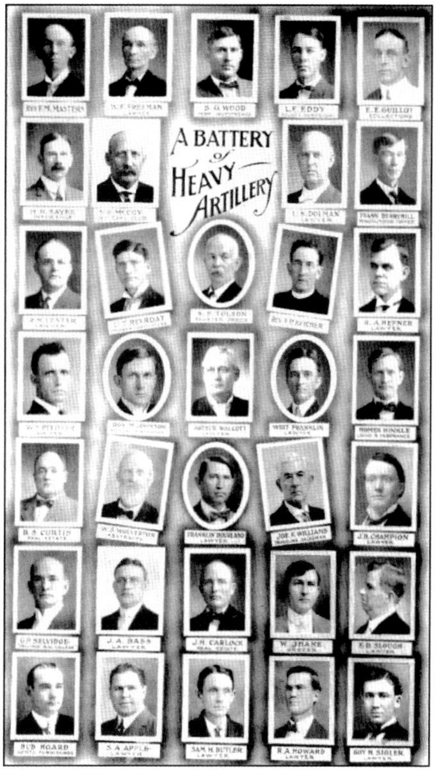

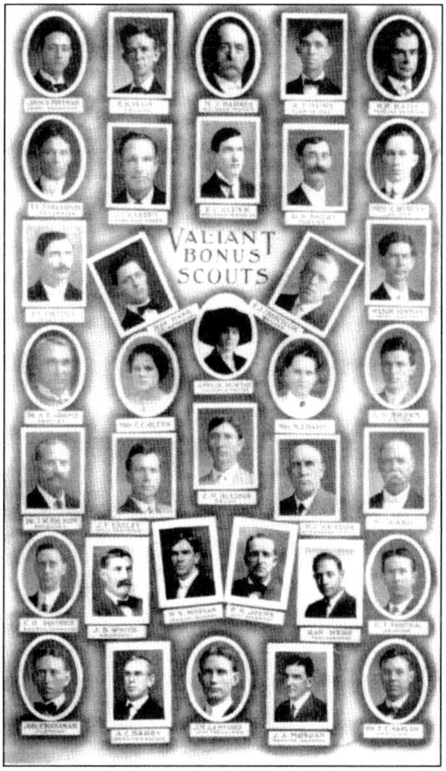

"Valiant Bonus Scouts" is another poster used to raise money for the Ringling Spur. Ardmoreites have always been willing to raise money for desirable projects. This railroad, proposed and financed by John Ringling, Jake Hamon, and the citizens of Ardmore, originally was intended to connect Ardmore and Lawton with construction by the Oklahoma, New Mexico and Pacific Railroad to provide transportation for agricultural products. (Courtesy of Ardmore Main Street Authority.)

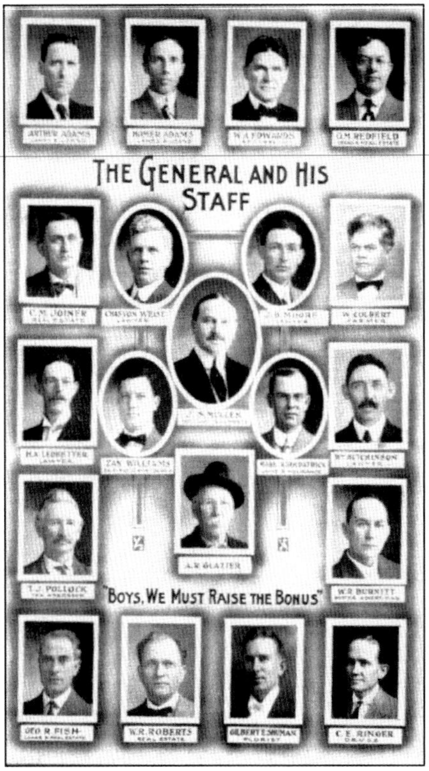

"The General and His Staff" was another bonus poster stating, "Boys We Must Raise the Bonus." The bonus was the amount of money it would take to pay for the Ringling spur, which began on May 1, 1913. It never reached Lawton because, with the Healdton Oil Strike, Ringling changed his plans, but the town of Ringling was born at the western terminus of the spur. (Courtesy of Ardmore Main Street Authority.)

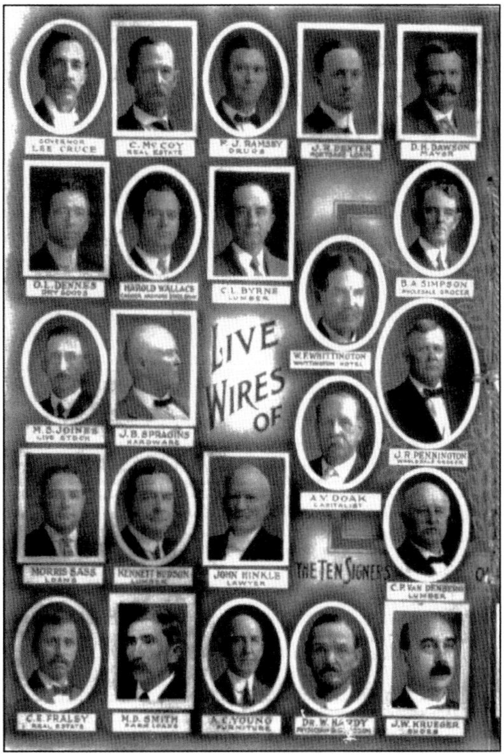

The Ringling spur also built track south to an area just west of Wilson, where the Ringling Brothers Circus established its winter resting grounds. On January 17, 1914, John Ringling named the town New Wilson in honor of Charles Wilson, manager of the Ringling Brothers Circus. On January 28, 1920, the town was renamed Wilson. That railroad spur was active until 1976. (Courtesy of Ardmore Main Street Authority.)

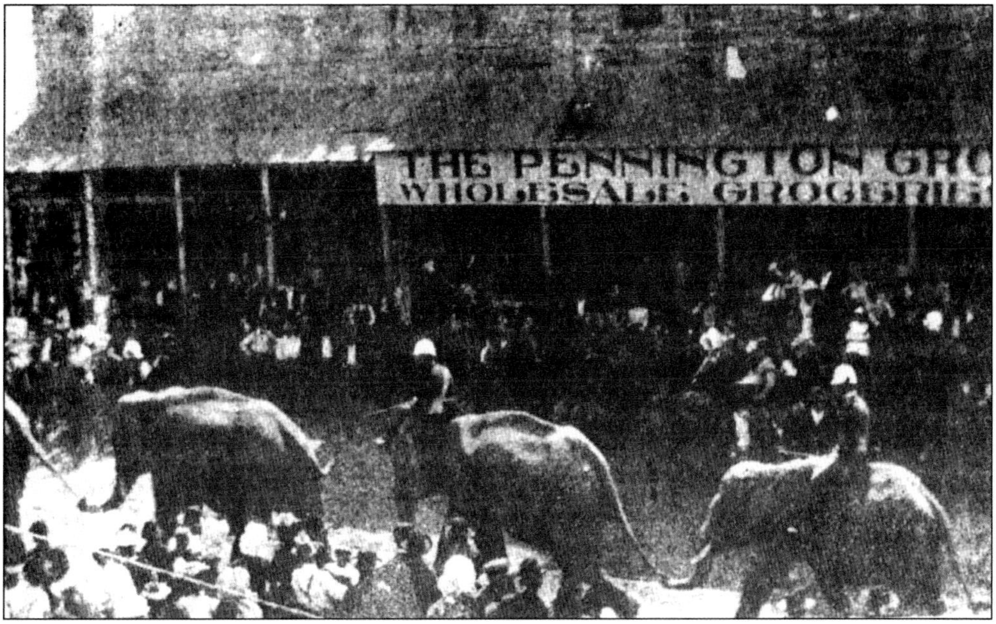

Once the Ringling spur was completed, John Ringling brought the Ringling Brothers Circus to Wilson each year to its winter headquarters. The circus came regularly to Ardmore, and elephants were a usual sight in parades throughout the winter months. People throughout the area traveled to Wilson to see the animals and visit with circus performers. (Courtesy of Ardmore Main Street Authority.)

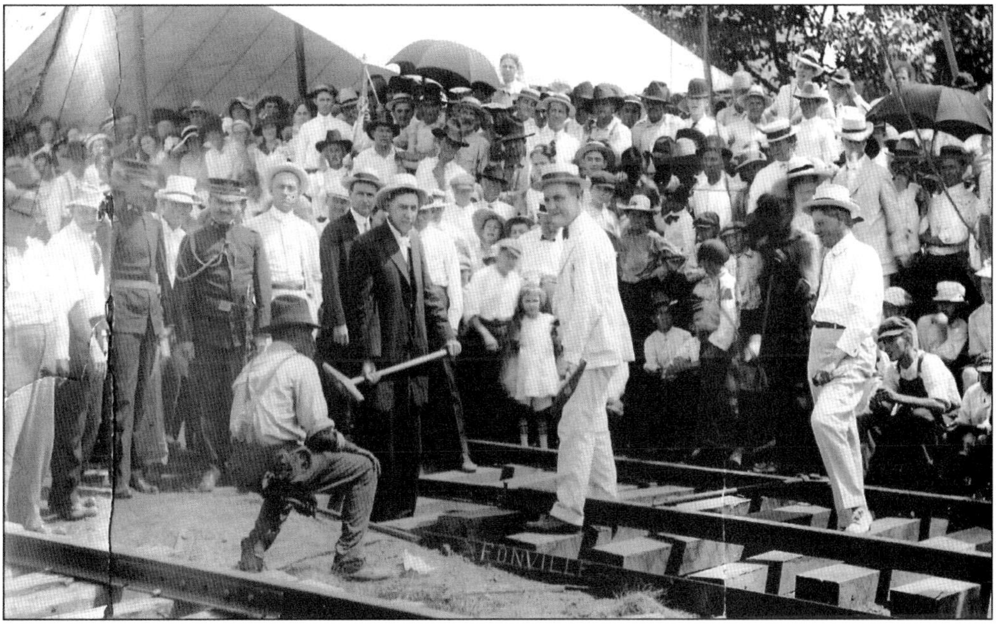

A large crowd came to witness the birth of a railroad spur that would connect Ardmore with Ringling. On August 4, 1913, after a tremendous local effort to raise money for the spur, Gov. Lee Cruce drove the first spike. Beginning at C Street and Grand Avenue NW, the Ringling spur was built straight west to Ringling. John Ringling's partner, Jake Hamon, is seen in the white suit. (Courtesy of Sally Gray.)

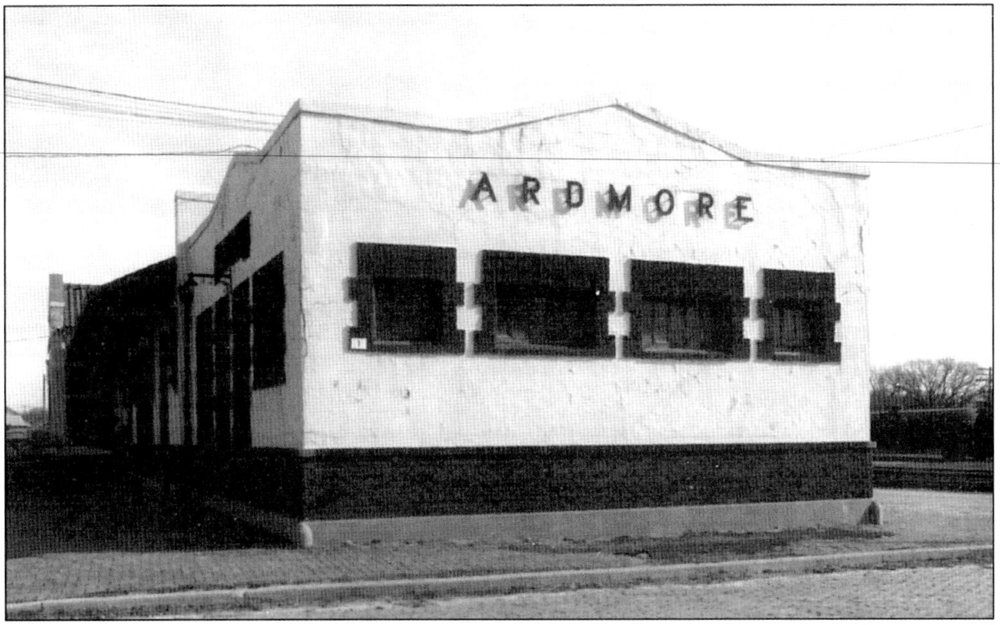

This is the south end of the refurbished Santa Fe depot at Ardmore. The original depot opened on the south end and on the east side onto a broad platform where passengers loaded and unloaded. During renovation, the building was covered with stucco and the main doors were moved to the west side. Passengers for the *Heartland Flyer* still board the train at this depot. (Courtesy of Ardmore Main Street Authority.)

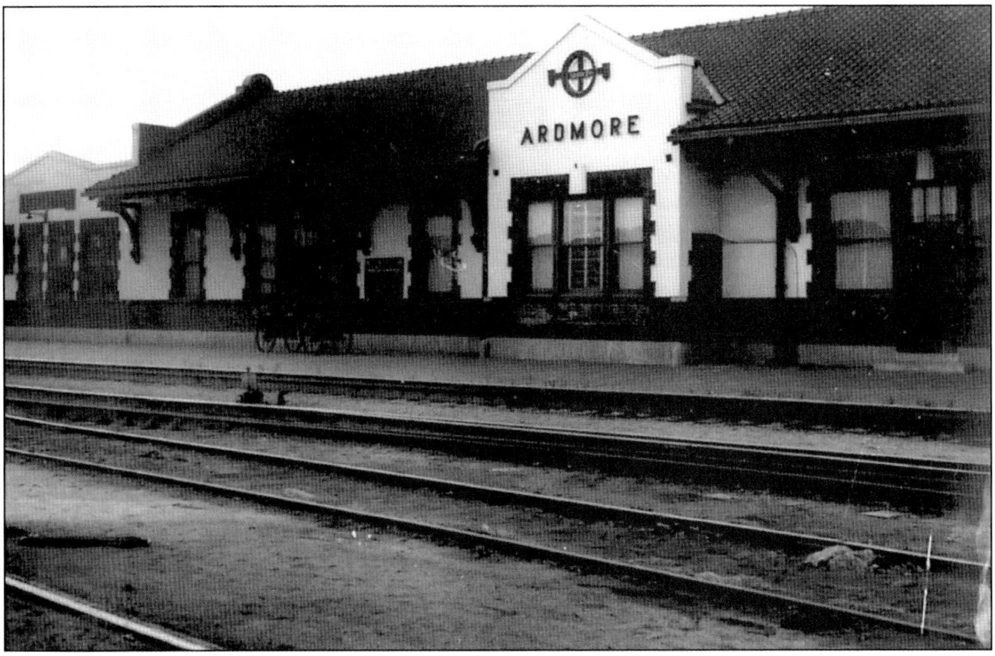

The current Santa Fe depot opens to the east for passengers to enter and exit. There are several sets of tracks. Ardmore has always been a railroad town even though passenger service was suspended. After the restoration of the depot, it seemed only natural that passenger service would be reinstated. (Courtesy of Ardmore Main Street Authority.)

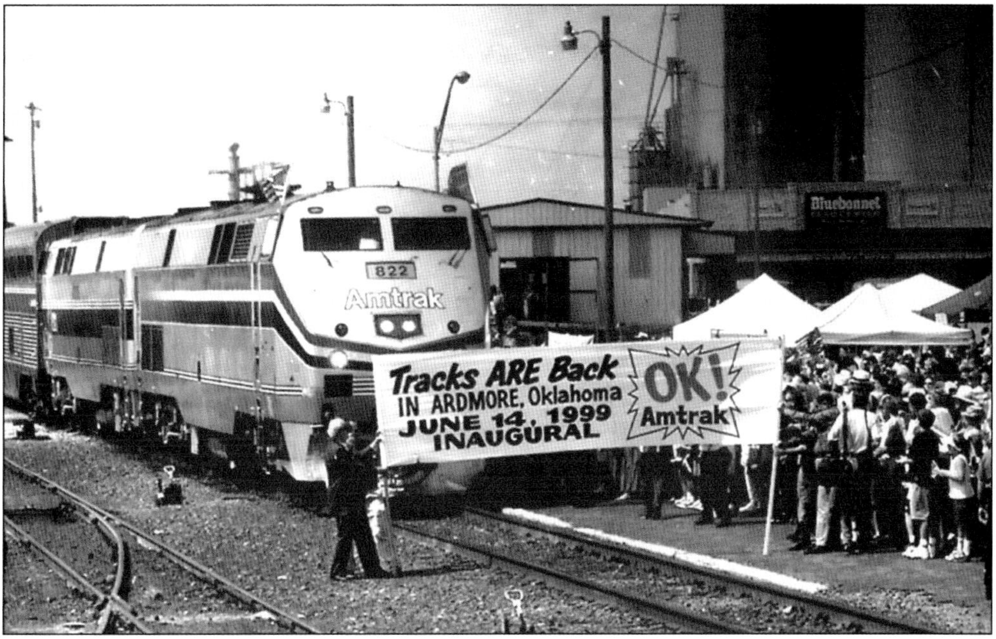

In 1999, passenger service was reinstated at the newly refurbished Santa Fe depot. The train, dubbed the *Heartland Flyer*, carries passengers between Oklahoma City and Dallas, Texas, with stops at Gainesville, Ardmore, and Pauls Valley. The *Flyer* stops in Ardmore at 10:30 a.m. traveling toward Oklahoma City and at 7:30 p.m. traveling toward Dallas. (Courtesy of Ardmore Main Street Authority.)

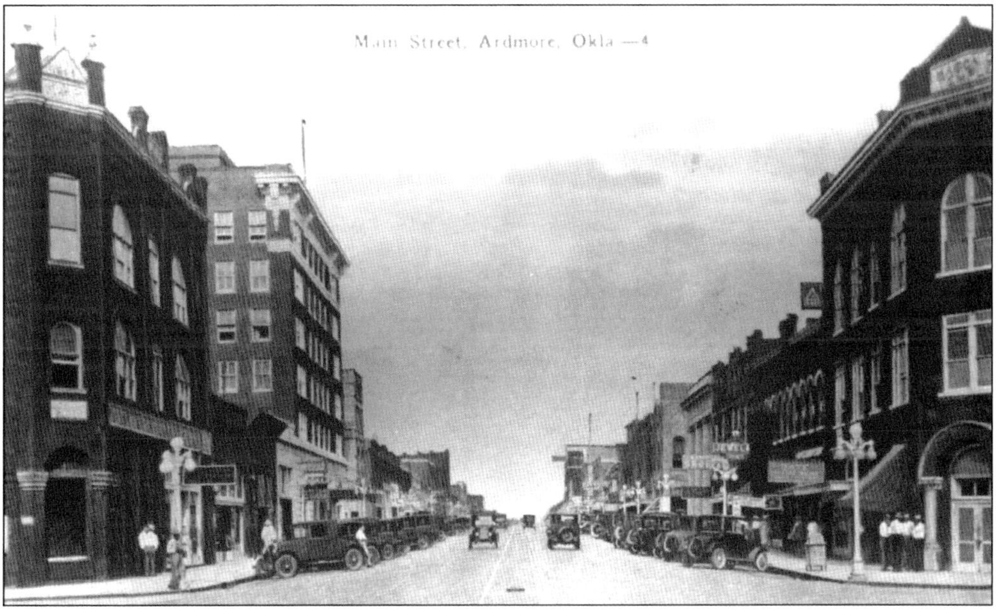

Streetcars came to Ardmore in 1907. Some 15 miles of track were laid in April of that year. Main Street and several main thoroughfares received the tracks laid by the Ardmore Electric Railway Company, owned by Joe F. Robison. This photograph shows the tracks down the middle of Main Street. Automobile traffic continued on either side of the tracks. (Courtesy of Ardmore Main Street Authority.)

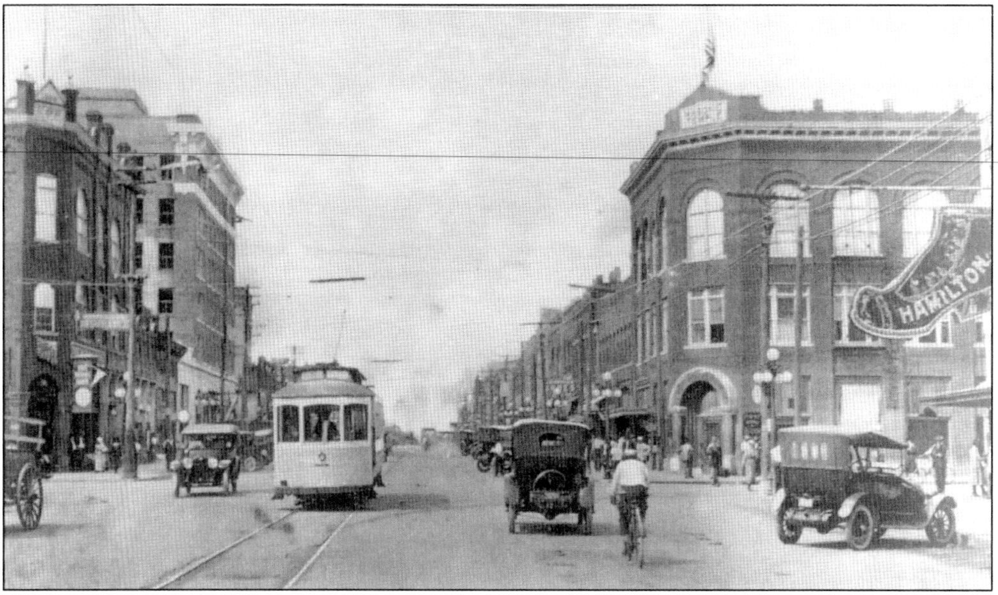

This street scene postcard was made after statehood, about 1910. The trolley is passing between City National Bank and First National Bank on the right. The original photograph was made by Webb Studio. The information for this postcard came from the McGalliard Collection. (Courtesy of Ardmore Main Street Authority.)

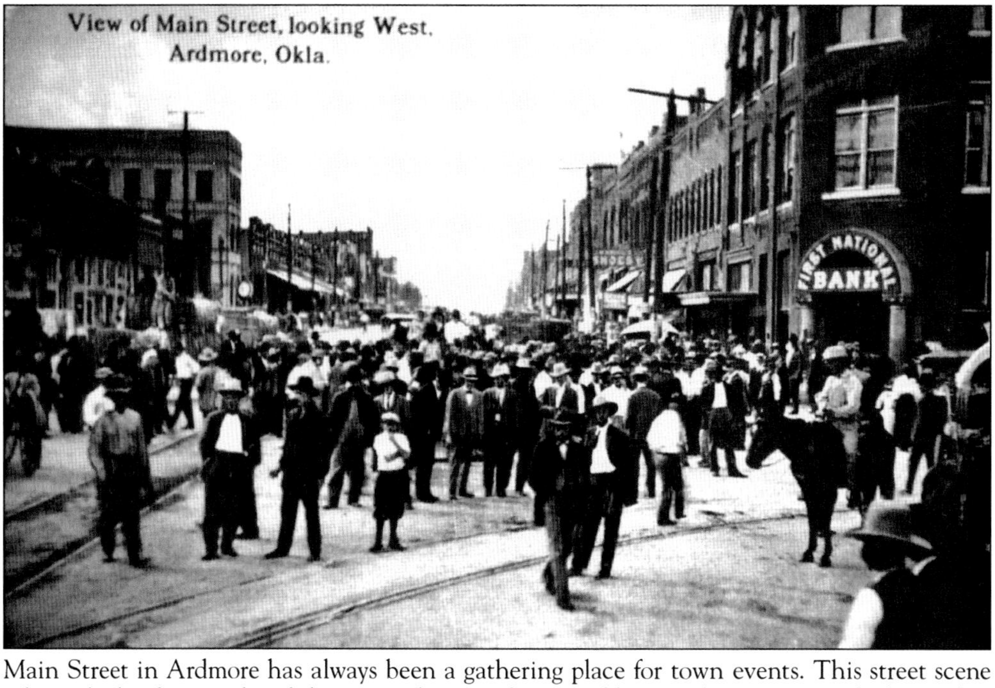

Main Street in Ardmore has always been a gathering place for town events. This street scene taken a little after statehood shows a gathering of men and boys with carriages parked on either side. Note the young boy in the center wearing knickers. The landmark Masonic lodge building on the right is City National Bank at this time. (Courtesy of Ardmore Main Street Authority.)

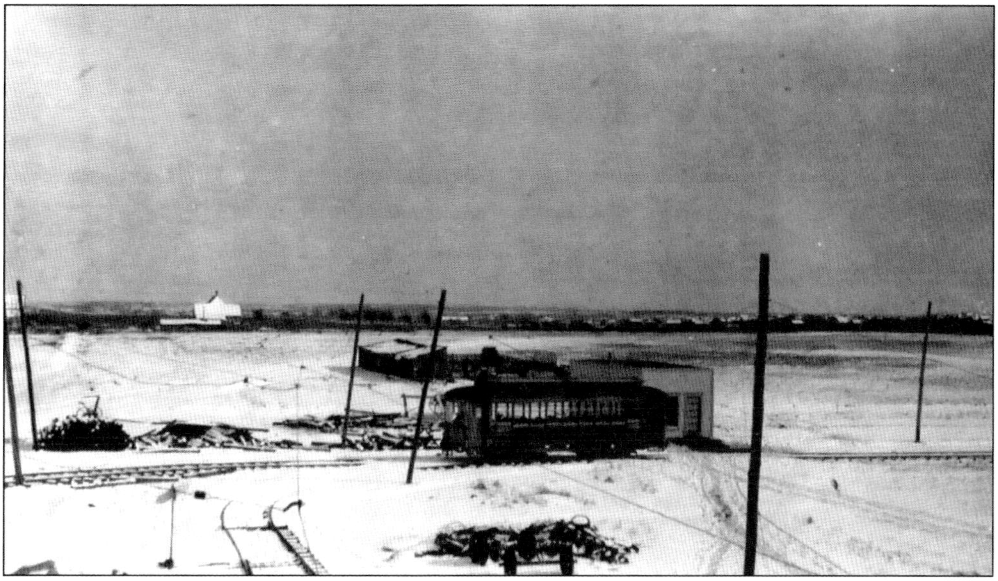

The carbarn was located northwest of Ardmore. In this photograph, one of the cable cars has gone to the carbarn probably for regular maintenance. The scene is in winter, and snow is on the ground. The estimated date of this photograph is 1917. (Courtesy of the McGalliard Collection, Ardmore Public Library.)

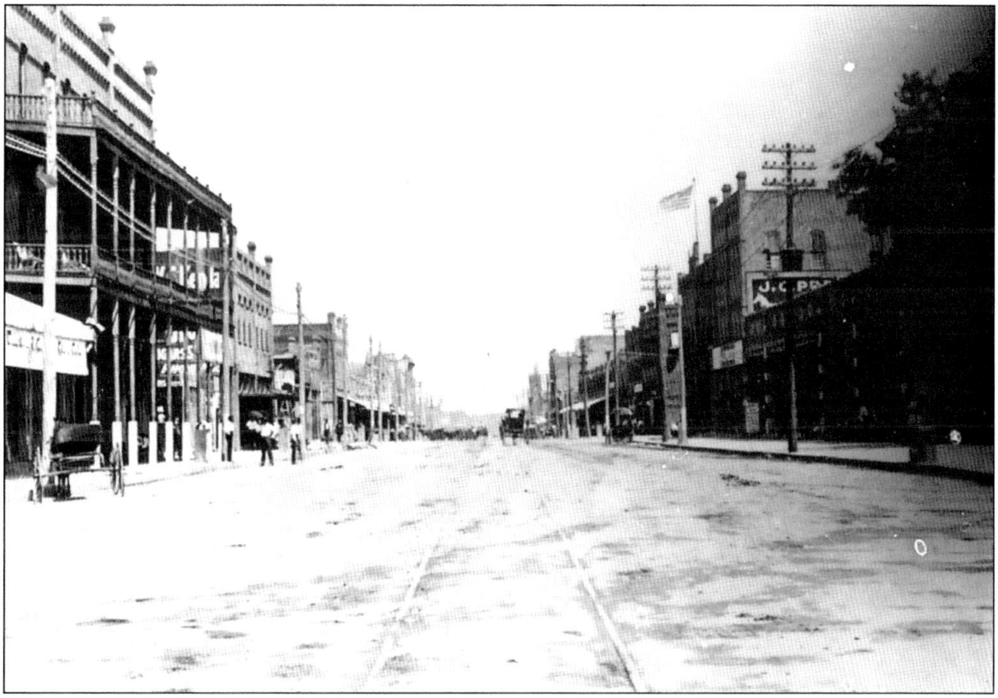

The Ardmore Electric Railway Company was organized by Joe F. Robison. The tracks were laid on Main Street and several other streets in order to provide public transport throughout the city. In this photograph the Randol Hotel with its wide verandas can be seen on the left. It was here that Jake Hamon was murdered by his mistress. (Courtesy of the McGalliard Collection, Ardmore Public Library.)

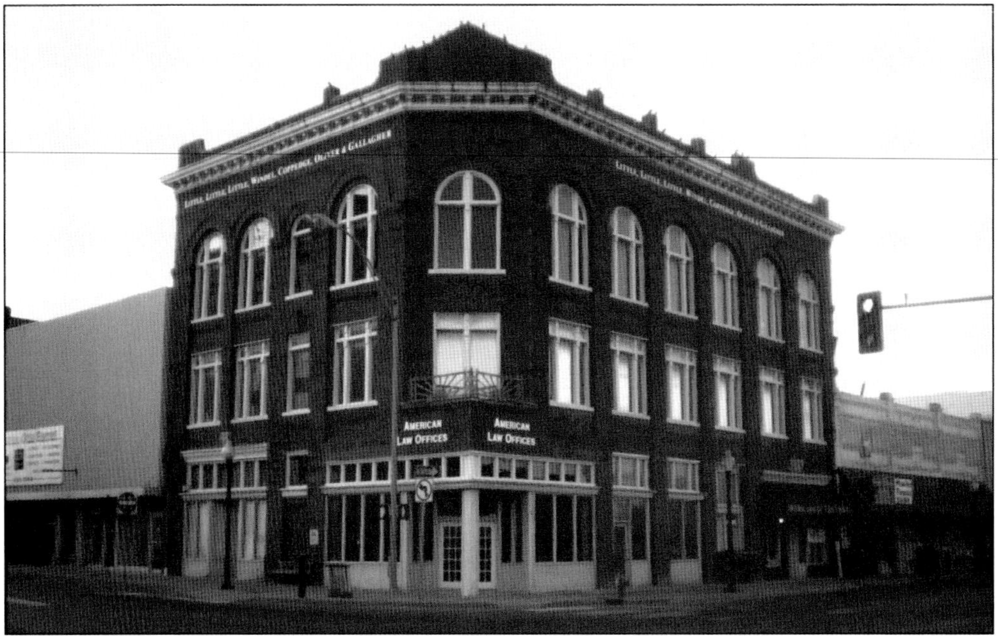

Currently this grand old building houses the American Law Offices. Much renovation was done to restore the building to its former glory. The ballroom floor still exists on the third floor, but it is not used as such currently. The cupola was damaged by lightning many years ago, and when it was repaired, the "Masonic Temple" plate was not replaced. (Author's collection.)

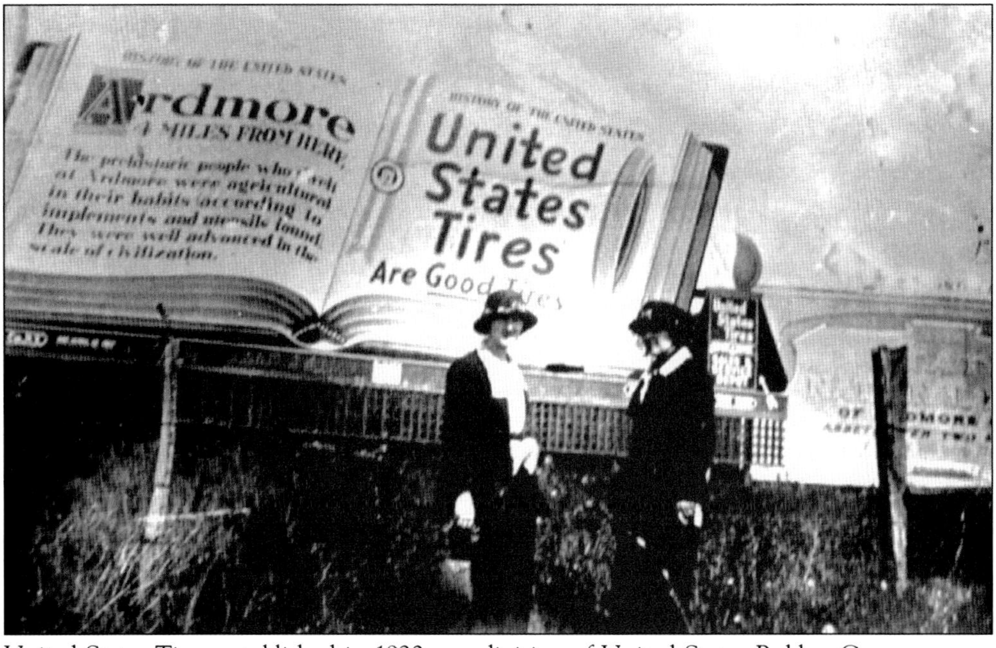

United States Tires, established in 1920 as a division of United States Rubber Company, one of the 12 original stocks in the Dow Jones Industrial Average, billed itself as the oldest and largest rubber organization in the world. Ardmore apparently had either one of the 53 factories or 235 branches. In 1961, the company became Uniroyal, Inc., and later was acquired by the French-based Michelin Company. (Courtesy of Sally Gray.)

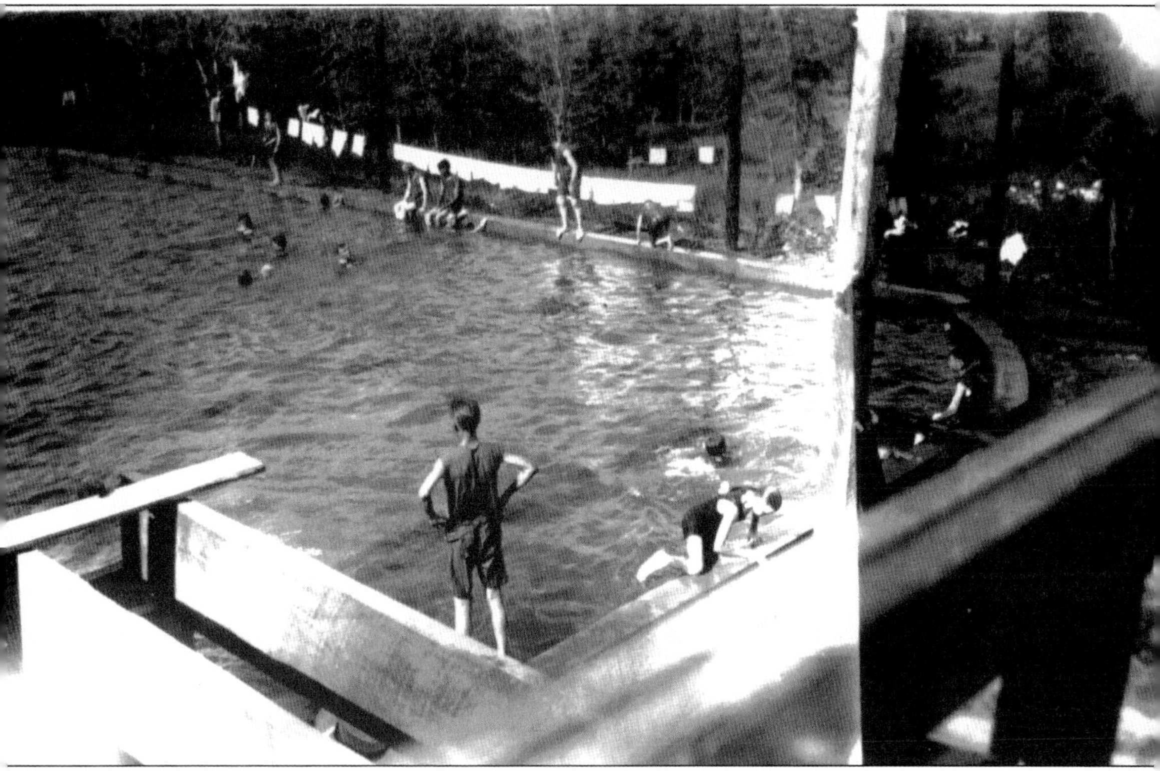

Lorena Park had a large swimming pool for the pleasure of young and old alike. In addition, there was also a lake with a double-decker diving platform. The park was open from 1908 until 1930 and was the scene of many picnics and social gatherings by Ardmore citizens who lived in a more gracious time when people took pride in courtesy, poise, and elocution. (Courtesy of Sally Gray.)

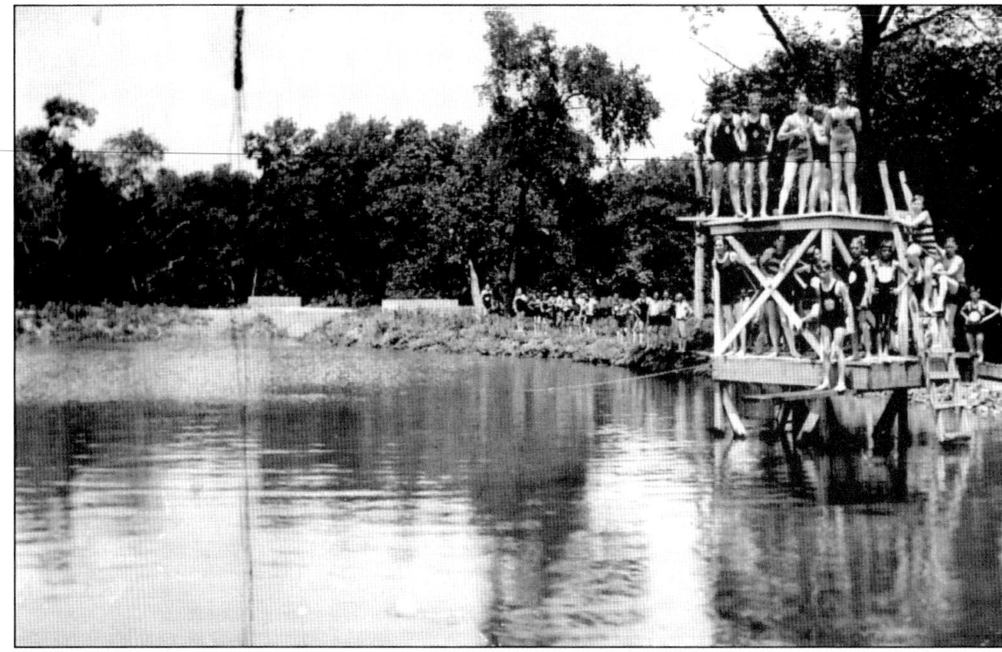

The lake at Lorena Park had a diving platform that was popular with young men and boys. In this photograph, approximately a dozen young men prepare to dive into the friendly waters of Lorena Park Lake. Nothing of the popular park remains today except for a few photographs, which elicit memories of a more formal social era. (Courtesy of Ardmore Main Street Authority.)

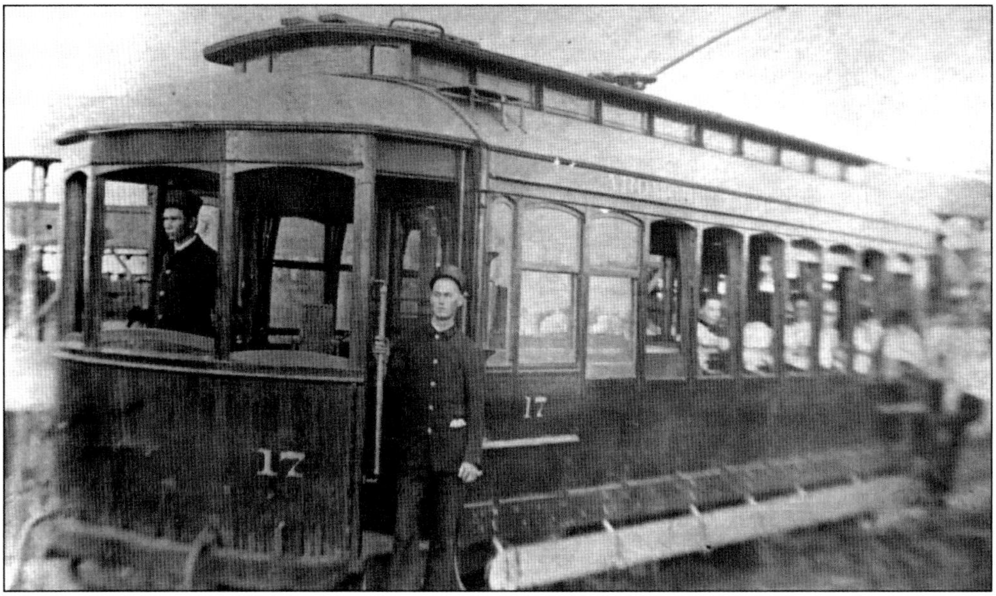

Streetcar No. 17 is again on its way to Lorena Park, as the destination sign states. Cable car No. 17 on the Ardmore line made daily trips north of the city to Lorena Park, named for Lorena Cruce, daughter of Lee Cruce, second governor of Oklahoma. The park was located north of Ardmore in the Dornick Hills area. Conductor of No. 17 was the father of longtime Ardmore grocer Dorn Moore. Fare from Ardmore to the park was 5¢. (Courtesy of the McGalliard Collection, Ardmore Public Library.)

These young ladies are identified as Alta Smith McKenzie, left, and Zelda Gremen. They are aboard the summer car of the Ardmore streetcar line. A notation accompanying the photograph indicates they are "in route to Lorena Park, perhaps." The photograph is dated 1915. (Courtesy of the McGalliard Collection, Ardmore Public Library.)

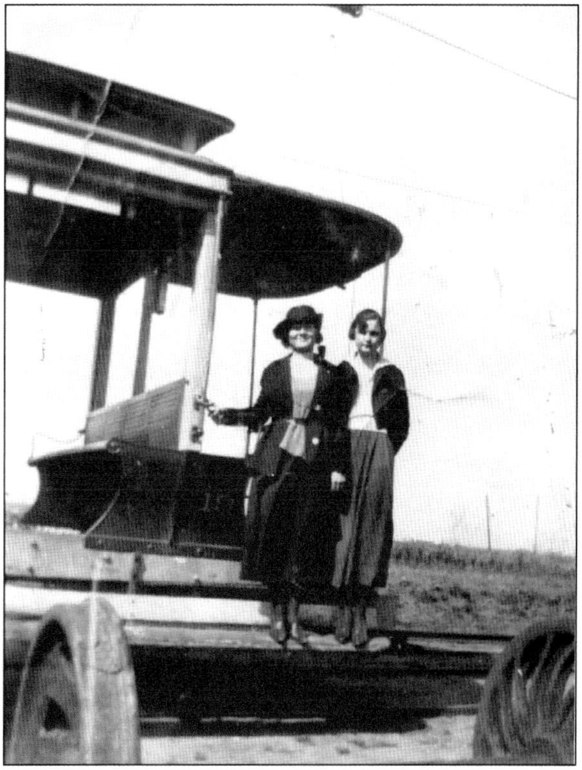

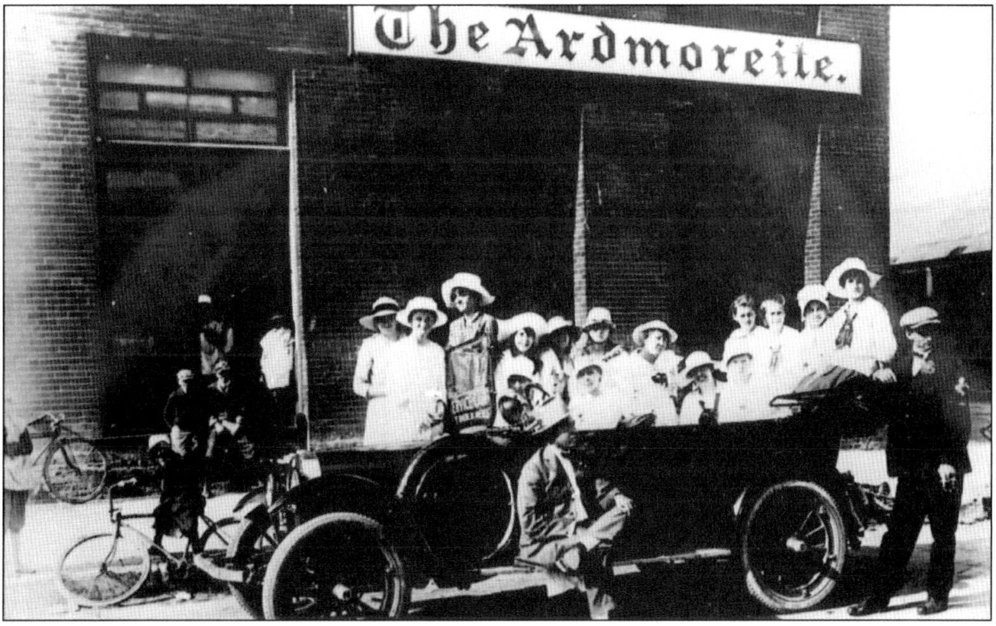

The people in the car and the event in this 1916 photograph are unknown. This *Ardmoreite* office is in the Odd Fellows Building on North Washington Street. The newspaper's first home was upstairs at the Moss Dry Goods Store. This location was heavily damaged in the great fire of 1895. Other offices included the Elks hall on West Broadway and the Joiner Building on Mill Street. (Courtesy of Sally Gray.)

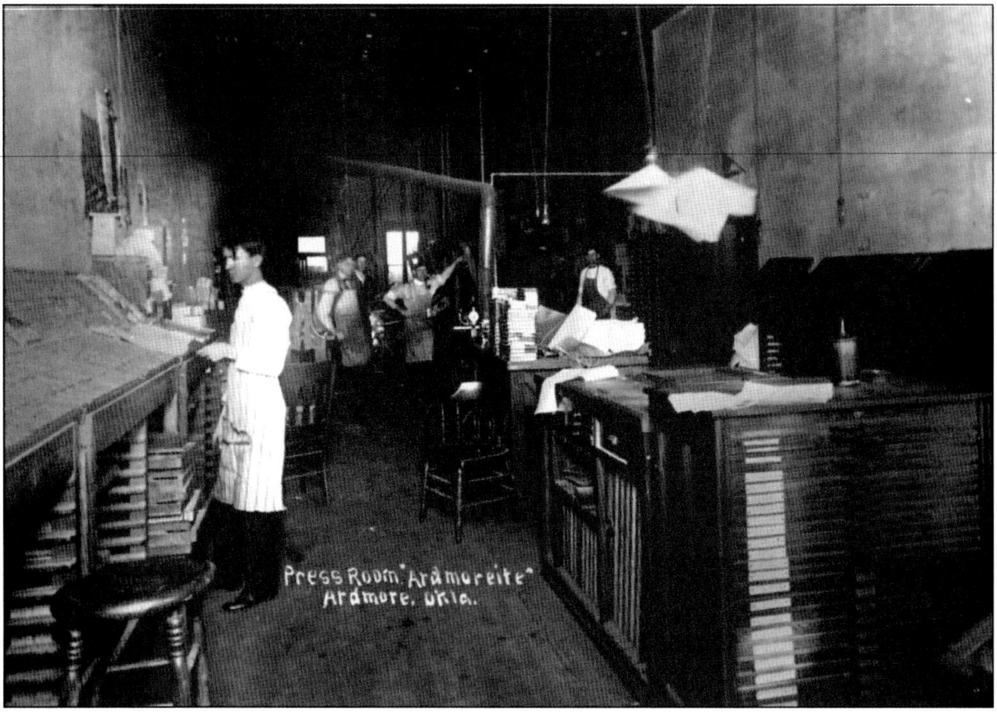

This photograph shows a *Daily Ardmoreite* pressroom. Leadership of the *Daily Ardmoreite* began with attorney R. S. Denee and hotel owner W. F. Whittington, who fronted money for D. P. Cloyd, Charles Kessler, and Laurine McWhirter to run the new enterprise. The *Daily Ardmoreite* purchased equipment from the *Daily Advertiser* and may have moved into that facility. F. E. Wilson and R. S. W. Parker purchased the paper within weeks. (Courtesy of Sally Gray.)

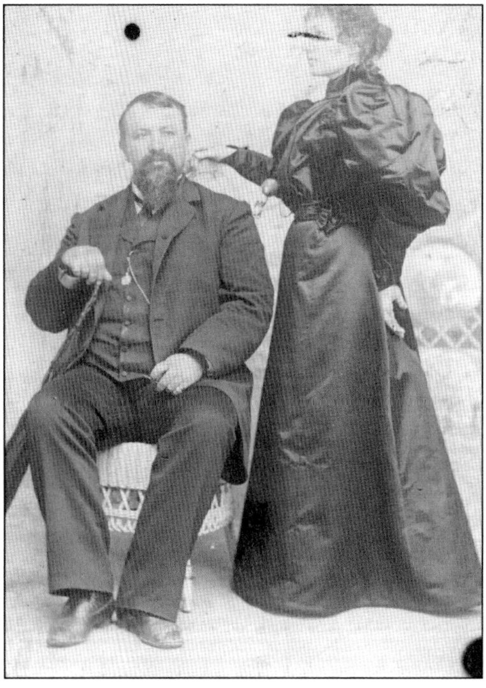

Sidney Suggs purchased the *Daily Ardmoreite* in June 1897. Although he had no newspaper experience, he did have the ability to locate capable employees. He also invested in technology and installed the first linotype machine in Indian Territory. He saved money by buying newsprint in bulk, a whole boxcar load at a time. Suggs owned and published the paper until 1917. (Courtesy of Greater Southwest Historical Museum.)

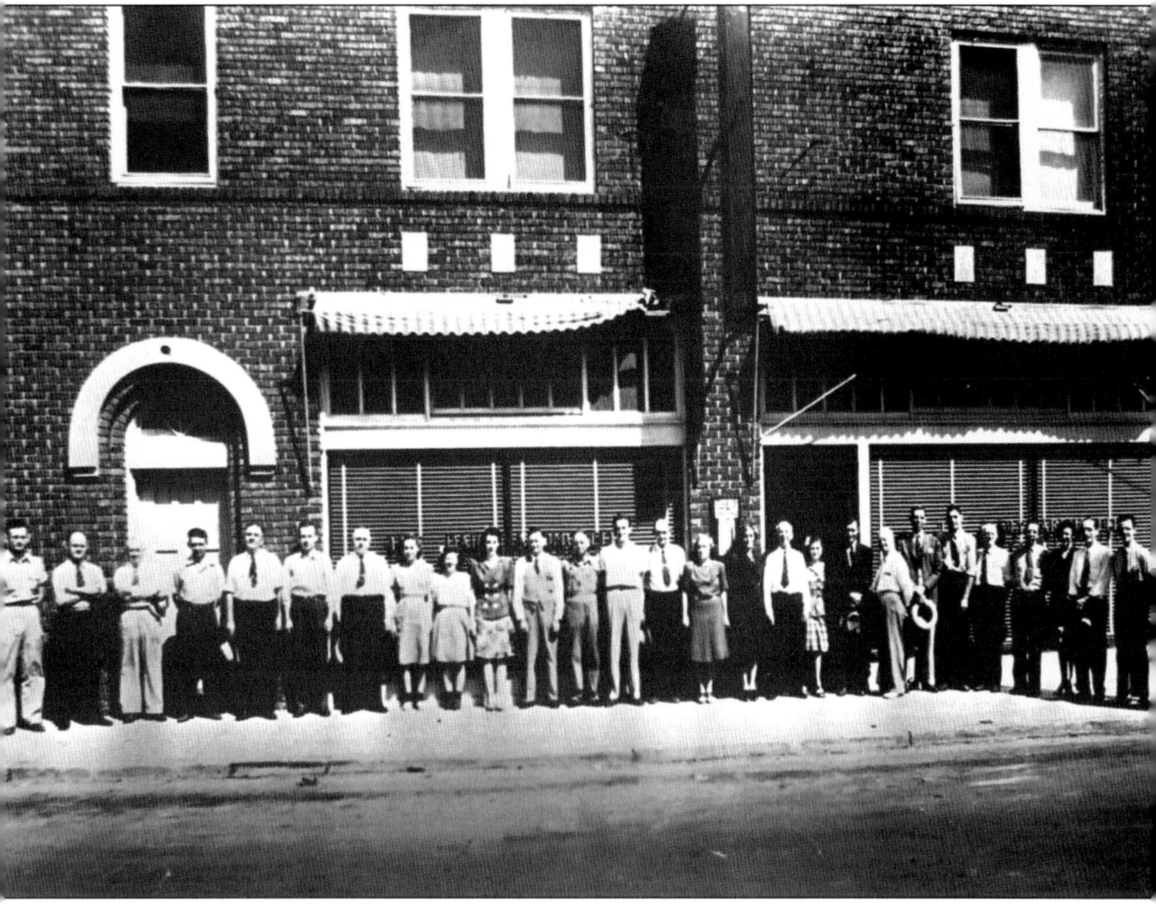

The staff of the *Daily Ardmoreite* is lined up in front of the office when it was located in the Odd Fellows Building on North Washington Street. The young woman in the plaid skirt standing in front of the blackened doorway at right is Sally Gray, author and local historian. The paper was first housed in Moss Dry Goods on Main Street, which was destroyed in the great fire. It moved to its current location in 1966. In 1896, Stephan A. Douglas and Richard Cearnal bought out Wilson and Parker and hired D. T. Nisbett as managing editor. Sidney Suggs bought the *Daily Ardmoreite* in June 1897 and remained its publisher until 1917. In 1919, John F. Easley became publisher and editor and held that position for several decades. On January 28, 1954, Easley was elected to the Oklahoma Historical Society Board of Directors based on his devotion to printing Oklahoma history in the *Daily Ardmoreite*. As editor of the *Daily Ardmoreite*, Easley was followed by Albert Reisen. (Courtesy of Sally Gray.)

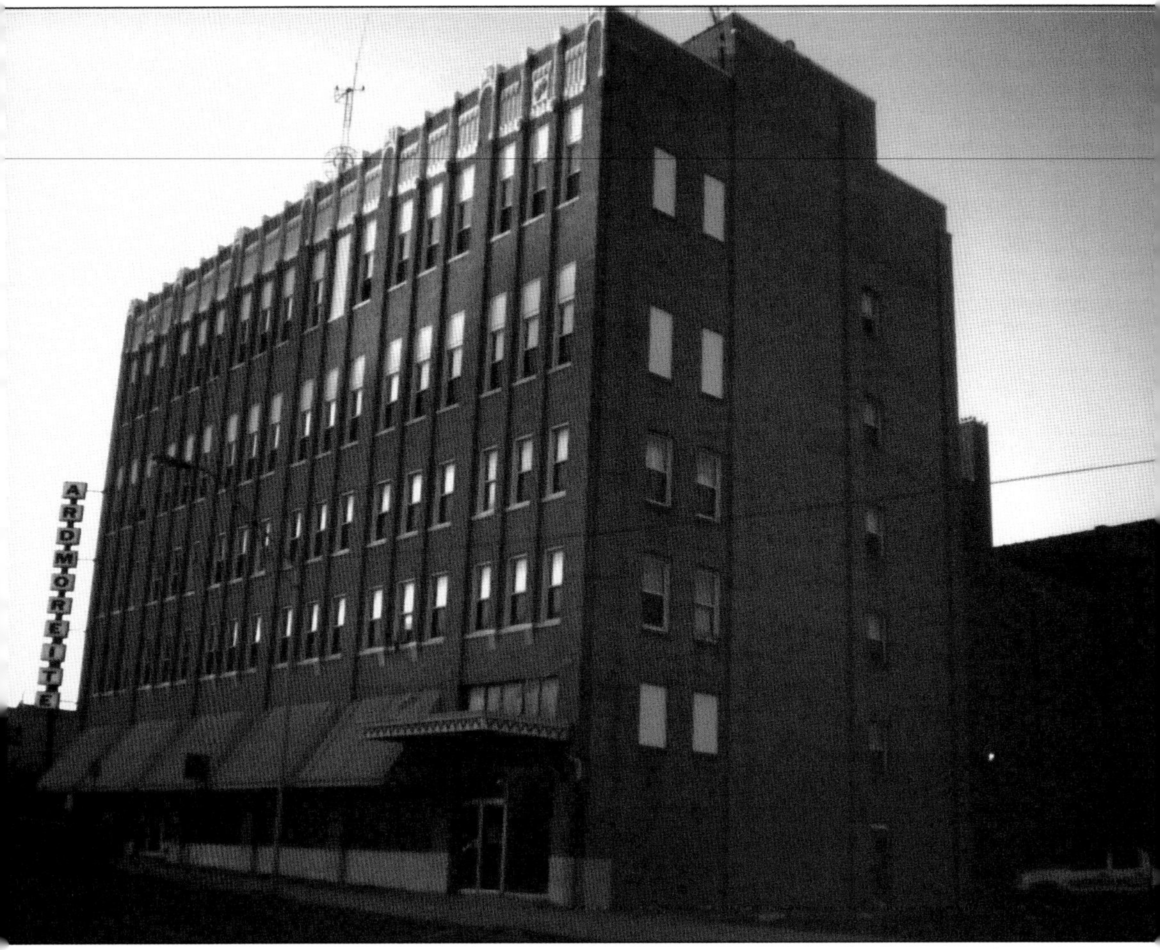

In 1888, Ardmore's first newspaper, the *Ardmore Weekly Courier*, was a six-column, four-page paper published on Thursday with a circulation of 1,800 at its height. The *Alliance Courier*, 1888 to 1896, was a Populist paper, eight pages, with a circulation of 1,000. In 1890, a newspaper from Oklahoma City moved to Ardmore, changing its name from the *Oklahoma Chieftain* to the *Chickasaw Chieftain*. Its main goal was promotion of noncitizens' rights and dissolution of the Chickasaw Nation. Its circulation was about 2,400. It became the voice for the need to provide legal standing to the intruder population, which had grown to more than 50,000. Other weekly papers included the *Ardmore State-Herald* and the *Ardmore Chronicle*, which combined in 1897. In 1891, Ardmore's first daily paper, the *Daily Advertiser*, began publication. In 1893, the *Daily Ardmoreite* purchased the *Daily Advertiser* and some equipment from the *Chickasaw Chieftain* and published its first edition on October 28, 1893. From that point, the *Daily Ardmorite* was the premier newspaper in Ardmore. (Courtesy of Sally Gray.)

The Tyler Simpson family came to Ardmore in the early years. The business was located in the rock building that now houses Bluebonnet Feed and provided a variety of merchandise at wholesale. One of the little boys in this photograph is William Simpson. (Courtesy of Sally Gray.)

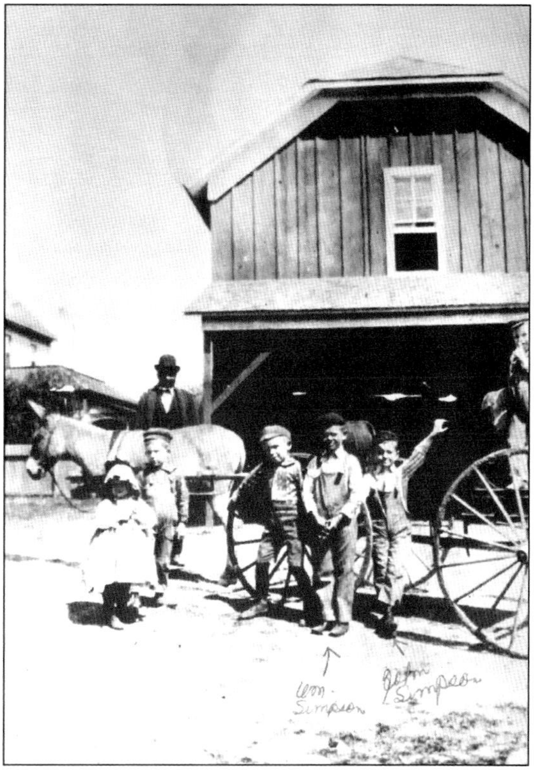

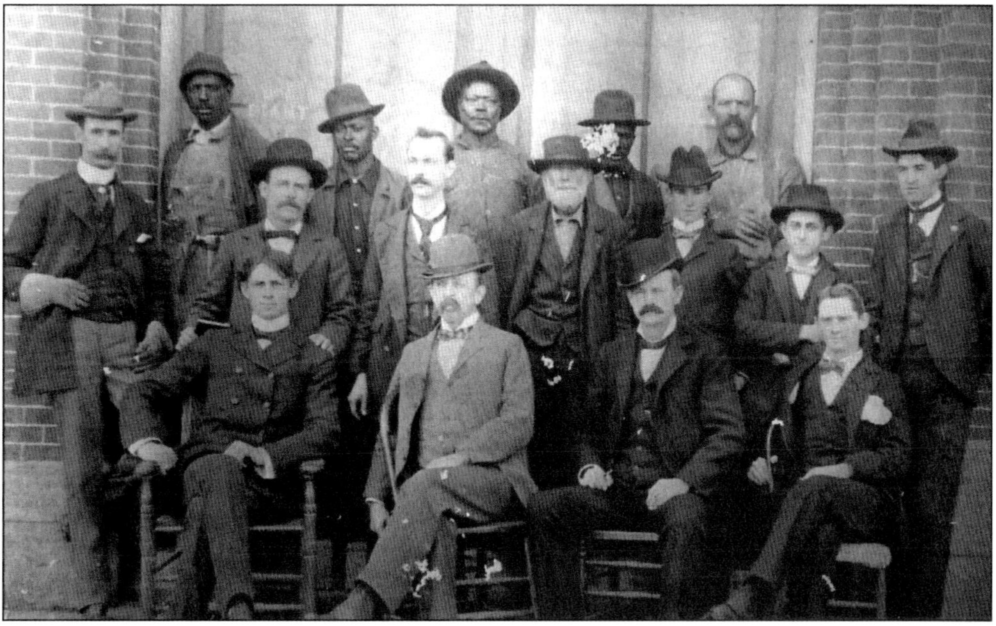

This Tyler and Simpson Company crew dates from about 1910. They provided wholesale groceries, especially canned goods, for several decades. The beginnings of the Tyler and Simpson Company were in Gainesville, Texas, in 1884 when a 50,000-square-foot, two-story building was constructed. Renovated, that building remains one of the largest pre-1900 buildings extant in northern Texas. (Courtesy of Sally Gray.)

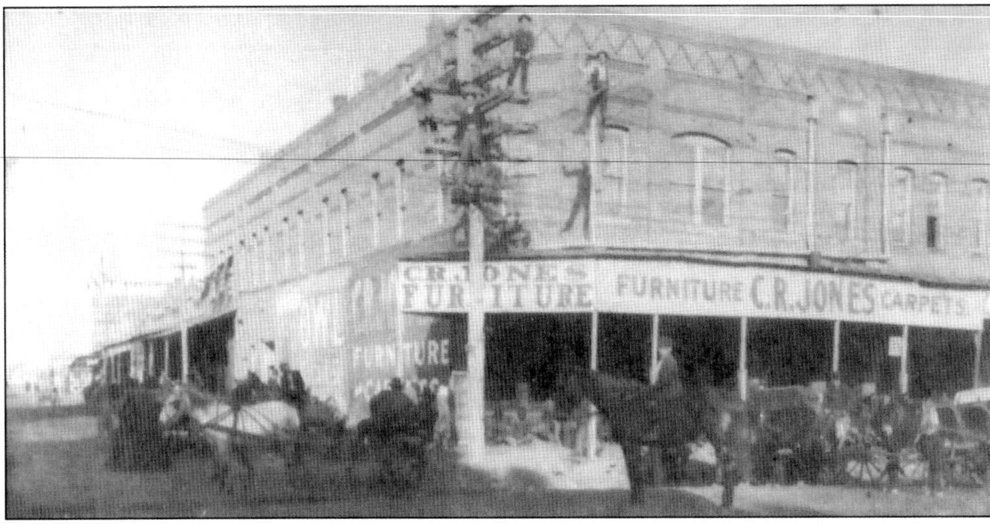

Old wooden telephone poles with numerous crossbars carried wiring for the Chickasaw Telephone Company, which provided the first telephone service to Ardmore. The photograph is probably dated 1900 because the *Daily Ardmoreite* is still located in the Odd Fellows Building on North Washington Street. The building housing the C. P. Jones furniture company burned in 1964, and the lot was turned into a parking lot. (Courtesy of Ardmore Main Street Authority.)

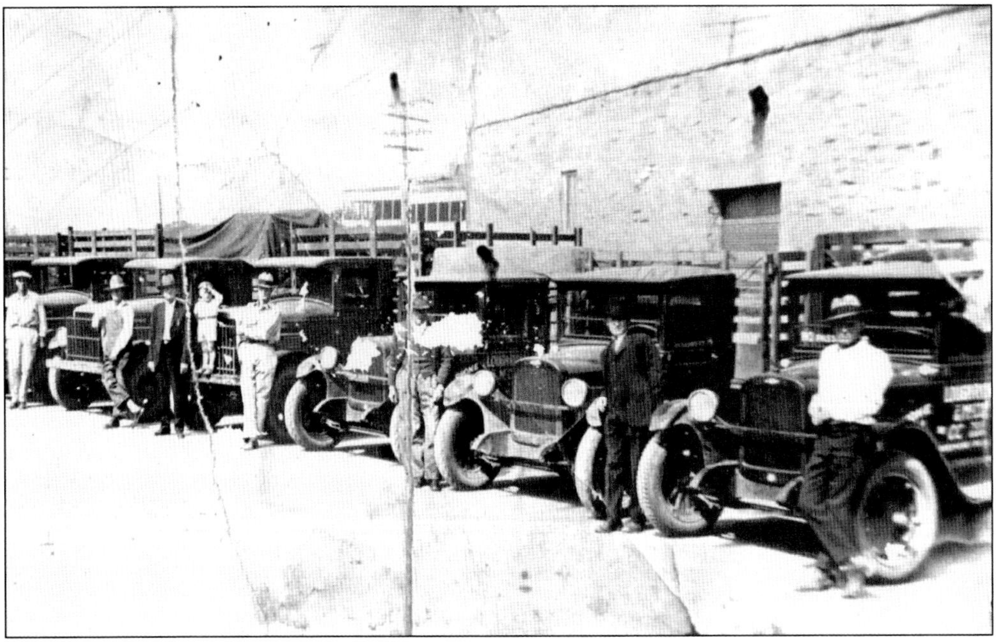

This fleet of trucks belonged to the Loughridge Company. With Ardmore being a railroad station, literally tons of equipment, supplies, furniture, and mercantile goods were unloaded at the depot each day. All these goods had to be delivered. The Loughridge Company is only one of the many companies that unloaded and distributed goods shipped in as well as goods shipped out of Ardmore. (Courtesy of Sally Gray.)

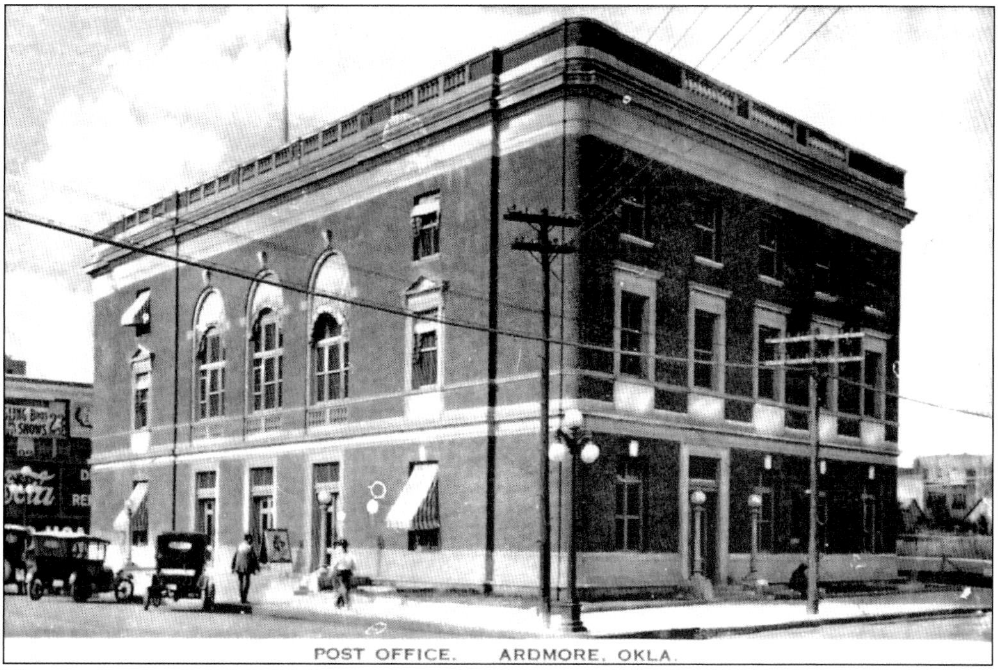

The first postmaster in Ardmore was Dr. Hillard J. Yarbrough, who was also a physician. According to Paul N. Frame's book *A History of Ardmore, Oklahoma, From the Earliest Beginnings to 1907*, "Dr. Yarbrough distributed the mail and doctored his patients all in the same room and quite often at the same time." This building housed federal offices that are still there and the post office until it moved to its current location. (Courtesy of Sally Gray.)

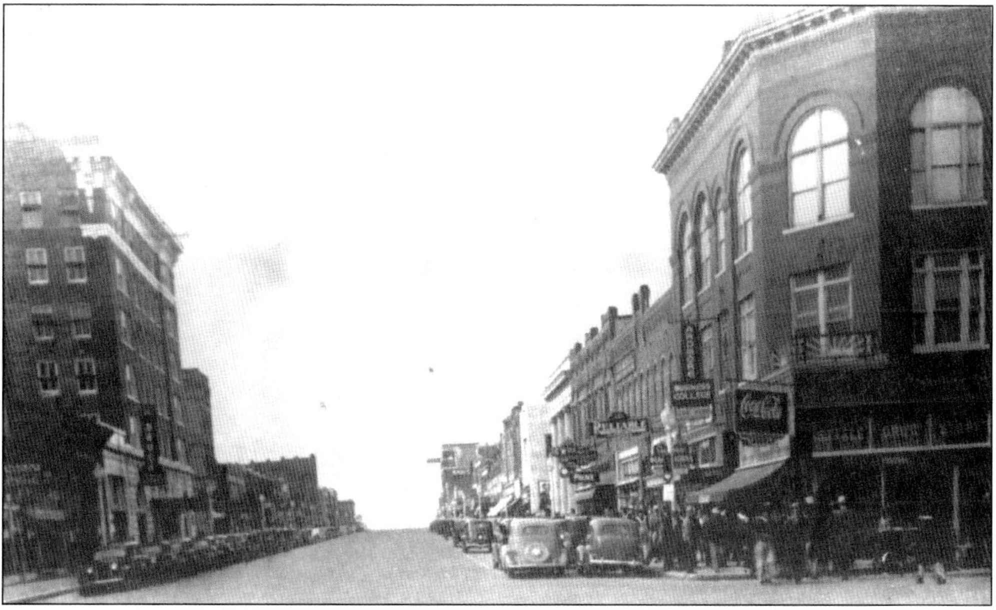

At far right is the landmark building that has served as a bank, the Masonic lodge, and, in this photograph, Steele Drug. The next building to the west is the Ardmore Business College. Notice how cars are double-parked on the right side of the street. (Courtesy of Ardmore Main Street Authority.)

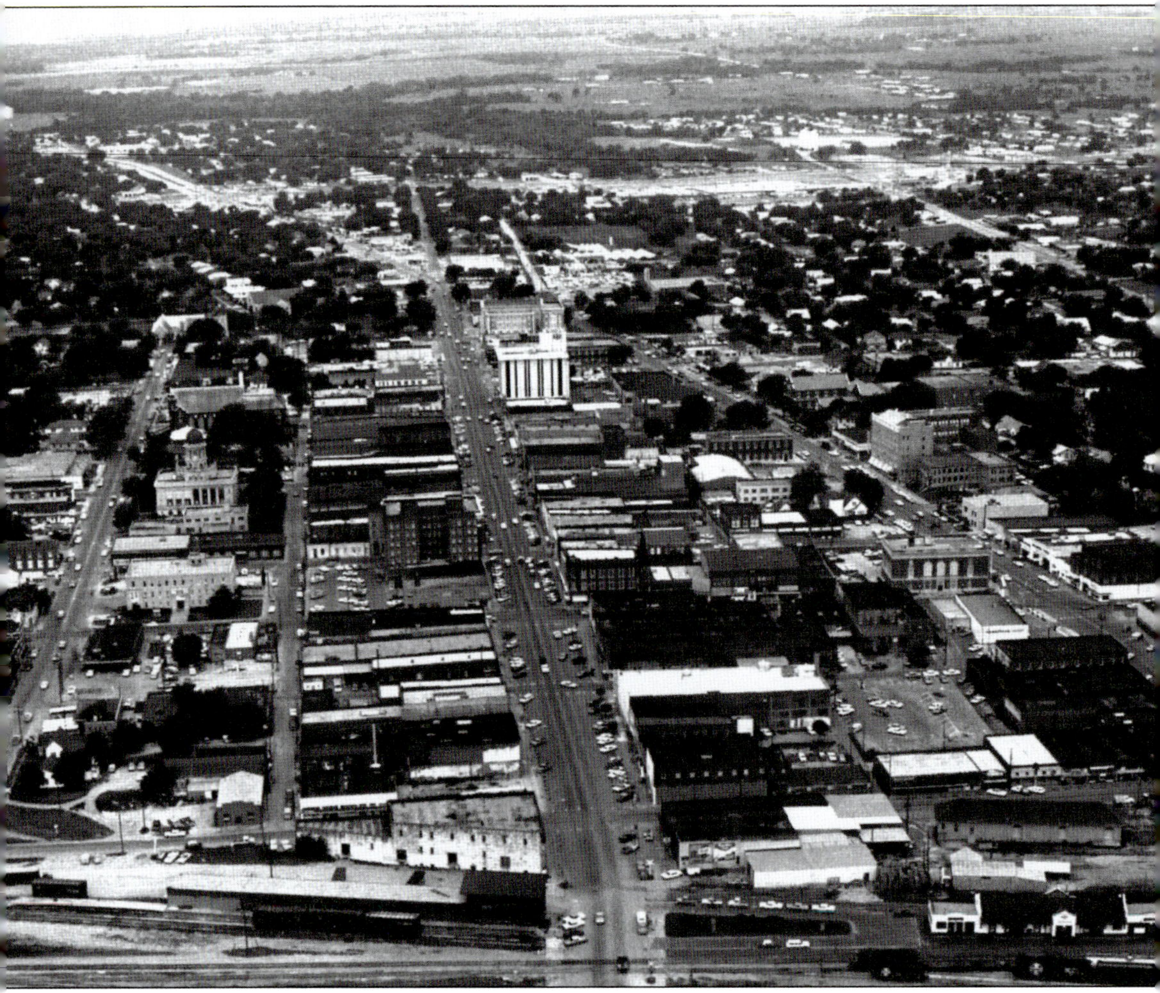

Ardmore began as a city of tents arranged on either side of a ditch dug into the earth by Jim Staples using a tongue plow. The earliest citizens of the infant town were merchants and attorneys. The merchants came to provide food, clothing, furniture, and household goods to the flood of people they knew would follow the railroad. The attorneys came so they would be in place when the Chickasaw tribal lands became open to white settlement. Within a few short years, the tents had been replaced by buildings made of wood and placed irregularly along a dusty Main Street that became a muddy quagmire in the rainy season. After the great fire of 1895, the burned structures were replaced by brick and rock buildings. Many of these buildings survived the explosion of 1915 even though they were heavily damaged, and several buildings in downtown Ardmore were repaired with different-colored bricks than the original wall. Ardmore was determined to survive, and it continues to be determined to repair and grow after every disaster that comes along.

Five

The Players

Ardmore was first peopled by intruders, immigrants who came into Pickens County. At first intruders such as Samuel Zuckerman and Bob and Frank Frensley came legally, that is, with a permit from the Chickasaw Nation. As more businessmen and settlers arrived, they began to ignore the tribal requirement of a permit. Businessmen did continue for a time to pay rent on the land on which they built their stores. As the city continued to grow, the entrepreneurs became concerned about their investments, and the names W. A. Ledbetter and Clarence B. Douglas are linked with efforts to represent Ardmore with the noncitizen protective leagues that were meeting in Ardmore, Chickasha, and Purcell. These men were sent on two occasions to Washington, D.C., to lobby for the rights of noncitizens in Pickens County. Their dreams were finally realized when the Curtis Act of 1898 ended tribal governments and provided for individual allotments to citizens. Ardmore was immediately surveyed, and current occupants were allowed first option to purchase lots. By 1903, all land had been purchased. It was a time of new birth for Ardmore. With legal ownership of land established, noncitizens at last felt that their capital investments were protected.

In addition to new construction, the social fabric of the city began to bloom as well. Churches were built in abundance. Numerous social clubs provided opportunities to experience personal development and enhance community progress. Civic groups continued their efforts to improve the city, and that same attitude continues to make Ardmore a progressive city. Under the leadership of Sidney Suggs, publisher of the *Daily Ardmoreite*, and H. C. Potterf, president of the Ardmore City Schools Board of Education, Dr. Charles Evans was hired as superintendent. Under his leadership, the five-month school term was expanded to nine months, new brick buildings were built in each ward, and enrollment increased from 900 to 1,900. The high school moved for a short time into the second floor of the Carnegie Library building before moving in 1912 to the new brick building on North Washington Street.

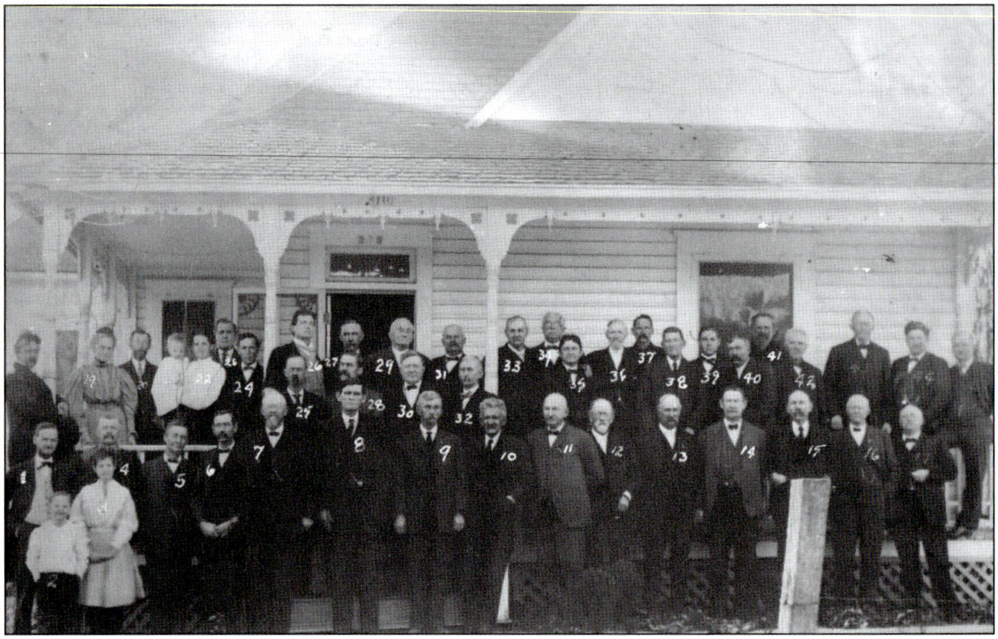

Although the event of the photograph is unknown, there are many well-known personages among this numbered group: Dr. Walter Hardy (1) and his children Charles (2), Minnie (3), and Milton (21) with Mrs. Walter Hardy (22); J. B. Spraggins (16); W. B. Frame (13) and Lon Frame (35); R. W. Randol (32); Judge Hosea Townsend (34); Dr. Henry (20); Dr. McCoy (25); R. W. Dick (28); and A. D. Chase (29). (Courtesy of Sally Gray.)

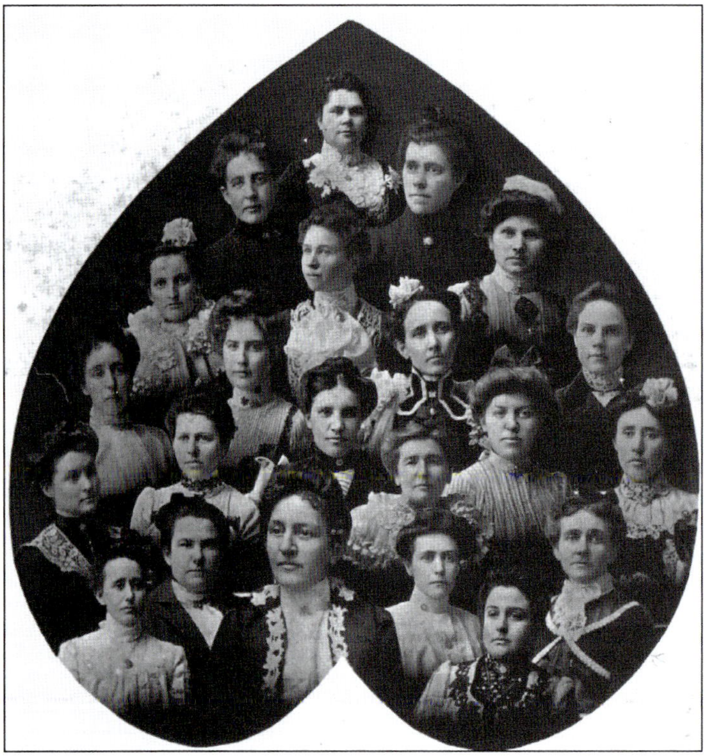

The Orio Club was a ladies literary club that read and discussed a variety of literature. It was organized in August 1901 by Mrs. George H. Webb. Most likely members of the club enjoyed Mrs. Webb's private library collection, which was extensive. In 1906, the Orio Club donated 350 books to the newly opened Carnegie Library, bringing the library's total circulation to 700. (Courtesy of Sally Gray.)

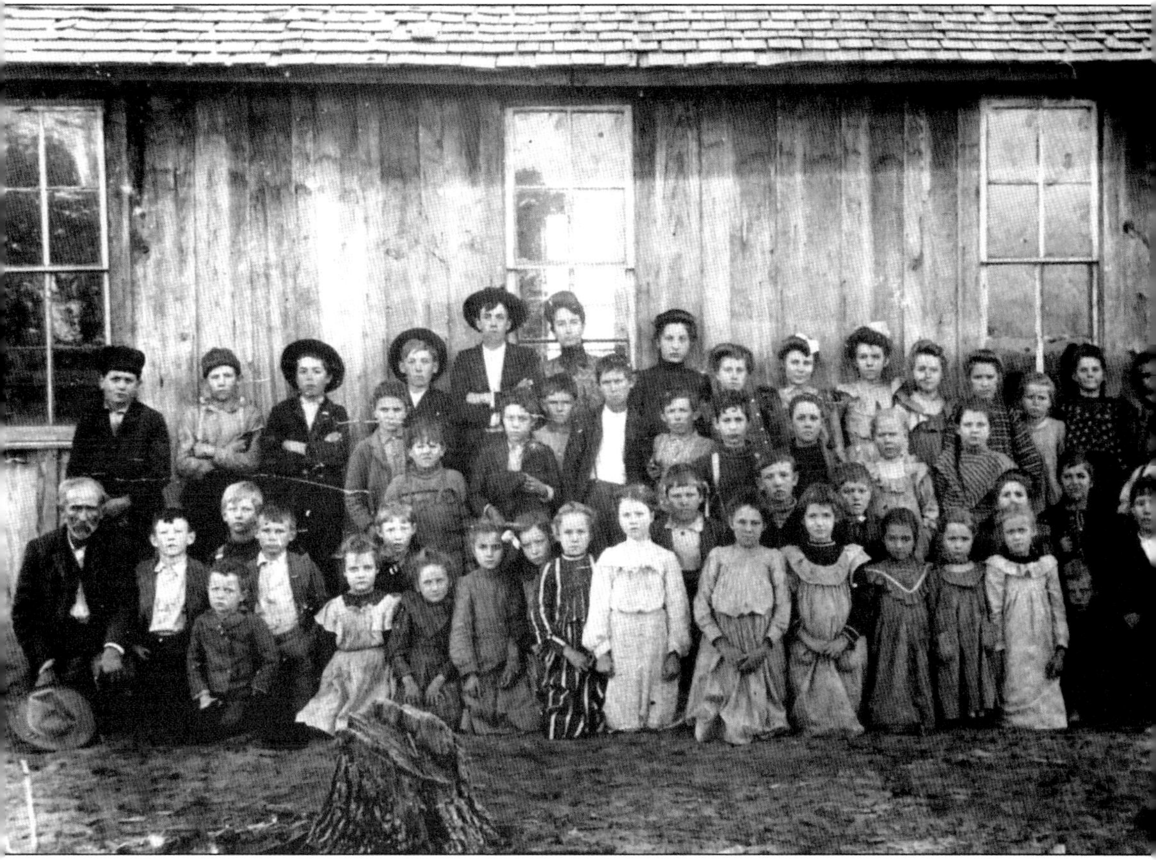

This photograph could have been taken at any one of a dozen neighborhood schools established shortly after statehood. Prior to that time, noncitizens sent their children to subscription schools, which were actually private schools with tuition ranging from 3½¢ a day at the primary level to 10¢ a day for high school. The school term ended in April, at which time students graduated or were promoted. There was no legal basis for intruders to levy taxes for support of schools. Therefore Ardmore residents sought donations with which they built a one-room schoolhouse and hired a teacher. Several ladies, including Mary V. Niblack, opened subscription schools. The teachers operated independently using whatever texts were available. Several larger schools operated, including King's College begun in 1888 for grades one through eight. St. Agnes Academy, started in 1897 by the Sisters of Mercy, boarded 120 children at its height. Hargrove College opened in 1895 and educated children until 1913 at three different locations. (Courtesy of Sally Gray.)

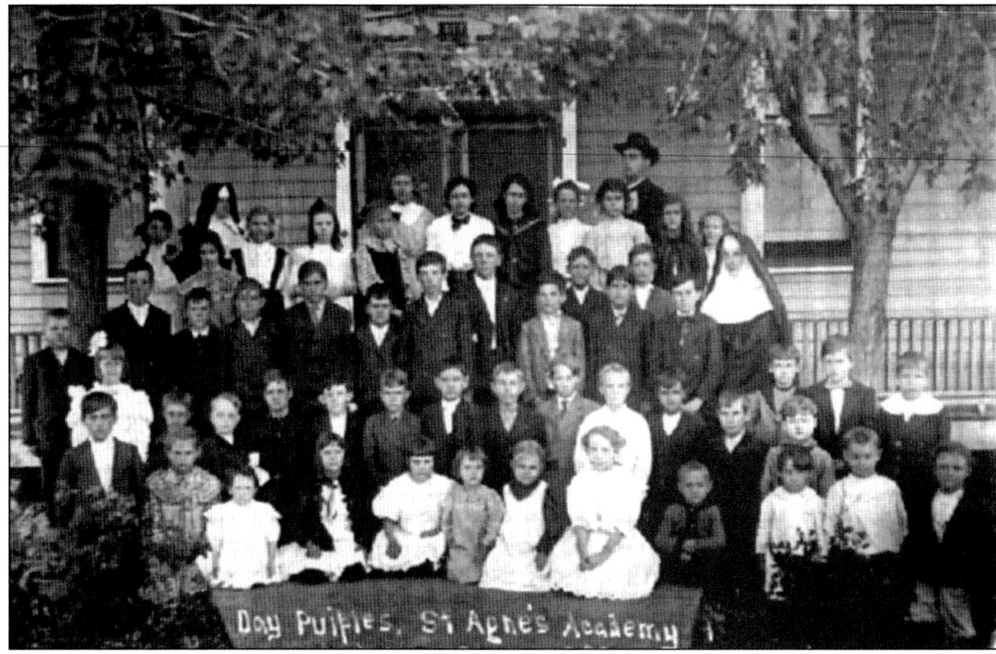

St. Agnes School first opened in Ardmore in 1898 as a boarding school for young women. It was operated by five teachers who belonged to the Sisters of Mercy. Eventually the school became the St. Mary's Catholic School, which closed down operation in 1968. Notice the spelling on the handwritten label, which identified this 1908 photograph as the "puiples" of St. Agnes. (Courtesy of Ardmore Main Street Authority.)

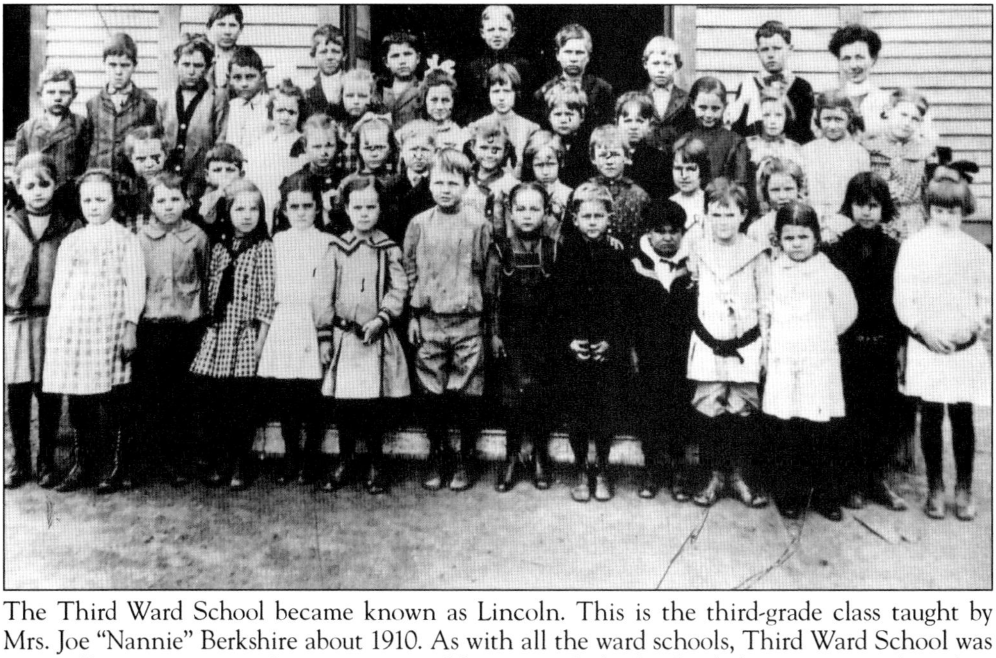

The Third Ward School became known as Lincoln. This is the third-grade class taught by Mrs. Joe "Nannie" Berkshire about 1910. As with all the ward schools, Third Ward School was originally a two-story wooden structure, and for a time, the high school classes were conducted on the second floor. Third Ward was replaced by a two-story brick building and later by a one-story building. (Courtesy of Sally Gray.)

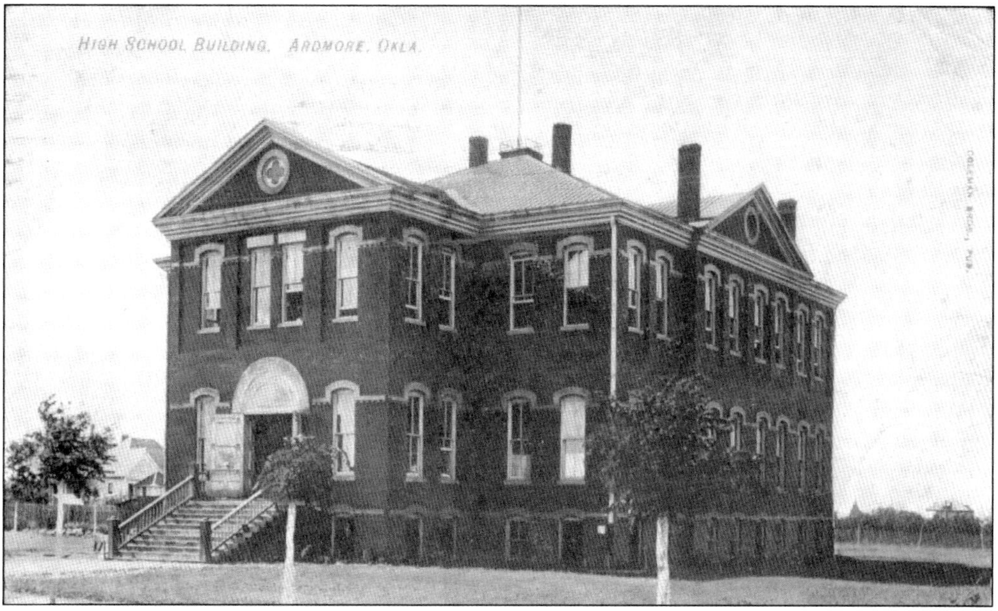

Ardmore built four wooden schools for grades one through eight, replacing them with two-story brick structures by 1906. Third Ward was also home to the high school with classes on the second floor. For a time, high school classes were held on the second floor of the Carnegie Library across the street from Third Ward. In 1912, the three-story high school on North Washington Street was completed. (Courtesy of Greater Southwest Historical Museum.)

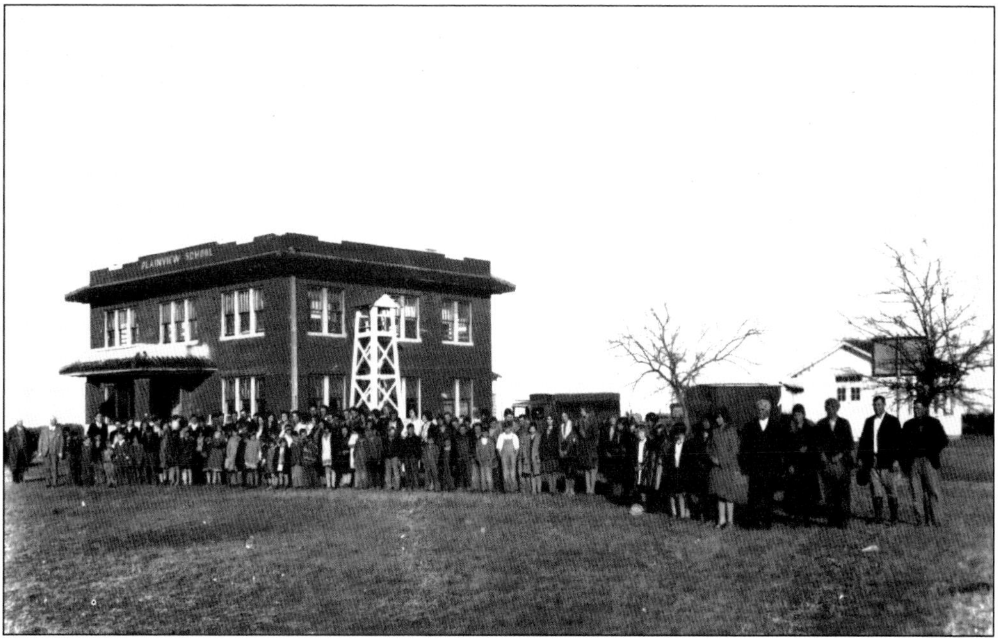

An early view of Plainview school and students shows a two-story brick building sitting on a small rise of land southwest of Ardmore. Today more than half a dozen buildings are spread across a campus more than half a mile wide; and the curriculum, faculty, and students make Plainview one of the highest-performing schools in the state. (Courtesy of Greater Southwest Historical Museum.)

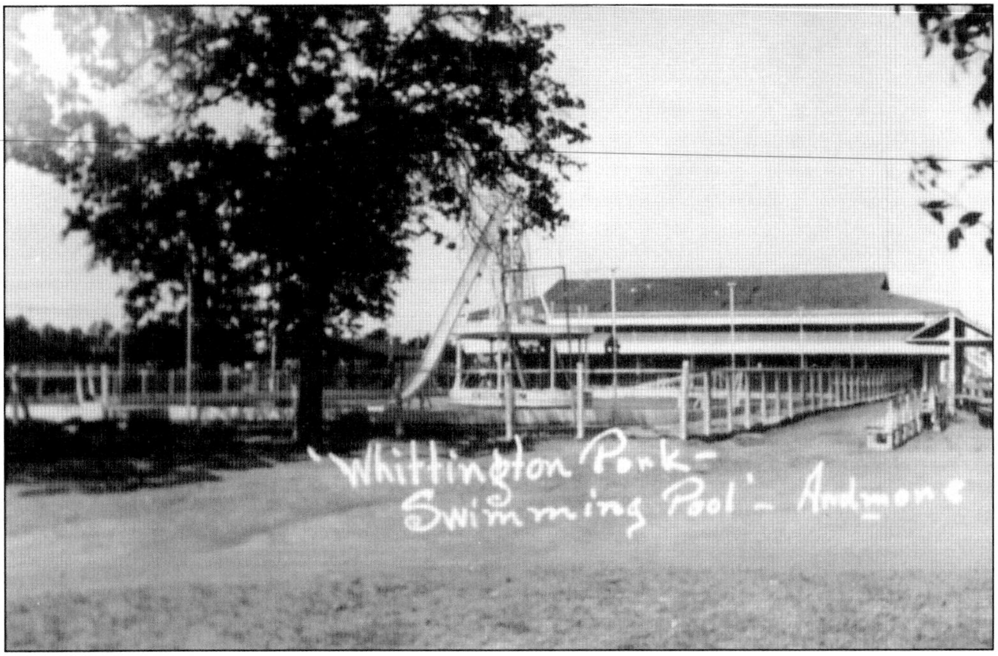

Whittington Park at one time had a huge community pool with a tall slide over the water. There was a large bathhouse with changing rooms for both men and women. Across the street to the south was a roller-skating rink. For most of the 20th century, a Founder's Day Breakfast and celebration were held at Whittington Park each year on July 28. (Courtesy of Sally Gray.)

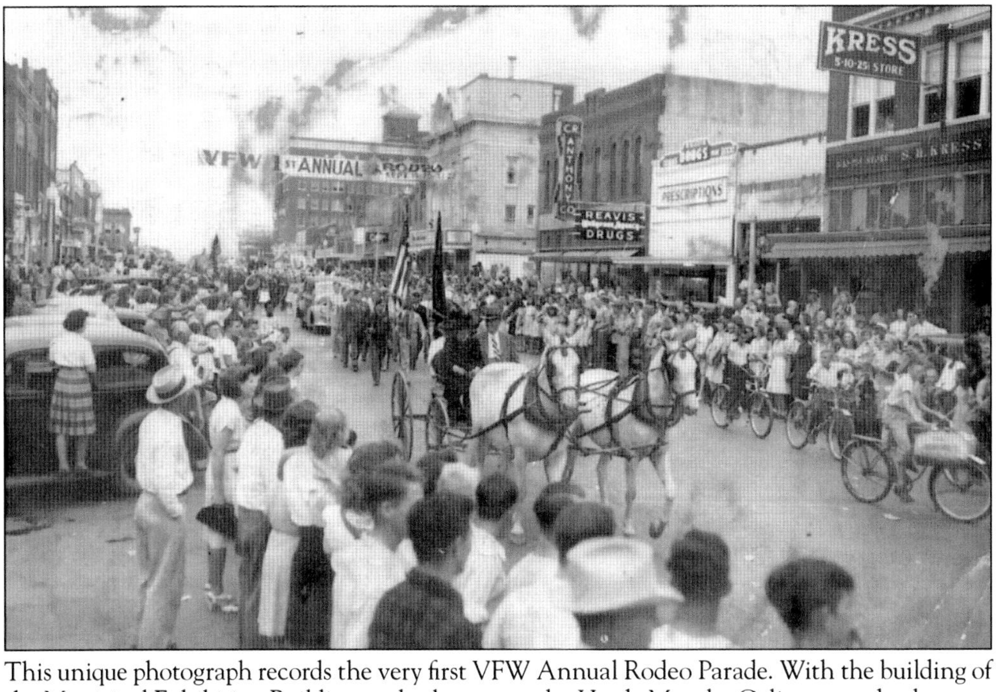

This unique photograph records the very first VFW Annual Rodeo Parade. With the building of the Municipal Exhibition Building, today known as the Hardy Murphy Coliseum, rodeo became big business for Ardmore. The VFW Annual Rodeo was later replaced by the Shrine Club Rodeo, and the parades continued. (Courtesy of Ardmore Main Street Authority.)

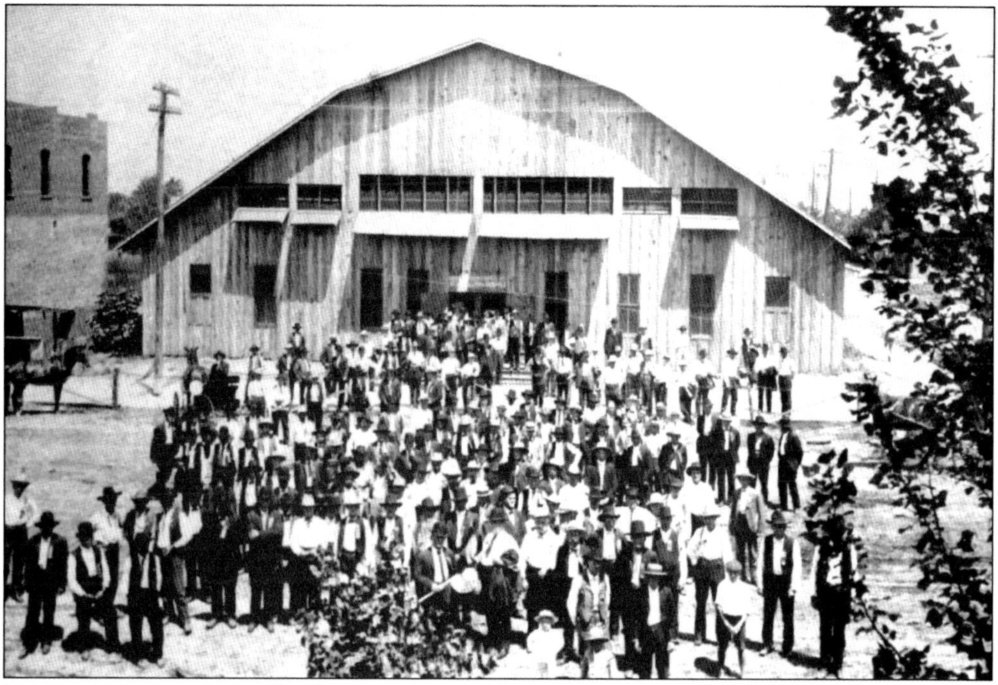

Here is Ardmore's first roller-skating rink, the Royal Roller Rink, famous for its peaked roof. It was located at the corner of C Street and West Main Street. This photograph is dated 1900. A large group of men and boys poses in front of the roller rink. The building on the left houses the Mansfield Grocery Store. (Courtesy of Ardmore Main Street Authority.)

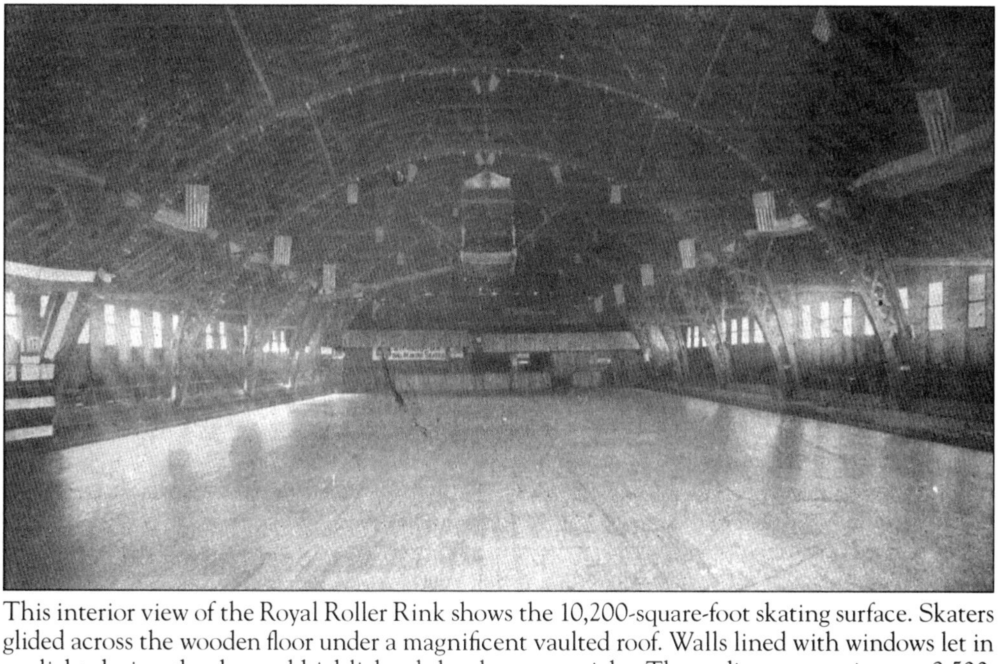

This interior view of the Royal Roller Rink shows the 10,200-square-foot skating surface. Skaters glided across the wooden floor under a magnificent vaulted roof. Walls lined with windows let in sunlight during the day and highlighted the skaters at night. The audience capacity was 2,500. Skating equipment included 500 pairs of skates with curved ends. (Courtesy of the McGalliard Collection, Ardmore Public Library.)

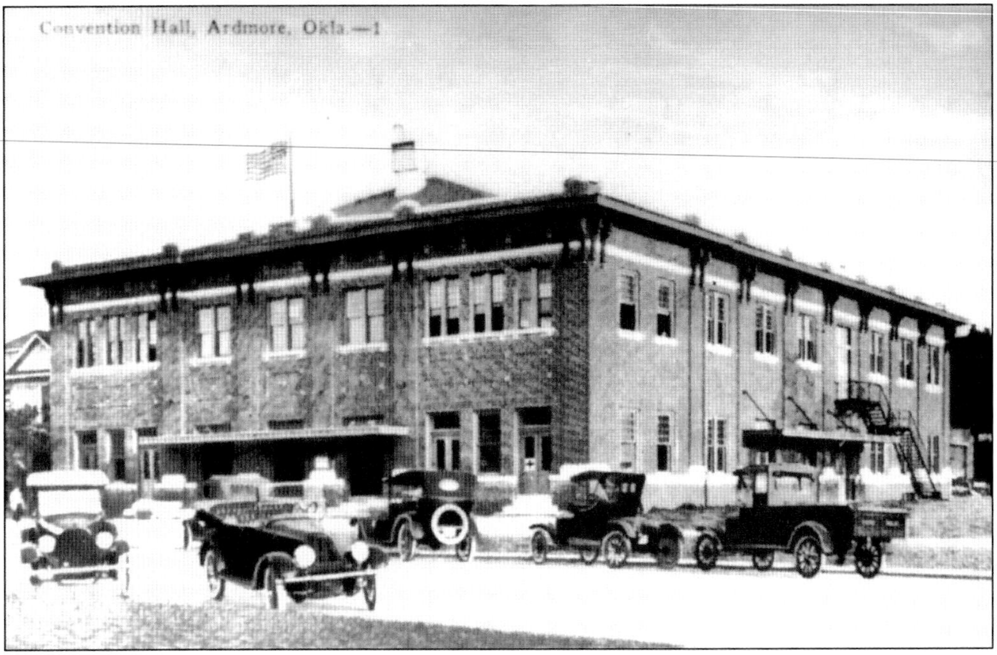

The convention center was built in 1916 in order to provide a venue for large audience events. It was constructed of red brick and was also called the Ardmore Auditorium. It fell into disrepair during the 1930s and developed major problems with the roof. (Courtesy of Sally Gray.)

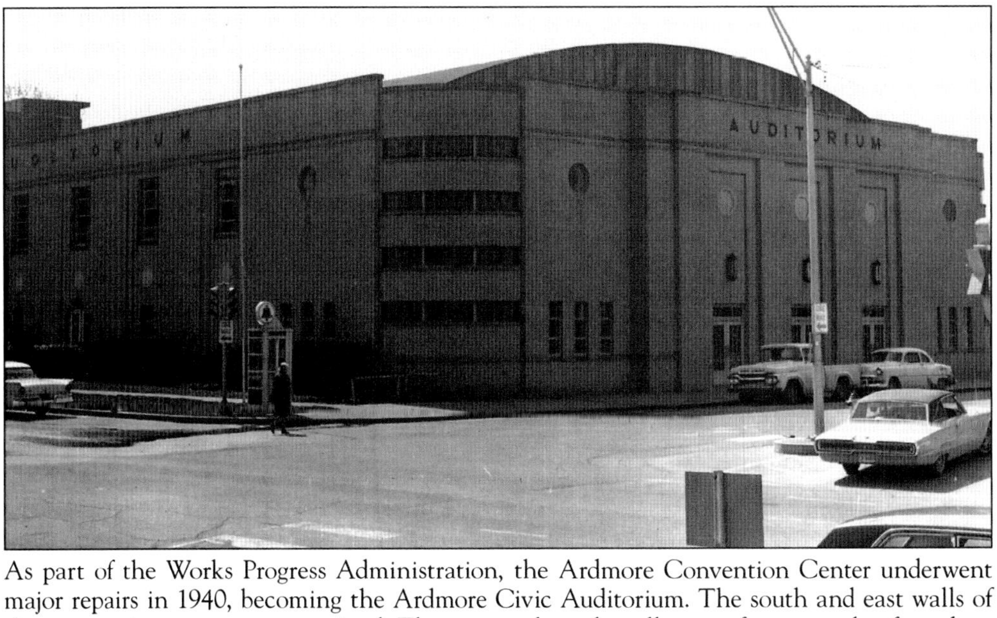

As part of the Works Progress Administration, the Ardmore Convention Center underwent major repairs in 1940, becoming the Ardmore Civic Auditorium. The south and east walls of the convention center were retained. The west and north walls are a fine example of art deco made of blond brick with curved corners, a combination of round and multipane windows, and fleur-de-lis motifs on the second-floor facade. (Courtesy of Sally Gray.)

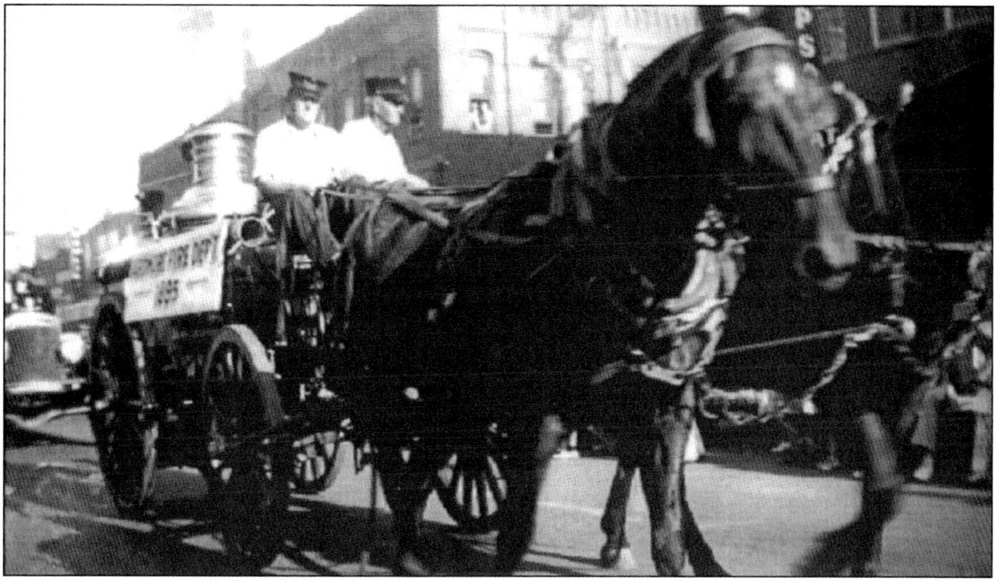

This photograph shows a team of horses pulling the fire wagon and the Ardmore Fire Department's first steamer pumper, which was purchased in 1896 after the great fire of 1895. Because Ardmore was not yet an incorporated city, the Ardmore Board of Trade, the forerunner of the chamber of commerce, raised donations of $1,800 to purchase the steamer. This parade is from the mid-1900s. (Courtesy of Ardmore Main Street Authority.)

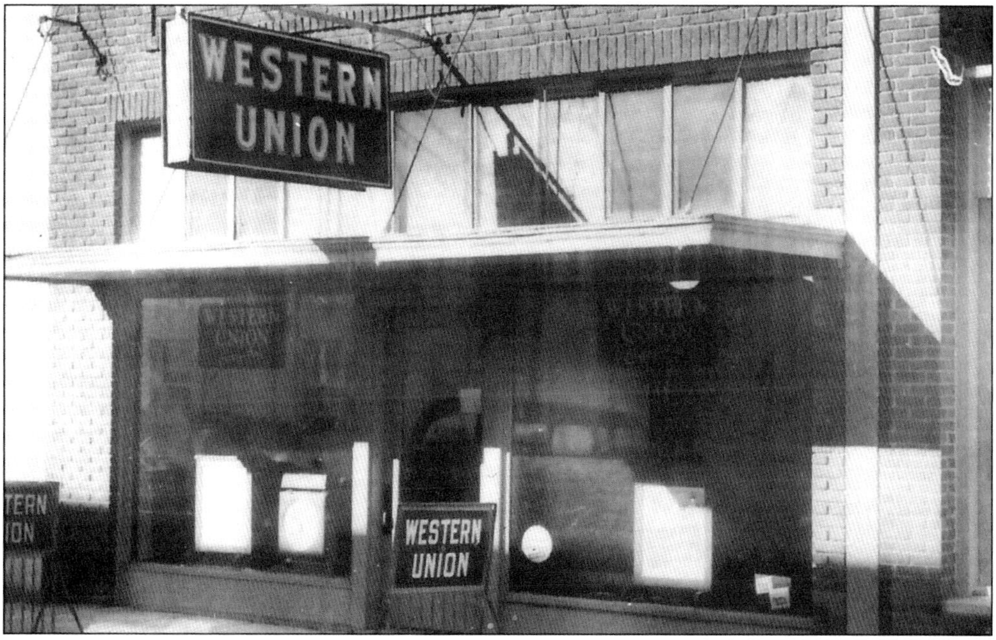

Western Union was founded in 1851 as the New York and Mississippi Valley Printing Telegraph Company, becoming Western Union in 1856. By 1861, the transcontinental telegraph was completed with service to all continents by 1896. In 1871, the money transfer was introduced, and in 1884, Western Union was an original stock in the first Dow Jones Average. In 1914, Western Union introduced the first consumer charge card. (Courtesy of Ardmore Main Street Authority.)

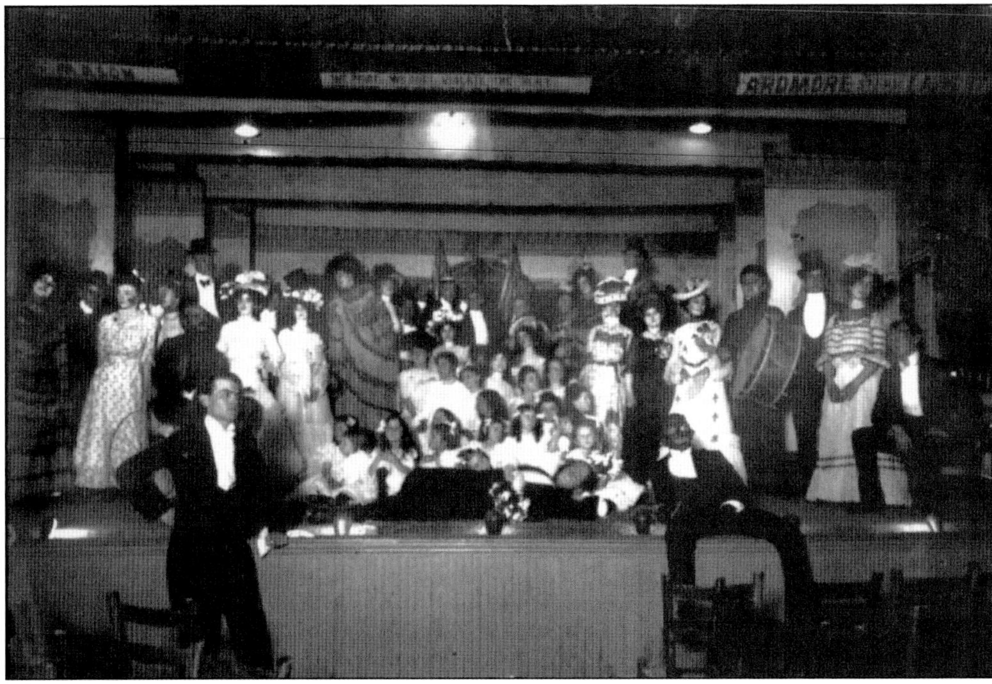

Since the earliest days, Ardmoreites have craved and enjoyed entertainment. During the first five years, citizens built three opera houses, two of which were destroyed in the great fire of 1895. Schools and social clubs have traditionally entertained the populace with plays. This photograph is from the Elks lodge in 1921 when it presented "A Night in Bohemia." (Courtesy of Ardmore Main Street Authority.)

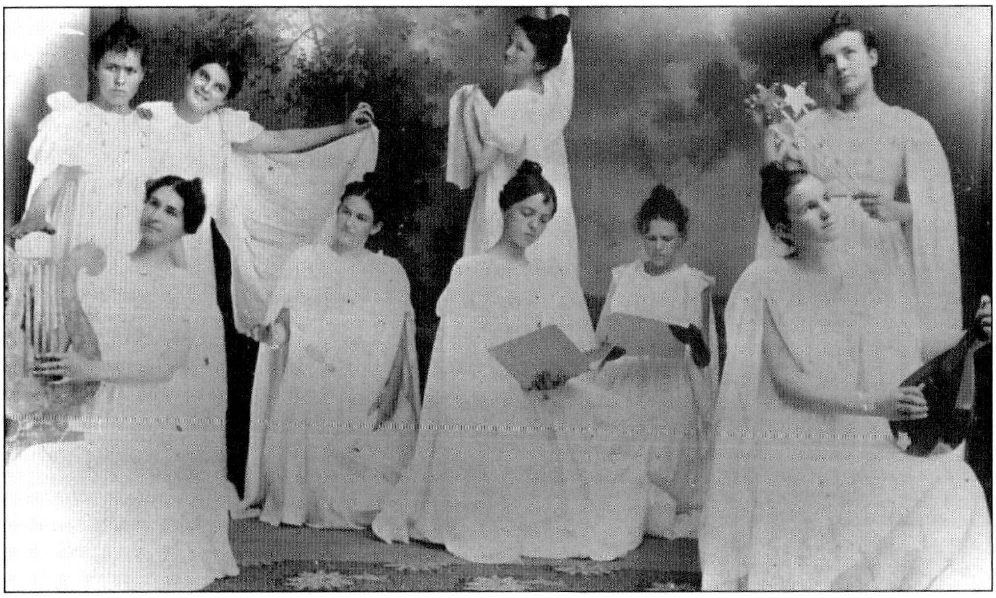

The Robison Opera was built in 1898 after the great fire, but he Anderson-Burch Opera House and the Kloski Opera House both burned. In addition to performances by local talent, acting companies entertained standing-room-only crowds for two to five days before moving on the next town. Drum and bugle corps also performed in Ardmore. (Courtesy of Sally Gray.)

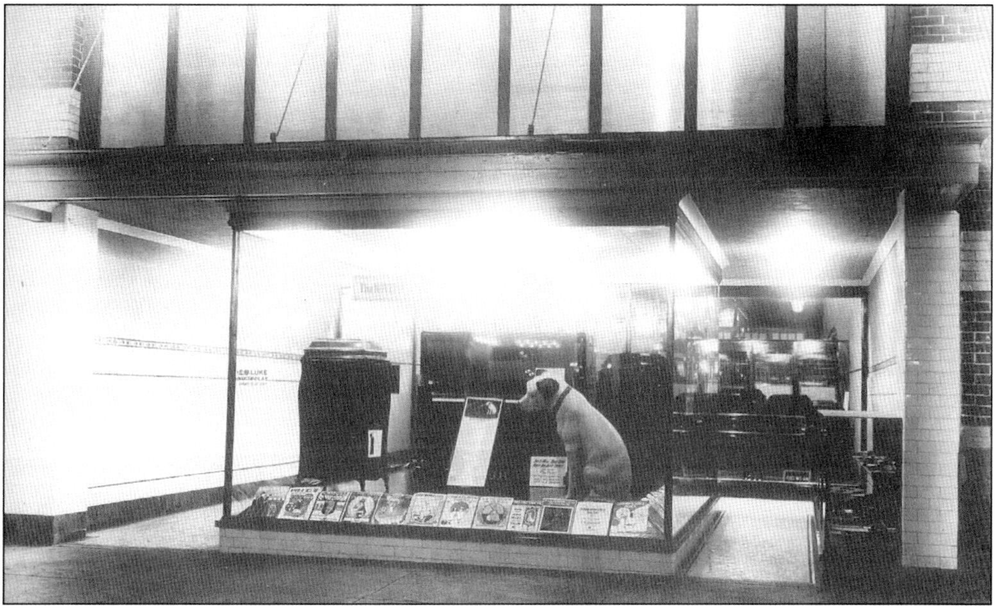

E. B. Luke established a music store on Main Street in 1896. A couple of times a month he would load several cottage organs into a spring wagon and travel through the countryside selling them to farmers who were becoming prosperous in the young state. He also took fiddles, guitars, and strings for these instruments on his journey. Inside the window of his store sat an RCA icon. (Courtesy of Sally Gray.)

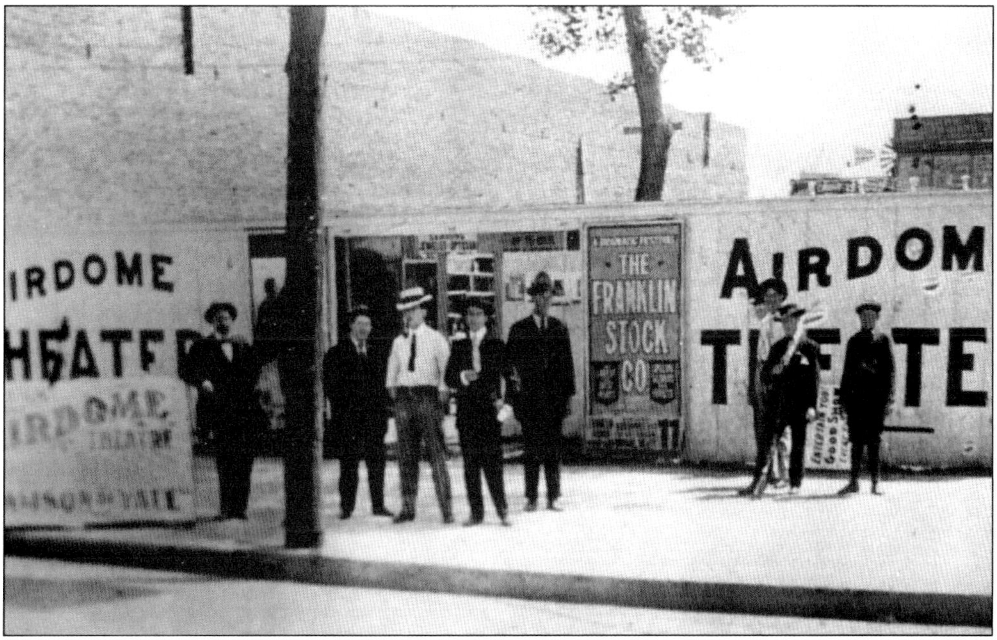

The Ardmore Airdome had a tall wall in front for a reason. The Airdome was an outdoor theater. That is, people could sit out of doors in nice weather and enjoy a movie. The high wall prevented passersby from getting a freebie show. Indoor movie theaters included the Gem, Park, Majestic, and Tivoli, all of which were located on Main Street. (Courtesy of Ardmore Main Street Authority.)

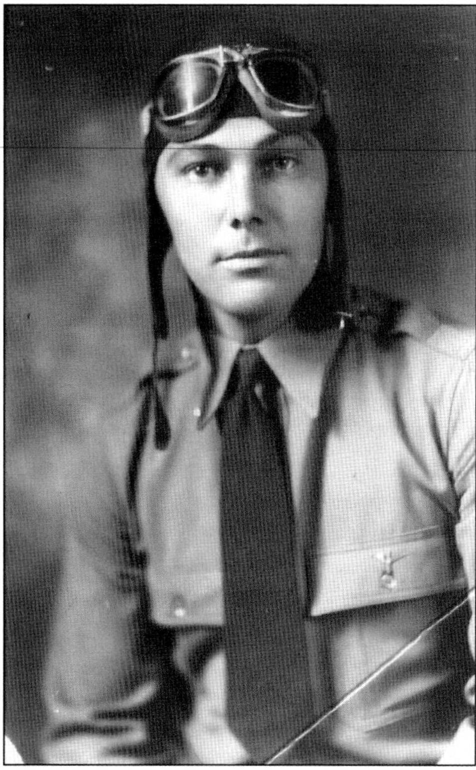

Art Oakley was a fighter pilot in World War I. He opened the first flying school in Ardmore and operated an airport in north Ardmore near Locust Street and Chickasaw Boulevard. From 1921 to 1926, he partnered with Dorsey Askew in the airport. In 1933, the hangar burned and was not replaced. Oakley worked for United Airlines and later became the private pilot of Lloyd Noble. (Courtesy of Sally Gray.)

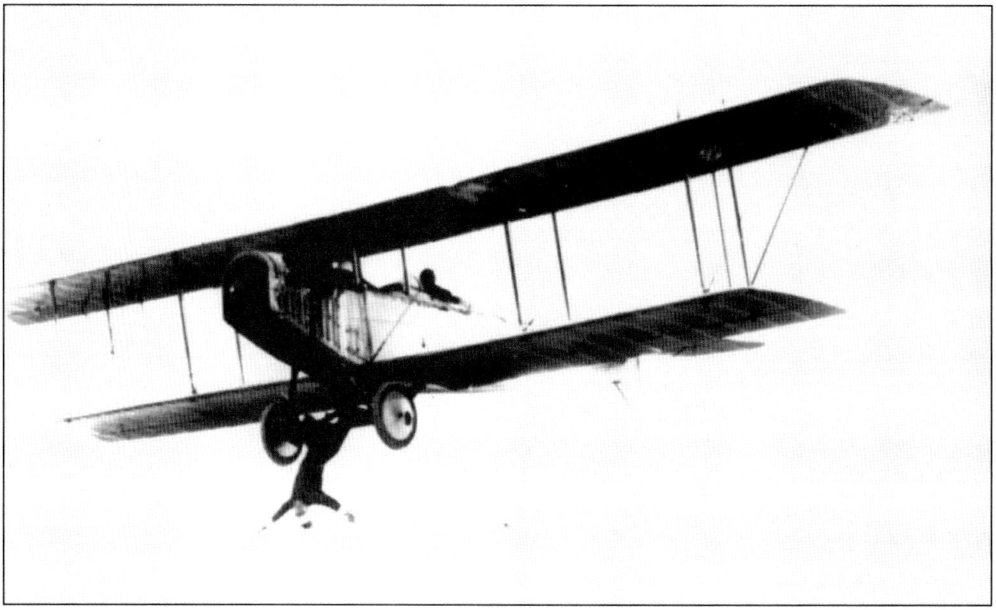

Art Oakley could qualify as a barnstormer. He loved doing aerial stunts. There is a picture of him hanging upside down with his knees wrapped around the landing gear. In this photograph, Oakley, hanging from a cable beneath a biplane, hovers above a railroad boxcar. He actually landed on the moving train and then was pulled back into the air by the plane. (Courtesy of the McGalliard Collection, Ardmore Public Library.)

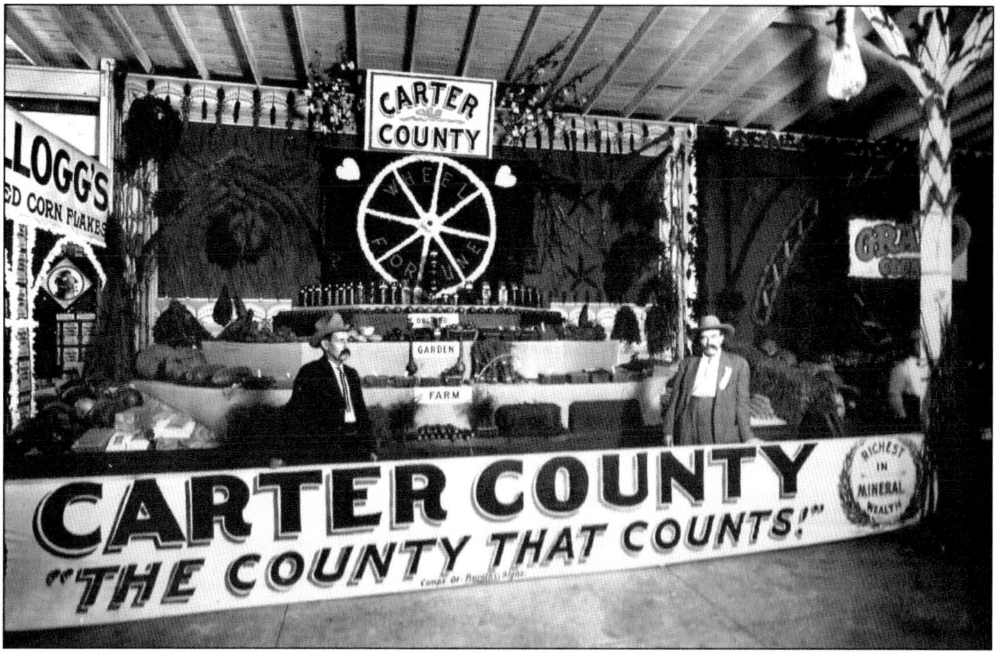

This photograph taken by P. Stone shows the 1914 Carter County State Fair exhibits in Oklahoma City. Carter County had a booth displaying fresh and canned fruits and vegetables and crops and a variety of crafts along the back of the display. Quilt making was a favorite activity of ladies involved with home extension clubs through the Oklahoma State University extension programs. (Courtesy of the McGalliard Collection, Ardmore Public Library.)

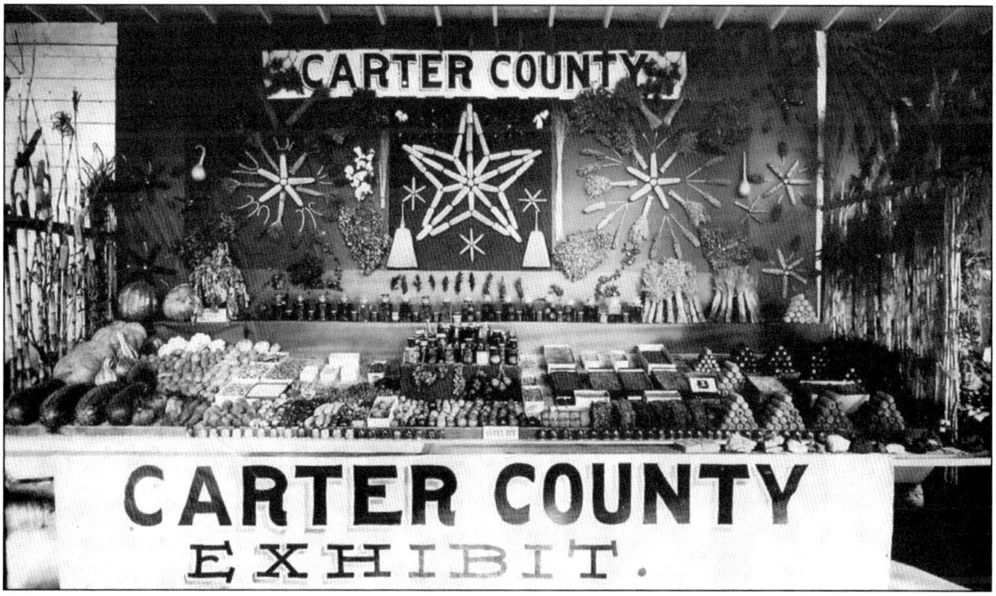

Again in 1915, Carter County State Fair exhibits were photographed. Both of the exhibit pictures came from the estate of Felix Knox West, who was the first secretary of the Carter County Free Fair. He was also secretary of the Ardmore Chamber of Commerce, a farmer, and a deputy sheriff. He lived in Ardmore from 1898 until 1917. (Courtesy of the McGalliard Collection, Ardmore Public Library.)

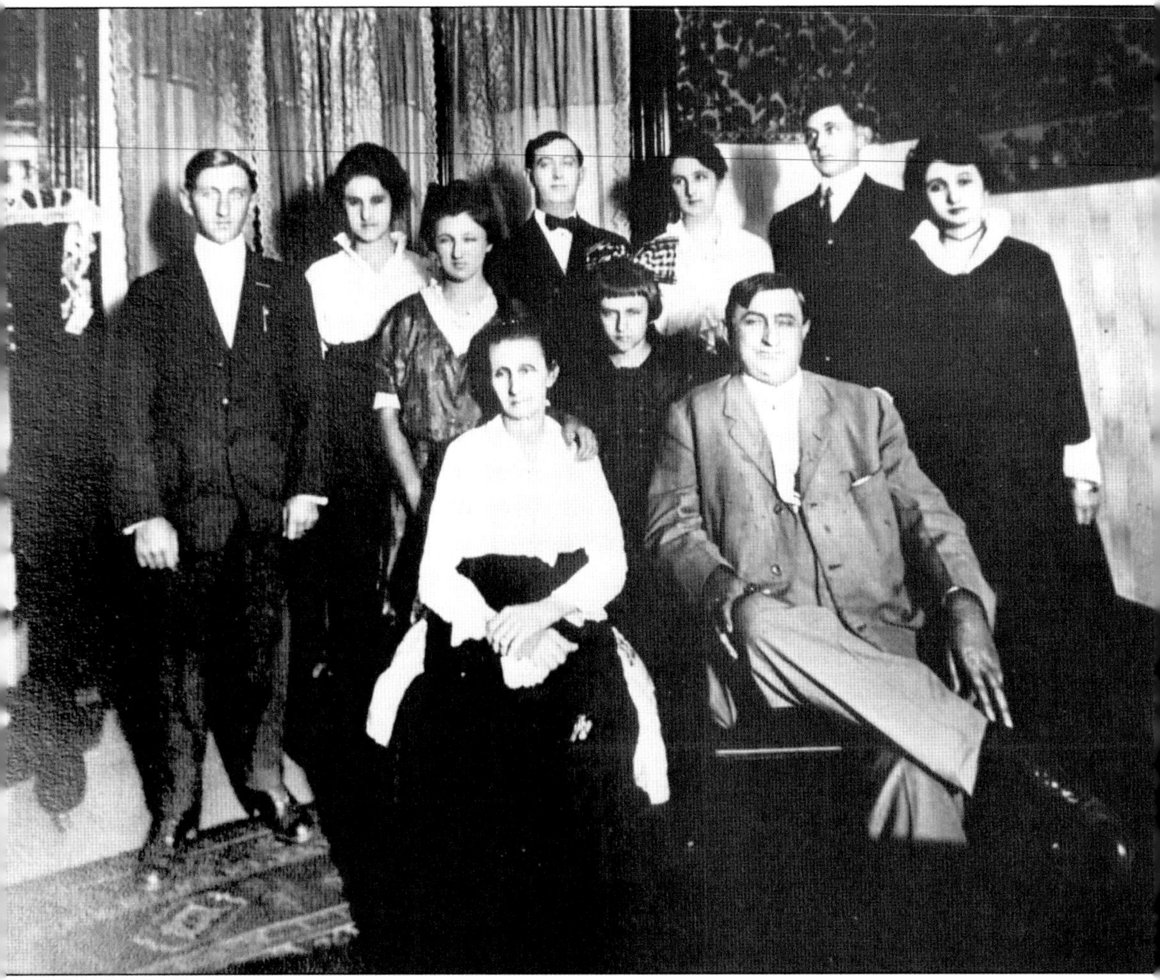

Columbus Marion Joiner and Lydia Ann Beaver Joiner pose with their children. Mary Louise stands between her parents. From left to right are Verne Snow, Frances Sue, Ruby Nell, James Best, Willie Mae, John Lee, and Martha Marie. Columbus was an oil man. He discovered the east Texas field in Rusk County, which was the largest field at that time. The Joiner family made its home in Ardmore. (Courtesy of Sally Gray.)

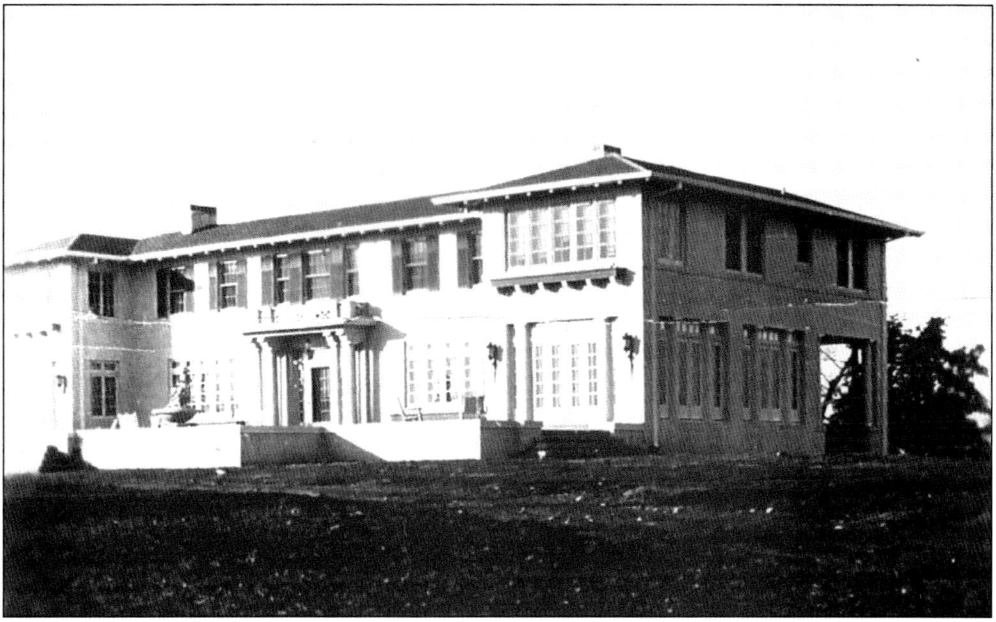

This is the Wirt Franklin home at Dornick Hills. After striking oil in 1913, Franklin was very active in the Healdton oil fields. He wanted a toll road between Ardmore and Healdton to facilitate traffic to the oil field. It is estimated that more than 1,000 teams of horses, mules, and oxen were used each day to transport equipment from Wilson and Ringling into the oil field. (Courtesy of Sally Gray.)

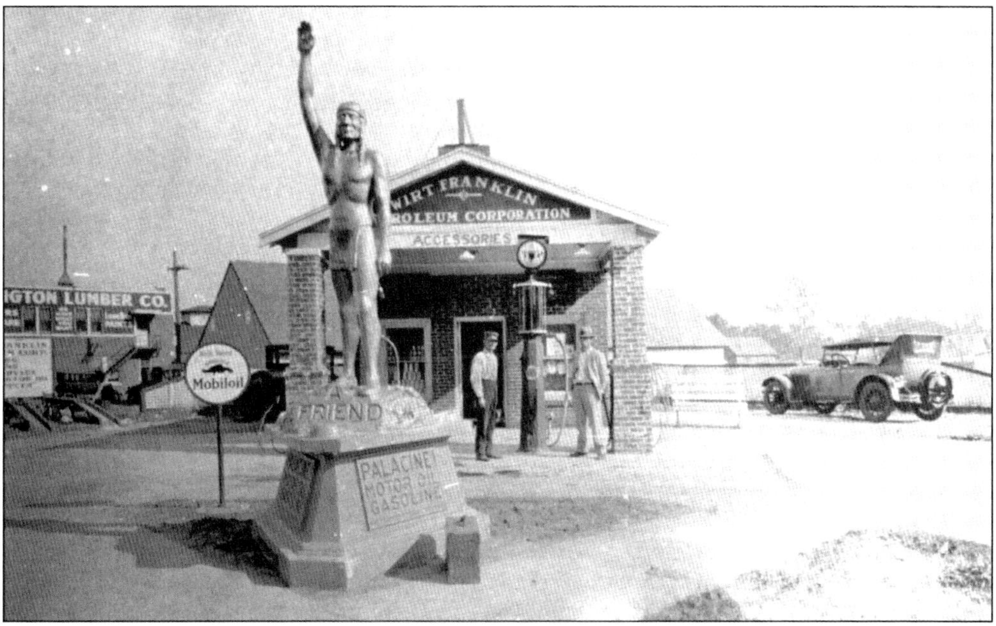

The Wirt Franklin Oil Company was headquartered in Ardmore where Franklin helped establish the Independent Petroleum Association of America. He was active in the oil fields of western Carter County where Franklin's service to the Healdton area is memorialized in the Healdton Oil Museum. His favorite car sits on the showroom floor along with many pictures and samples of oil field equipment. (Courtesy of Greater Southwest Historical Museum.)

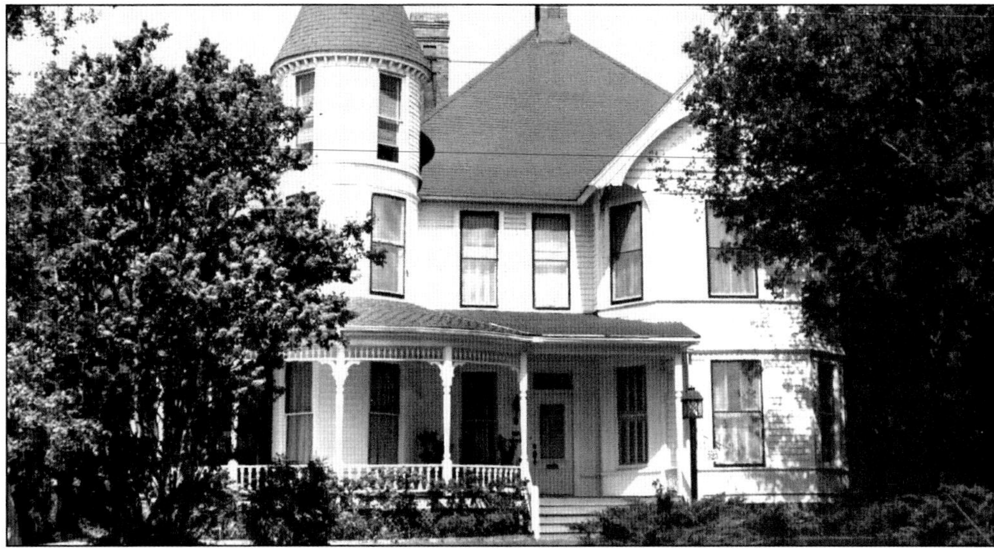

This house typically known as the Sayre-Mann mansion was originally built in 1887 on the north side of Main Street between D and E Streets, east of the railroad tracks. It was built for the Munzesheimer family. In about 1902, the house was purchased by J. M. and Gertrude Dodson, who had it moved to its present location at 323 F Street SW. To see that house with its three-story turret being hauled across town must have been a sight indeed. It was secured on its new foundation, and the Dodson family lived there for seven years. In 1909, Horace and Pearl Sayre purchased the house and lived in it until 1969, a total of 60 years. Noel Mann purchased the house in 1969. The building is in the Queen Anne style. It has fish scale shingles and clapboard siding. There is a large entry hall, and both the first and second floors have a great hall. In 1982, the house was placed on the National Register of Historic Places.

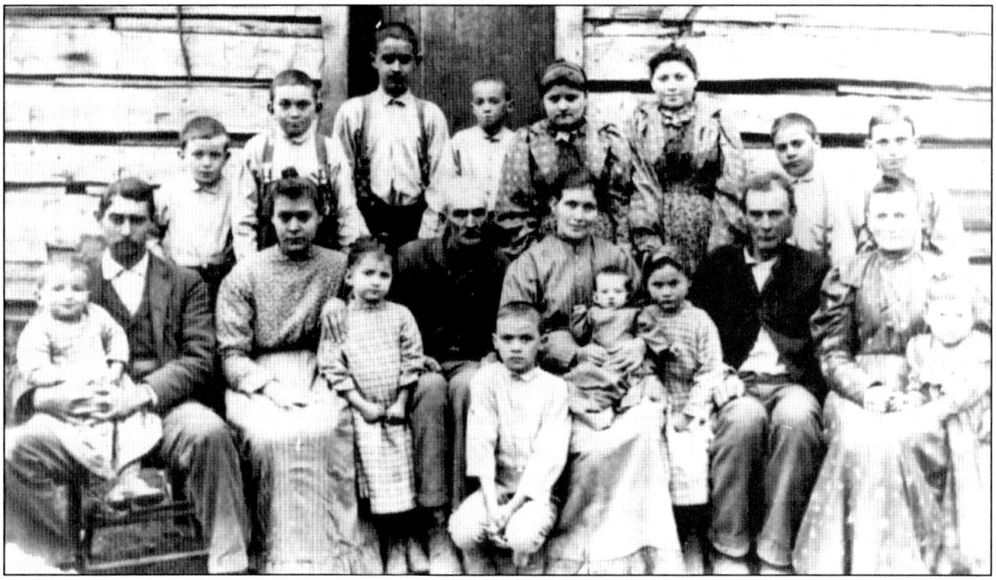

It is believed that the greater part of the family in this pre-1900 photograph belongs to a sister of either Jerry Collins, seated far left, or his wife, Diretha Barnes Collins, seated next to him. The baby in Jerry's lap is one of his children. The girl with Diretha's hand on her shoulder is believed to be Clemmie Collins, who died of diptheria on her wedding day. (Courtesy of Flora Palmer Foust.)

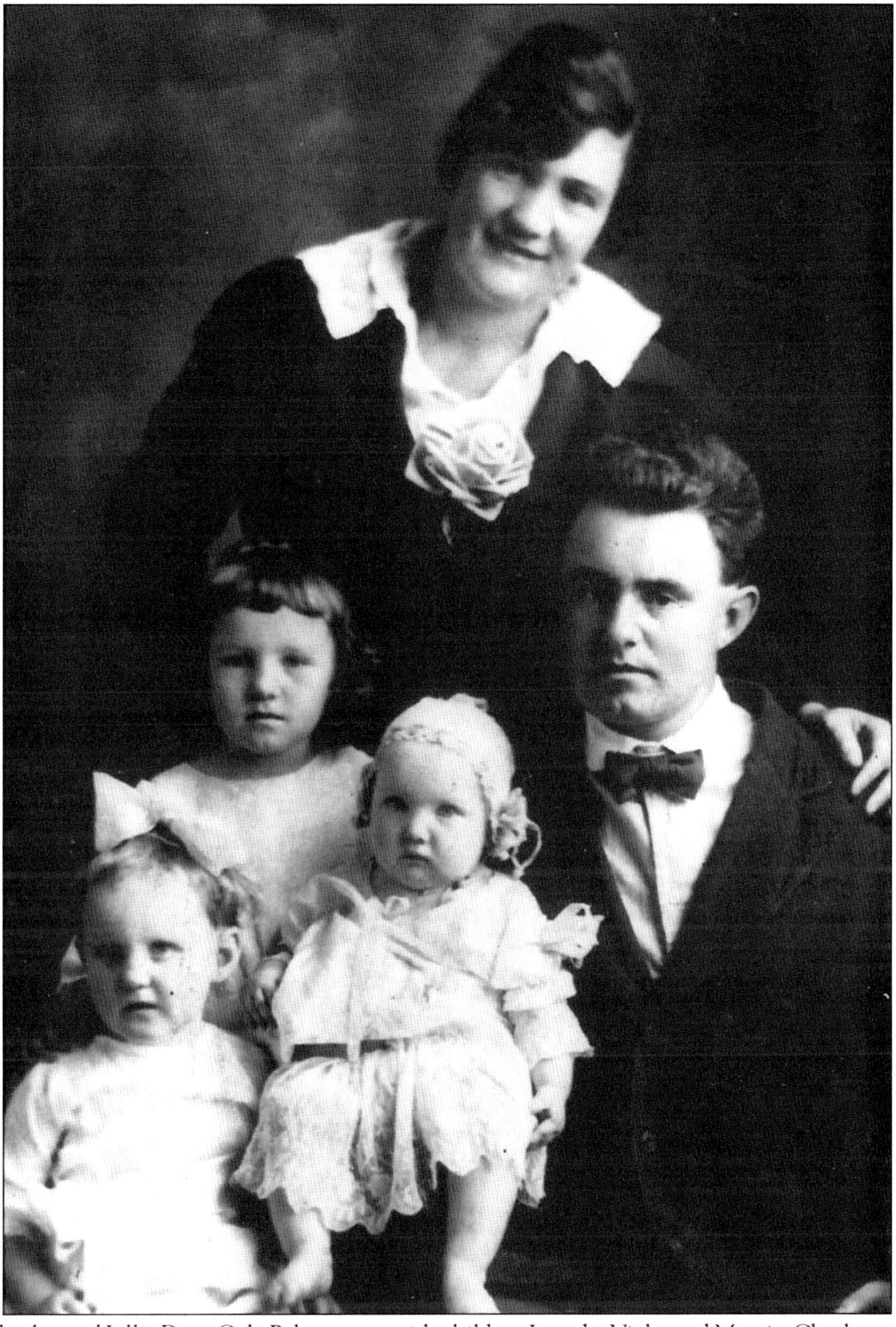

Charley and Lillie Dove Cole Palmer pose with children Lavada, Viola, and Margie. Charley told how his family came to Ardmore when he was just about three years old. He remembered being carried by his father as Sam Palmer walked along the station platform seeing to the unloading of his family's furniture and trunks. Charley and Lillie lived in Ardmore during the explosion of 1915. (Courtesy of Flora Palmer Foust.)

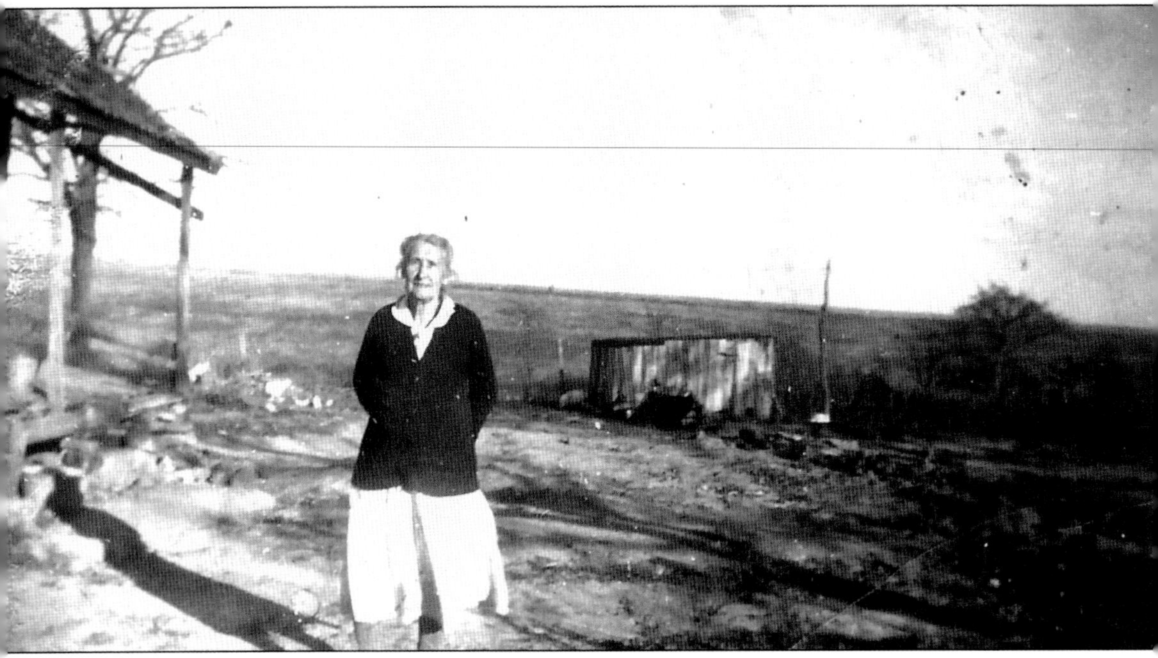

Nancy Jane Williams Cole was born in Pickens County, Chickasaw Nation. She was the daughter of an intruder in the Jimtown-Leon-Ryan area. Nancy Jane was the only girl in a family of 10 children, and she was her father's favorite child. She married George Washington (G. W.) Cole, and they farmed near her parents. Nancy Jane was in such pain when her first child was born that her father held her in his lap while her mother delivered the baby. Several children later, little Molly was born. As Nancy Jane and G. W. drove toward Ardmore one cold morning, they stopped to let a train pass in front of them on the tracks. It was customary for the engineer to toot his whistle in greeting when the train passed through the countryside. On this day when the whistle blew, Nancy Jane felt little Molly stiffen and shudder and go limp. Whether she had an unknown health defect or whether the train's whistle literally scared her to death, Nancy Jane never knew. Nearly every pioneer family remembers their own "little Molly." (Courtesy of Flora Palmer Foust.)

Bibliography

Ardmore State Herald. April 19, 1895.
Bridges, Butch. *This and That Newsletter.* Vol. 5–12, 23–27.
Frame, Paul N. A *History of Ardmore, Oklahoma, From the Earliest Beginnings to 1907.* Ardmore, OK: Greater Southwest Historical Museum, 1995.
Gould, Chas N., Ph.D. *Geography of Oklahoma.* Ardmore, OK: Bunn Brothers, 1909.
Robinson, Gilbert L. "Transportation in Carter County 1913–1917." *Chronicles of Oklahoma* Volume 19, No. 4. December 1941.
www.geocities.com/rickw_123/hist2.htm
www.rootsweb.com/~okgarvin/ipp/tusseyhenryipp.htm

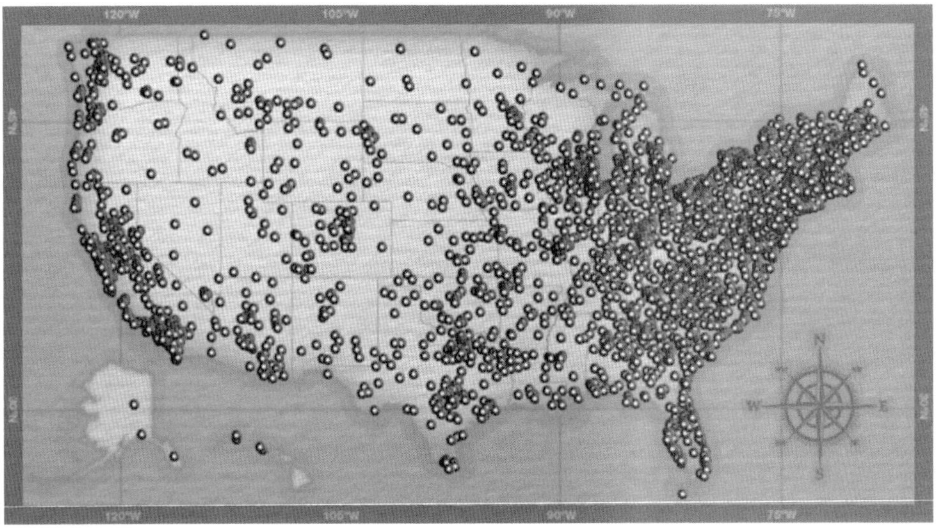